"Never, never, never give up."

—Winston Churchill

Evolution of a Revolution: From Hope to Healing

How Thinking Parents Are Recovering Their Children And Uncovering The Truth

Collected by
Helen Conroy and Laura Hirsch

Team Thinking Moms' Revolution Press, an imprint of Rainbow Books

This book may be purchased in bulk at a special discount for sales promotion, corporate gifts, fund-raising or educational purposes. For details, email info@teamtmr.org.

Visit our website and donate to our grant program at www.teamtmr.org.

Library of Congress Cataloging-in-Publication Data is available on file.

ISBN: 978-0-9776653-4-1

Printed in the United States of America

10 9 8 7 6 5 4 3 2 1

Cover Design by Kimberly Ruckman

Interior Design by Louisa Swann

DISCLAIMER: The materials in this book are for informational or educational purposes only. It is not intended or implied to be a substitute for professional medical advice, diagnosis or treatment. It is the sole responsibility of the user of the information indicated in this book to consult a licensed medical professional to determine if procedures or recommendations are appropriate for yourself or others. If you do use the information contained in this book without the approval of a competent health professional, the authors cannot assume any responsibility for your actions. The authors have no liability whatsoever for direct or indirect damages relating in any way to the use of the information in this book.

To all of those who are still fighting: Only forward from here...

CONTENTS

PREFACE

Through a variety of avenues, both happenstance and intentional, each of us at Team TMR came to know and love The Thinking Moms' Revolution. We wake up to their blog posts in our email boxes, and read them over morning coffee. Those mothers and one dad provide us with a much-needed voice and we live vicariously through their epic adventures in the world of autism and related childhood disorders.

TMR has passed the proverbial torch, and we have been brought together and given the opportunity to share our stories of the emergence from struggle into hope and recovery. Now, the ties that bind us — to each other and to TMR — extend beyond our affected kids. We need each other like air and water. We share in each individual's successes because they might not have happened without each other's steadfast support and mountains of knowledge. The belief we hold in recovery only serves to make us stronger and make healing more realistic.

Our hope is that readers will find themselves in these pages, much in the same way we found ourselves mirrored in The Thinking Moms' Revolution. We want our stories to give you strength to keep up the fight one more day and give you the confidence to overcome this unique, but shared challenge. We would like you to turn to our words when you think you just can't do it anymore. We aspire to instill in you the faith and knowledge that TMR gave us, because it was this faith and knowledge that kept us from surrendering. We believe to our very core that all children deserve to live free from physical and emotional pain, in whatever way they manifest, and collectively we can make it happen.

INTRODUCTION

Not very long ago, the friends behind the Thinking Moms' Revolution wanted to share the support they had found in each other and decided to write a book. That small idea became a blog, and eventually a social thought movement. TMR is known for demanding action, so it felt natural to shift from offering hope and support to offering financial assistance as well. Team TMR, a 501(c)3 not-for-profit organization was born. The women that contributed to this book volunteered their stories without compensation because they believed in hope, in supporting others on this path, and in the Thinking Moms' Revolution. I am awed and humbled to be in their company. When I read their stories of faith and recovery I feel deeply connected to each of them. The funds generated from the sale of the book will benefit the Team TMR grant program and will fund treatments for children with autism and other related disorders. Thank you for supporting our mission. We remain committed to turning the tide of this epidemic, and your help is greatly appreciated.

Helen Conroy, Executive Director, Team TMR

Our goal with The Thinking Moms' Revolution was to help parents understand they were not alone. We wanted to share our stories in the hopes they would inspire others to pursue recovery with the same fervor and tenacity we did. We dared to dream that in doing so, we would inspire a thought revolution! Along came these incredible Thinkers. Moms who have done the work, some having attained the magical "R" word we all strive for with each waking moment. So honored and blessed I consider myself to be, among such genuine greatness. We hope you see yourself in these pages. We hope the truth written here settles in your bones and becomes a part of you. Recovery is real. Believe it.

Lisa Joyce Goes, Board President, Team TMR

Evolution of a Revolution: From Hope to Healing

BLING

On January 5th, 2001, I gave birth to a beautiful healthy baby boy named Gannon. It was a planned C-section delivery and I was very calm and excited to meet my second son. When he rolled into my room in the hospital bassinet, I remember so clearly looking at him and being overwhelmed with the feeling that I needed to protect him. I called my friend who had three children and asked her if she had ever experienced this with any of her children's births. She told me that she had not, and I told her I was puzzled as to why I had this feeling with Gannon, and not with my first born son. I now know why I had that feeling...my son had a compromised immune system that I would not learn about for another four years.

Over the next nine months, Gannon developed normally, meeting all milestones ahead of or on schedule. He rolled over, sat up, crawled, and walked, all the while babbling and looking at us, and communicating with his sounds and his eyes. Then around his first birthday, we noticed that he was not responding to our voices and he was not looking at us as much either.

Fast forward to his 15 month well visit with his pediatrician where he was given five vaccines. Over the next few months, we noticed that he was losing more eye contact and no longer had solid stools. We also watched him become more agitated and he stopped all progression with his speech. He no longer turned his head when we called his name, and he became very disconnected from us. I remember taking him to our "mom and tot" class and noticing that he was the only child who could not sit still at circle time. He also did not play with any of the other children in his class. I was exhausted running after him and bringing him back to the circle only to find him running away again after I sat down.

I asked my pediatrician about his behavior, his lack of speech, and his loose, very smelly stools. He responded by telling me that Gannon's loose stools were the result of him eating a lot of fruit, and his lack of speech was due to the fact that he was a boy and boys spoke later than girls — WHAT? I was uneducated at the time, and had no idea how to question him more effectively. We had NO CLUE what was really happening to our son.

At the age of three, we had him evaluated by our local school and after his testing was completed, we were told that he was "speech and language impaired" and we would need to enroll him in an early education classroom. This required our boy to take a bus every morning so he could attend this school. The school said it was best and that the bus would help eliminate his anxiety and reduce his inattentive running. I was completely shocked; he was only three! I was frightened and sad.

After he began attending his ECDD classroom, his behavior became worse. He was biting and pushing down little girls, and becoming even more anxious. I was afraid to answer the phone because I did not want hear any more bad news. During this same time, my older son was experiencing extreme separation anxiety in kindergarten, and I had also given birth to our third child, a little girl who refused to take a bottle and was attached to me for a good part of the day. Because she refused the bottle, my husband couldn't help with night feedings. My world was crashing and I remember pulling over into a church parking lot and saying out loud, "God, I know you won't give me more than I can handle… WELL, I CAN'T HANDLE ANY MORE…I AM GOING TO DIE!"

I picked myself up, recharged and ready to fight. The Lord had answered my prayers and had given me more strength. I dove into research and noticed that diet kept coming up on many of the internet sites that I had visited. The gluten intolerance really stood out because my sister-in-law had just been diagnosed with a gluten intolerance and she had shared with me that she never knew how sick she felt until she removed the gluten. She had grown up feeling ill and had come to view it as "normal." I thought to myself, "My poor little boy is in pain and he doesn't know how to communicate with me."

Alright, let's clean out the pantry! I removed everything from the pantry and called his teacher to let her know that Gannon would be following a strict diet. He was not allowed any food other that what I sent for him. There was a moment of silence on the phone after I gave my instructions and then I heard, "Mrs. Scheer, I just need to tell you that there is no scientific proof that a special diet will help Gannon." I told her that I didn't need scientific proof; I needed proof from families that had experienced improvements through diet. Well, this turned out to be one of our most important protocols. Within three months, our baby spoke his first complete sentence. That sentence was, "I love you too, mommy!" JOY! We knew that we were on the right track, and we made an appointment to see a DAN! (Defeat Autism Now) Doctor. That same teacher told us that she was a believer in the gluten-free diet now after witnessing Gannon's speech explode and his ability to finally potty train!

Over the next two years, we implemented protocols for yeast, bacteria, and viruses. Gannon was speaking more, however he was still a runner and full of pain and anxiety. We couldn't go anywhere in public with him for fear that we would lose him; he was fast on his feet and could vanish in only a moment's time. He knew no fear and would go away with anyone. We became prisoners in our own home.

I needed help, so I found an autism support group meeting. Off I went. I walked into a room with about twenty moms who had children with autism. Throughout the evening, I would see photos of children at Disney World, and hear about adventures at Chuck E. Cheese. I left the meeting, got in my car, and CRIED my eyes out! Disney and Chuck E. Cheese…how??? We couldn't even think of going to any of these places because our son might hurt another child, get lost, or go with a stranger and never come back! I felt so alone…I didn't even fit in at an autism support meeting! Again, I prayed for help and later found another group with families more like ours. I finally felt like I was not the only person alive that was going through this!

Age five-and-a-half brought our worst day ever. It was a summer's day and I was upstairs doing laundry. My phone rang and a lady on the other end said, "I have your son." I lost my breath for a moment and then starting running through the house to find Gannon. My last stop was the back door, and there I found two boxes stacked up…boxes that Gannon had put there to climb on and release the dead bolt…and he was gone. The lady then told me that she was at the entrance to our subdivision with Gannon.

I jumped on my bicycle and raced to the front of our subdivision which is three blocks from our home. When I approached, I saw two police cars, four police officers, and my son in his underwear, no shoes, and no clothing. I ran up to Gannon and picked him up and in that moment, my mind raced. Was the police officer going to question my parenting? Was he going to take Gannon from me? What was going to happen? I must have had a horrified look on my face because when I made eye contact with one of the officers, he looked at me and nodded that is was okay for me to leave with my son. I took Gannon home and put him on the couch to talk to him. He was like an empty shell and looked like someone had stolen his soul. He had no fear, no remorse, and no idea what had just happened. I remember saying, "Gannon, where are you?" He mumbled the words, "I don't know." I left the room and sobbed. I was numb with worry of what the future would hold for him. I knew we had to do more for this child.

It was now time to enter kindergarten and we had no idea where to enroll our son. We searched and searched, and finally decided to try him in a Christian school and see how it went. The teacher was not equipped to handle Gannon and it was very obvious that we needed to move him.

Next stop was a kindergarten classroom with a one-on-one aide. This did not work either. He was throwing chairs, eating dirt, and urinating on the playground. The stress level in my body was reaching an all-time high and I needed to find a solution. I spoke with the school district's autism consultant, who told me about an incredible teacher in another school who ran an emotionally impaired (EI) classroom. I did not want my son in a classroom with children who might teach him more bad behaviors. She assured me that this would be a great fit for Gannon and that this particular class had two children with autism in it, as well as nine other children with only mild behaviors. She assured me that the teacher had a handle on it.

I called the director of special education and left an urgent message regarding this new classroom. I left three messages total, and then decided to call the superintendent, as I knew there was only one spot left in this classroom and I needed to get it for my son. Sometimes you need to go to the top to get things done, and when it's your child, you can't hold back. I set up a meeting with the head teacher in the EI classroom. Gannon and I went to check it out. I told her ahead of time that Gannon had become obsessed with the color blue and elephants, and I needed a teacher that was strong enough to not to give in to his obsessions. Everyone at the other two schools had catered to his outbursts to keep as much peace as possible which was not teaching him anything.

She immediately challenged him by giving him a carpet square with a giraffe on it knowing that he would explode because it was not the elephant. She handled him beautifully and I knew this was the place for our Gannon. Her calm, yet firm approach was just what he needed. Finally, after three schools in three months, we had found our home.

I went to a DAN! Conference and heard a parent panel speak about chelation. There was one mom who really stood out to me after she showed the before and after video of her son. Her son reminded me of Gannon. I knew that this was a therapy that we were now ready to try. During the next two years we were fortunate to see many improvements. His world was opening up to other interests and his anxiety level was dropping. He could now sit with the family while we sang Happy Birthday, and not run screaming out of the room. We then added Hyperbaric Oxygen Therapy (HBOT) along with more new supplements, and had more improvements.

We were able to go to the movie theater for the first time ever without Gannon running out with his hands over his ears. In fact, when we walked into the theater, Gannon went down to the front of screen, spread his hands out and said, "This is great!" He was also able to ride his bike without training wheels, which he would not do just four months prior. He also made his way into the swimming pool for the first time ever. He would always run around the outside edge of the pool while all the other children played, and now he was going in with a swim toy, and kicking his legs all around the pool. He was making gains every day!

When Gannon was in third grade, he began to spend about twenty minutes each day in a general education classroom. He gradually increased his time in general ed to an hour each day, and then to two hours. We were very happy with his success, however he needed to become more independent and more socially aware and mature. We were switching things up with his protocols but somewhere along the way, we became stuck. We did not have any notable improvements over the next three years.

Then came the day that my dear friend SNAP! from the Thinking Moms' Revolution called me up to tell me about a new thing she had been trying with her son. I asked what the cost was because we were broke after all the treatments we had tried. She said, "Twenty-five dollars." I said, "Are you kidding me?" I immediately emailed the woman SNAP! referred me to who was helping hundreds of children recover from autism and told her I wanted to try her protocol. About a month into trying these drops we put in water, we were amazed that our son began to move forward again. His social skills increased tenfold. He was complimenting me, asking to help with chores, and becoming more responsible at school!

While on this protocol, we attended a social gathering and Gannon came back to the table and said, "Mom, I just did a good deed." "Really, what did you do?" "I was at the drink table and someone came up to the table so I poured their juice for them."

Next we went to a roller skating party with his school, and Gannon, who could barely stand up on skates, announced to us that he was going to be in the race. Holy cow, I was freaked out and happy at the same time. I did not want to discourage him but I did not want him to get run over either. The race began and we cheered wildly from the sidelines, "Go Gannon, go!" He came in last place and I began to make my way over to the other end of the rink to make sure he wasn't going to have a meltdown because he didn't win. The way Gannon handled defeat was one of our biggest struggles. He could not handle losing without having a meltdown. Well, not only did he maintain composure, he skated up to me and said, "It's okay that I didn't win, Mom. I had fun." I wanted to call Good Morning America right then and tell them that I had just witnessed a miracle.

We later added a parasite protocol to his schedule, and again we saw huge gains! He had now graduated from his self-contained EI classroom and was with his typical peers all day long. We were thrilled. We then did forty dives in a hard HBOT chamber and saw more incredible gains. He was now asking for different foods, and was not having attacks of anxiety. His busy days of school, math tutoring, and HBOT were being handled with ease and happiness. He became responsible for his own homework and did not get upset when we asked him to do it. In fact, he would go to his room and do it independently.

He became the star of his school talent show with his choreographed rendition of "Banana Phone" and was moved onto a competitive base-ball team at the Miracle League of Michigan. His social skills in school still needed work, but he was well loved by his peers. His personality was shining through. His hobby became joke telling, and at his 5th grade graduation he was awarded "Funniest Student" in the class elections.

September 2013 brought middle school! To say that we were nervous is a huge understatement. I was a complete wreck. Middle school is scary enough for any child, let alone one who had been through what Gannon had. He had shadowed a student during the prior school year's orientation and really liked the school. He was excited to get out of his elementary school but I'll never forget my thought on the first day. I felt like I was releasing him to the wolves. I was so afraid.

We went to orientation and then we went back in a couple of days before school began. We practiced his locker combination and his classroom route several times and he said he was ready. I realized that Gannon's locker was on the opposite end of the 6th grade hall and that he would probably have a hard time getting to his classes on time. I did not say anything to his teachers as I wanted to try my hardest to not be a "Helicopter Parent."

On the third day of school, Gannon came home and told us that he had been given a new locker and we needed to go in early the next day to learn his new combination. Gannon and I went to school early the next day. As we were approaching the lockers, I glanced down the hall to see locker number 54, a handicapped locker with a bright blue sign on it. It took all my strength not to burst into tears. I immediately began to peel the sticker off and I remained very calm for Gannon. The look on his face nearly broke my heart. After years of just wanting to fit in with everyone else, he had this locker that said he didn't. It may as well have had a big blinking light on it too!

A teacher walked by and told me that I was not allowed to remove the sticker because they had to have a certain number of lockers in the school for handicapped children. "Well, we don't need it, so it's coming off," I said. I then looked at Gannon and I'll never forget the words that came from his mouth. As he shrugged his shoulders and took a breath he said, "It's okay mom, it's just a sticker. I know I'm not handicapped." I said, "You're right Gannon, it's no big deal." My beautiful son had handled this situation better than I did. This time he was perfectly fit to handle a tough situation all by himself.

I went to the parking lot and sobbed. I was sad and happy at the same time, and so proud of my son! I called the principal and apologized for taking off the sticker and he told me not to worry about it at all. He felt very bad about what had happened and told me that they just gave him a number from a list, not knowing that it was a handicapped locker. I explained Gannon's history some more, and he felt really bad. He offered Gannon another locker and Gannon decided to keep the one he was given. "It's bigger than the others and easier to get my stuff in and out of," he said, "I think I'll keep it." I later noticed that all the handicapped stickers were removed from the larger lockers in the school.

I close this chapter with the words that Gannon spoke when he was near recovery. We were walking along the monuments in Washington D.C when he walked up to me and put his arm around me and shared these words with me. These are his exact words:

"Thank you for being the best mom in the world.

You love me and you heal me.

What would I ever do without you?

I want to go back in time to the good old days when I was little.

I am remembering those times when I was an infant and you held me all the time.

Oh mom, please don't ever leave this world,

I love you so much."

These are the words of a child who has beaten the odds and won his nine year battle with autism. He has "woken up" and he has taught our family more in the past 10 years, than we could have hoped to learn in our lifetime. I will be forever grateful for the support, encouragement and tireless help of my loving husband, kids, and Gannon's grandparents. I give all the glory to God for our strength and our son's recovery. Praise to you Lord Jesus Christ!

SHAWTY

My journey with autism recovery began like many others I am sure. I was the model of the OCD, type-A career woman that has become quite common in this day and age. I thought I had it all together. When we decided to try for a baby, I read all the books, took the courses, researched doulas and breastfeeding. What I didn't study at all were vaccines (everyone knows they are safe, duh!) or other toxic chemicals that we accept as "normal" nowadays. I made sure we killed every "dangerous" germ within a three mile radius through copious use of disinfectant wipes and bleach. I ate processed foods with additives, slathered my body with toxic lotions, body washes and perfumes. I micro-waved my food and had no concern for organic or the ramifications of genetically modified foods. I look back now and cringe at how much I didn't know when I thought I knew it all.

My pregnancy had a few issues but nothing major and although I wanted an intervention free birth, I got anything but that. I didn't go into labor on my own and my doctor was eager to induce. While I cancelled the first scheduled induction, I succumbed to the second when I was one week over due. What I didn't know at the time was the critical role cholesterol plays in activation of oxytocin receptors. Over the years, I was praised for my low cholesterol (112) and never was a word said about how levels that low are actually detrimental to physical and mental functioning. After 20-plus hours of Pitocin-induced labor, I stopped dilating at five centimeters and we went in for a C-section. My beautiful son came into the world screaming. Little did I know that would be the norm for us for years.

We deviate from the typical story here a bit. My son did not regress at 12 months like many do. He had reactions to his four month vaccinations where he received seven that day. He went from sleeping seven to eight hours a night to sleeping maybe four hours per night, no more than two at a stretch and screaming most of the day and night. I wore him in a baby sling and vacuumed to get him to sleep, the white noise was one of the few things that calmed him. I was assured that it was just "colic." But of course, it was brain inflammation as a result of vaccinations. He screamed so much immediately following his vaccines there was little I could do to calm him. Just as we would get him leveled out from the previous round of vaccinations it would be time for more and the cycle would start all over again.

Motherhood was something I prized more than life itself. I had always wanted to be a mother. And then I failed at it. I felt like a complete and utter failure. I had this tiny, amazing, beautiful child and I could not provide a world in which he would sleep and not scream. What was I doing wrong? Why couldn't I get him to stop screaming? Why do all the baby books say babies can feel their mother's emotions and yet when I sat sobbing from sheer exhaustion did my son look up at me and giggle? Why? I knew something was wrong, I just didn't know what. My concerns were brushed off as "That's odd" or "I've never heard of THAT happening before."

I quit my job because I feared someone would abuse him if we put him in daycare because of his screaming. I walked around like a zombie from sleep deprivation. I remember one morning my husband looked at me as I was in tears after yet another sleepless night and said "I'm worried about you." "You should be." I replied. When I asked our pediatrician about my son's lack of sleeping, I was brushed off with "We don't recommend giving infants anything to make them sleep, but give Tylenol if he's fussy from teething." Thanks for nothing. No trying to understand why he would not sleep, no looking into the underlying causes for the constant screaming, no help whatsoever was what we got from mainstream medicine.

By the time he was six months old he contracted chicken pox, and then again at three years old. His immune system was not functioning the way it was supposed to. Even with his first bout of chicken pox, he never ran a fever. His gaze was not on my eyes but rather my hairline. His other milestones were met until it came to language development. That was inevitably what got us early intervention at two and a half. Playgroups were a joke. He was in someone's kitchen cupboards looking for Tupperware lids to spin rather than being remotely interested in other children. He rarely acknowledged the presence of his baby sister. He still mouthed everything way past the age of appropriateness. Sleep was still nonexistent. He would alternate between screaming and giggling for no reason. The giggling was a sign of yeast overgrowth but we had no idea. We made modifications to our house to ensure his safety. My husband made a Dutch door so that he could not wander on the off chance I didn't hear him get up in the middle of the night. I learned to sleep very lightly and the slightest noise would have me up and bolting down the hallway towards his room. Our two story house scared me but the Dutch door at least slowed him down. He escaped everything; baby gates were a joke. Appropriate play was a mystery. Life was stressful to say the least, but that became our normal.

His diet was pretty "Standard American." He lived off of wheat and dairy. His favorites were cheerios and graham crackers. He was very schedule-driven and if we deviated, especially his nap schedule, there was hell to pay. He would not sleep in the car and anything other than his own environment caused colossal meltdowns. I mean colossal! We became "those" parents. We would rush out of gatherings to get our child to bed on time; we declined invitations, almost afraid to step out of our house for fear of sensory overload. Even trips to the grocery store resulted in hours long scream-fests and just as upset parents. I had a friend tell me I was "hiding" from the world. The stress took a toll on friendships and my marriage. My husband and I began to look to each other to place "blame." Those were dark days for our family.

The one good thing to come from a moms group I was a part of was a very special friendship. A mom I met had been an occupational therapist using DIR (Floortime) techniques before having her child. She was able to recognize very easily what I was struggling with. She helped guide me through our process of navigating early intervention and she opened the door to what would be an explosion of interest and knowledge when it came to food. She shared with me the opiate-like effects that both gliadin (wheat) and casein (dairy) have on the brain. She opened my eyes to the many and varied toxins, from MSG to addictive chemicals that are added to our foods. It was just the tip of the iceberg and I hit the ground running, first removing dairy and then wheat. Yes, it was hell at first but so worth it after a few months. That was the beginning of our journey of hope.

As a part of our state services through early intervention we needed a full evaluation for my son. I reached out to a local autism specialist at a renowned center. I was excited for my appointment and for some answers. After a long drive there, the stress of getting through the hours-long appointment with an infant and a toddler on the spectrum, we left dejected. We were given a diagnosis but nothing more. We were told to find a good speech therapist and she offered a prescription, but she would not even consider recommending enzymes. ENZYMES for shit's sake! Thanks for nothing! She would not speak of biomedical treatments, period.

After that, I searched out a DAN! Doctor in a neighboring state and attended my first DAN! Conference. I was soaking up every bit of information I could get my hands on. I learned about environmental toxicity, I listened to mainstream MD's speak about their OWN journeys with autism and how it changed their ways of thinking and practice. I read research study upon research study. I now had two children under three and every free waking moment was spent online or reading books. I was exhausted, stressed and overwhelmed, but at the same time, a fire had been lit and I would not stop until I made significant changes for my son, and for my whole family.

We did a full array of testing: urine, hair, blood, and stool. My child's bodily fluids traveled to more places than I did! We started piecing his puzzle together. We immediately started Methyl B-12 injections and logged our progress. There was significant gut dysbiosis, widespread inflammation, almost no natural killer cell activity. Our child had an immune system that had all but given up! Things started clicking, like how he got chicken pox twice and how he seldom ran fevers but on the rare occasion he did, his autism symptoms seemed to get better. We started Low Dose Naltrexone (LDN) for immune modulation, we started even more dietary interventions, low oxalate in addition to gluten and dairy free and we had many food allergies to navigate. We consulted with a nutritionist to help guide us through that maze. We tried many, many things. Some things worked really well, others didn't. There were ups and downs. We saw regression, we saw progress.

What also happened at that time was a transition from the "autism" classroom at my son's school to the integrated preschool class. He used to scream just walking by the integrated classroom, but now he spent the duration of his day there without issue. Teachers were stunned. They all saw his extreme reaction in the past, and to have him not only tolerate but flourish in the integrated class and not need the autism classroom was nothing short of miraculous. I shared with them that we had started a targeted biomedical approach after extensive testing, dietary fine tuning and supplementation.

We also found that my son was very low in cholesterol and yet had a very high IgG allergy to egg. We started a cholesterol supplement which resulted in pretty big cognitive and emotional gains. Things were clicking, yet we still had more work to do. Language was finally coming along. His sensory system appeared to be able to handle more input without major meltdowns. My husband and I celebrated once we got to the point where we could run more than one errand in a day without issue! That was huge for our family. Therapies started becoming more meaningful; he participated more and made progress faster once we started biomedical interventions. His anxiety was dramatically improved with supplement support. Putting him to bed would take hours before we added supports. My husband or I would have to lay with him until he fell asleep and then creep out of the room. If not, it would be a constant interplay of him calling out for us or coming to see if we were still there. He had compulsive thoughts about us leaving him (we rarely ever left him with anyone). He freaked out if he could not see us.

Our state coordinator regularly noted how well he was doing and how impressed he was at the changes. He also took copious notes on the various supplements. It is important to note that this is our journey and each child is different. We also tried a lot of stuff that didn't work, and some things had negative effects. Trial and error is going to happen until someone invents that darn magic wand.

We also did homeopathy. Each piece was a layer, peeling back and getting to the root issues. It took time. But thanks to methylation support and yeast treatments my son was sleeping (hallelujah!!) and that meant we were sleeping too. I felt like some of my sanity returned. His language made dramatic improvements. Gone were the repetitive behaviors like sitting on the floor spinning Tupperware lids. He responded when his name was called. We would see a re-emergence of that "foggy" behavior when his yeast would flare. We would see the aggressive, short fuse behavior when Clostridia was high and the two would "teeter totter." So when we treated one, the other would grow to fill its spot. We had to be smarter than the bugs. By God, I was going to beat these things that had such an impact on my child's brain. We started to see a light at the end of the tunnel. Options for kindergarten loomed in front of us and a highly academic charter school was a possibility after all! That was my own deadline I had given myself, I had to get him recovered enough by kindergarten. Looking back now, that was so silly but I wanted to make significant progress to give him the best start in school.

We did more work, I listened in on webinars, I picked other mom's brains, I cornered doctors in hallways at conferences, and I made it my job to learn as much as I could. That drive also opened career doorways for me in this field. I have also tried to mentor, blog and just give back as much as I can along the way. I remember what it was like in the early days, staring bleakly at a computer screen, wishing someone would respond to my post already! And then being frustrated when what worked for their child did not work for mine.

So where are we now? My son turned 10 six months ago. He wanted a Star Wars themed party with all of his friends. Yes, he has friends. He has play dates, loves Legos and Star Wars. He loves reading and playing basketball. He still gets speech and OT in school but we no longer have any outside therapies. When I meet new people and they have read my blog they assume I must be speaking about a different child when they meet him. They cannot accept that he had a diagnosis of autism, especially one as severe as it was. He and his sister have a "normal" sibling relationship, whereas before I don't even think he knew she existed. His recent report card notes a "stellar" year from his teacher. Riding home the other day he called my name. I turned to look and he had made a heart symbol with his hands and he says "I heart you mama." That's my boy! I think back to when all I was told was to "find him a good speech therapist." F U A!

What do we still see? A little remaining anxiety, fear of failure, he does need coaching on navigating certain issues that come up with friends and of course there still is residual damage resulting in some learning disabilities. We keep supporting him nutritionally as much as we can to keep repairing his brain and body. But, now he gets sick appropriately, his body fights off a bug and gets over it. We still do a special diet. It has actually morphed into a Paleo/SCD hybrid which is working really well for him. He still takes supplements. But, as of this writing we managed to resolve his yeast and Clostridia overgrowth. It took seven years but we did it. His beautiful blue eyes are clear. Moms, you know what I mean. There is no fog; there is no "out of it" look. I see my SON. The child who was in there all along but was held down by toxins, food allergies, dysbiosis, and who knows whatever other shit. I broke him out. AND YOU CAN TOO!

What we did is not extraordinary, others have too. Don't let anyone tell you otherwise. Recovery is happening, and my son is proof. We need to stand strong in our convictions that we are a generation of parents doing what many have said is impossible. We are recovering our children and undoing the damage done to them by man. My son was not born with autism. I hope my story serves as fortitude. Read it when you are exhausted and your child is in his or her room screaming, or giggling hysterically at nothing at 3:00 am and you are at your wit's end.

Know that while you may feel alone, you are not. There are thousands of us out there, and we know what you are going through. We know the exhaustion, we know the frustration, we know the RAGE you feel at the lack of help for your child. You are not crazy, you are not a bad parent, and you are not a failure. Read my son's story and know this can be your child's story too. Is it tough? It sure as hell is. But there is nothing more worthwhile in this world than to see my child flourish and love, be loved, laugh, connect with others, show affection, cry over hurt feelings, be alive and FEEL emotions. The road is long but we are beside you. Keep marching, keep reading, searching, asking, questioning, THINKING. We are here for you, we are sisters and brothers on this journey and we will not stop talking until we get our children back. Each and every one of them.

And most of all, cut yourself some slack. Get off the guilt trip and quit blaming yourself. I know you are doing it. I did it. I still fall into that trap sometimes. Guilt doesn't help anyone and it doesn't move your child forward. Let it go. Move forward and don't look back except to savor the good times. Keep your eye on that prize, go with your gut and never lose sight of what could be. Don't accept anyone's definition of your child's capabilities. Only your child will determine how far he can go, no damn test score should limit him. Roll with the punches, but don't forget to throw a few when you need to. You are your child's best advocate and savior. You know what is best; whether you think you do or not.

A few years ago, I went into my son's first grade classroom and spoke to the students about autism. We were still fairly new to our biomedical protocol and he was being bullied in that school. It was incredibly hard to have the conversation with my son about his autism and how his brain works differently. But a few years later he reminded me of that visit and he looked at me and said "I used to have autism but now I don't." He can recall certain aspects of those early days. It still brings me to tears, but instead of sorrow, they are tears of joy at the future that lies ahead of my amazing, sweet, loving son!

HOPPY

Over two years ago now, I was sitting in the basement with my 21 month old son Jack, my husband, and Jack's developmental therapist. My five week old baby boy was asleep upstairs. Jack had just finished his third weekly therapy session and run off to throw toys on the floor, as he did very often back then. Since we had not yet had a real conversation about what was going on with him, I decided to bring up autism with his therapist.

I knew the answer already, but having my fears confirmed by an expert broke my heart into a million pieces. She sat with us patiently, giving us little pieces of hope as she described seeing other kids improve by eliminating dairy and gluten. She mentioned Jenny McCarthy's book, which I immediately discounted ("Isn't she, like, anti-vaccine?"). Still, I read the book when she brought it to me the next week. I was desperate. I am so grateful to this day that our therapist was open-minded enough to put me on the right path.

The beginning of my story is not so different from that of most mothers of special children. My son was born vulnerable. He had lots of stress, was sick a lot, and received all of the recommended vaccinations. Around 18 months, we realized that something was wrong because he wasn't talking and barely looked at us anymore. He entered our state's Early Intervention program and started speech, occupational, and developmental therapy. That first day his therapist mentioned "autism" to us, I thought my life was over. I felt like I didn't know this beautiful boy at all anymore, and maybe never had. It seemed like the end of a dream. Really, it was just the beginning of a better life for all of us.

My son has been under stress his whole life, beginning with his conception. A year before Jack was born, our first baby was stillborn at 32 weeks. It was unexpected, unexplained, and unbelievably devastating to my husband and me. We decided to move forward quickly to try to ease the pain, and conceived Jack about five months after losing her.

It was a wonderfully uneventful pregnancy, but it was very stressful. I constantly worried that it would happen again. I had over 20 ultrasounds to monitor my son and ensure that all was well. My OB and high risk specialist agreed that I should be induced at 37 weeks. I was grateful for all of the interventions and just wanted him out and alive. I had no idea what I was setting him up for.

My induction lasted for three days. I was given drugs to dilate my cervix, then massive amounts of Pitocin to push him out. He needed vacuum extraction after I pushed for two hours and was too exhausted from the induction process to keep going. I was so unaware of these issues back then, and about the huge amount of stress I was putting my baby under by forcing him out early.

He was a beautiful baby, just shy of seven pounds at birth. He had a ton of dark hair and big dark eyes. But he was a tired baby. He could not stay awake long enough to nurse. He had terrible jaundice that required an overnight hospital stay when he was just three days old. I was instructed to give him formula or else he would never be able to excrete the bilirubin. I did as I was told.

The first several weeks of his brand new life were, again, stressful. He cried a lot. He would curl up like his tummy was just killing him. He would only sleep while moving, so he spent a lot of time in the swing, and we took a lot of car rides. I asked questions about dairy allergies, reflux, and why did he have so much gas? Our pediatrician brushed me off and said that there was no research to support any of my ideas. I cut out dairy from my diet anyway and it seemed to help. We found a new pediatrician.

Then, of course, the shots. He got them all. Once I counted up 29 different vaccinations between birth and 18 months of age. My son did not have an obvious regression after his vaccines. He was, however, constantly sick. He had colds, RSV, two ear infections, and a sinus infection before he was nine months old. He was in daycare and everyone told me this was to be expected, that it was building up his immune system. He never slept during the day; he was so stressed by the noise and commotion. They said he was a happy baby, which made me feel better, but now I know he was just in his own world. He spent a lot of time in the jumper as he got bigger — he would jump all day if we would have let him, trying desperately to organize his body and get the input that he needed. I wish I'd never put him there — I was so distracted by work that I didn't see what was happening.

When he was nine months old, my mom retired and started watching him full time. He seemed to catch up then. He started crawling, rolling over, and babbling a little, and the sickness faded. He was still a cranky little guy. He spent a lot of time jumping, playing with toys that lit up and played music, and watching TV — the only things that seemed to calm him. I stopped breastfeeding when he was 13 months old and I was pregnant again. After that, he steadily lost touch, and his developmental progress had slowed to a halt by the time he was 18 months.

I've never been able to pinpoint the moment or day or week that it happened. I've looked at photos, watched videos, and searched my brain for memories of his eye contact, his engagement, his development. Where did it all go wrong? I believe now that it was happening all along, and started even before birth. Gradually life became too much for him, and he faded away into his own world of repetitive play and sensory seeking behaviors.

I try not to dwell on the diagnosis, or my feelings about the causes of my son's condition. The guilt still gets to me at times. I vividly remember completely ignoring my own gut instincts about many things — the induction, formula supplements, daycare, so very many shots — but back then I didn't trust myself. I went with the flow. All of my friends did what I was doing, and their kids seemed perfectly fine. It was very difficult to accept that my decisions had caused so much trauma for my son, but knowing that there were treatments I could try and actions I could take made it easier. My guilt propelled me to find ways to help him.

We removed dairy from my son's diet the day our therapist told us that it might help. Within two days, his eye contact was drastically improved. I needed no further reason to also remove gluten from his diet. By the end of the summer, I had learned how to read ingredient lists, make GFCF meals at home, and knew I should probably avoid the processed GF items and eat only whole foods. It was an easy sell for me, since I'd always believed that organic is best and had made all of his baby food. I decided that if it was good for him, it was good for all of us, so it became part of our lifestyle very quickly.

It took me several months to decide how I felt about the vaccination issue. While it was too late for Jack, I had a brand new baby boy to make decisions for now, so I got to work. He had already received the ridiculous Hepatitis B vaccine at birth, but I couldn't change that now. By his two month checkup, I had decided it would be best to do a delayed schedule, so I allowed the DTaP and Rotavirus vaccinations, and promised to come back in a month for two more. Instead of returning after that month, I kept doing my research. It was one of the most difficult beliefs to overcome during this whole process — I was surrounded by friends, family, the media, and my own beliefs that these horrid diseases would infect my baby if I didn't stick to the recommended schedule. I asked our pediatrician for advice, I read studies that contradicted other studies, and I searched my heart and mind for what truly felt right to me. During that time my baby received another vaccination for DTaP at four months and HIB at six months. By his nine month appointment, we were knee deep in supplements, biomed, probiotics, and therapy for Jack. I knew now that vaccinations were not right for my family, and I listened to myself.

I asked our pediatrician if I could delay any more until my son was at least in school. I told her that he was low-risk because he stayed home with me and I planned on extended breastfeeding. She tensed up and asked us to leave her practice. We left without argument, but some part of me felt rejected. I felt very alone, with no friends who had made this choice at that time, and I didn't like the feeling of being outside the norm. Still, I knew she had done us a favor. This was clearly not a person interested in partnering with me in the interest of my children's' health.

Around this time, I discovered the Thinking Moms' Revolution. I read the blog religiously every day, taking so much comfort in knowing there was a group of parents out there doing the same work and making the same choices as I was forced to make. I started to find more like-minded moms through Facebook groups that I could talk to about treatments, diets, and therapies, and life started to feel more "normal" again.

Just after his 2nd birthday, we started seeing a DAN! Doctor in our town. I felt lucky to have someone so close who could help him recover. As many other moms do, I was exhausting myself with research. I joined email groups, Facebook pages, read blogs, books, and other children's lab tests — trying to become a doctor and a chemist overnight to help my son. I understood most of it — how this vitamin helps that function, how to combine supplements appropriately, what his genetic mutations meant, how to kill yeast, bacteria, and parasites. The problem was, I didn't believe that any of these issues were the root cause of his problems. Every time the DAN! Doctor sent us home with a new supplement to add in, I felt a huge weight bearing down on me. I knew that if his little body didn't have enough of a particular nutrient, there was a deeper problem, one that would not be solved by giving him a synthetic version of it. We did a round of antifungals, along with a ton of probiotics and supplements, including B12 injections, and saw almost no improvement. We considered chelation and parasite protocols. My gut told me this was not the way for us, and this time I listened.

I started to understand that the stress we had caused him through his birth and experiences as a baby needed to be removed at a deeper level. For us it wasn't about metals, or parasites, or yeast. These issues were just symptoms of greater disease and dysfunction in the body. Our kids have problems with all of those things, but I firmly believe that our bodies should be able to balance themselves, when given the right environment.

Homeopathy entered my world in March 2013, when my son was 2 ½. Every time I saw it mentioned in one of my autism groups, I felt compelled to look into it. I did not fully understand how it worked, but I went with my instinct and made appointments with two different providers, which I cancelled when it just didn't feel right. Finally, I found Rudi Verspoor. At that point I couldn't find anyone who had worked with him, but when I read about his practice something really resonated with me.

The first time I talked to Rudi was over a year ago now. I listened to him explain that stress and trauma creates disease and imbalances in our bodies, but that Heilkunst (the medical system that he practices) can systematically remove these traumas. He told me that most cases take about two years to resolve, depending on the complexity of the situation. We were to create a timeline of my son's traumatic events, starting with the most recent, all the way back to pregnancy. Once those traumas were cleared, Rudi would then treat for the inherited disease patterns, or miasms, that are passed down from our ancestors and affect us all. He warned that there might be negative reactions to some of the remedies my son would take, but that it was all part of the healing process, likening it to the process of tearing down an old house and rebuilding a new one. Finally, an explanation that made sense to me! I knew now that we were on the right path.

We started seeing results within the first six weeks. My son had suffered from low energy and fatigue most of his life, but with Heilkunst he gradually perked up. He was better able to handle his therapy sessions, and he learned to jump and climb quickly. He started gaining new words and putting more words together. He was more engaged with us and more present in our world. Where he had previously wandered away or flat-out resisted social situations with noise, commotion, and strangers, now he was diving right in, watching the other kids and enjoying himself. I knew we had a long road ahead, but seeing all of these positive outcomes showed me that my instinct had been right.

Soon after I dropped almost all of the supplements that he had been on, and his energy improved even more. He still takes a probiotic, digestive enzymes, and cod liver oil, all of which help his digestion and immune system function. I hope someday he won't need these, but for now, it's working well. We've been able to add in some foods again that he had a high IgG reaction to just a year ago, with no apparent downside.

My whole family is being treated with Heilkunst now. We just endured a winter that sounded like it was of horrible illness magnitude from the constant complaints I heard from friends about their sick children, but my kids never had more than a sniffle. Removing blockages that damage our immune systems and eating whole, organic foods has kept us strong and healthy.

Jack is currently enrolled in a mainstream preschool, and he seems to love it there. He is obviously behind the other children in many ways, but having him enjoy school is my main objective for now. His social anxiety has completely disappeared, and he is slowly learning to express himself more and participate in classroom activities. My younger son is nearly two years old, and is wonderfully typically developing, even advanced for his age. There was a time when I lived in fear that he would be taken by autism too, but he's had the benefits of all that Jack taught us to keep him safe and healthy. Every new skill he develops and word he says is a blessing for which I never fail to thank God.

One of our recent challenges has been to find a therapy model that works for Jack. Though I wholeheartedly believe that Heilkunst is ultimately what will bring him back to health, I also feel it is important to be doing something to actively work on language, motor skills, and social connections. I'm also incredibly impatient for full recovery. Jack always resisted traditional speech and occupational therapy. We learned some great activities, but it was not time well spent for either of us, as he cried and fought all the things that were challenging for him. When he aged out of Early Intervention at three years old, we decided not to pursue therapy privately. He briefly received services from the school district, but it was more of the same — trying to force him to complete activities that he has no interest in, and not using his natural motivation to help him learn. I received a lot of criticism from his former therapists and teachers for discontinuing his therapies, but again I followed my instinct.

After spending the fall researching other possible programs that would help, I discovered Becky Blake, founder of Creating Super Kids. She travels around the world to families' homes to set up individualized programs for their children. Having had a child with autism herself, she spent the last 20 years learning techniques to help their brains and bodies work together better. Becky has developed a model for removing stress, strengthening motor skills, improving language and communication, correcting digestive issues, and more. It's truly amazing that she has figured out how to put together so many different therapies and methods to help children of all abilities. Even better, her theory that stress is the main cause of autism and related disorders corresponds perfectly with Heilkunst, and seems to work in much the same way, albeit on a different level.

Within a few days of starting Becky's program, my son was already speaking more. He is more observant, telling me what he sees and what he wants more frequently. His body seems less out of balance, and he loves the activities that she has set up for us. He is better able to imitate body movements and control himself. He finally learned to take off his socks, and is working on other clothing now too. Hopefully within the next few months I will have much more progress to report.

I have incredible hope for Jack and for our future as a family right now. He has taught me so much about life in the short time he's been here. Our family is stronger and healthier because of him. Most days now, I feel as though my son is healing me rather than the other way around. I wish that his life was easier and that he hadn't had to endure so much trauma, illness, and frustration, and I would give anything to take that away from him. But I can't say that I regret anything. I made the best choices for him that I knew to make at the time. When we know better, we do better — and I wouldn't know better if it weren't for my sweet little guy. So do your best, learn everything you can, and above all, TRUST YOURSELF. Your instinct will never lead you astray, but sometimes it can be hard to hear over all of the noise we have to sort through. Learn to hear that voice inside your head, and do what it says to do. You are wiser than you know.

BARRACUDA

When I was pregnant, I read the Mayo Clinic Guide to a Healthy Pregnancy. I was so excited that I was going to be a mom! It was a rough pregnancy, but Sophia was born healthy and that was all that mattered to me. She hit all her milestones, but the perfect storm was on the horizon. It didn't happen overnight, it was a slow regression into autism. Between 12 and 18 months she had eight ear infections, all treated with antibiotics and lots of Tylenol, plus all her vaccines. Sound familiar? I had no idea what was happening to Sophia. After she had tubes put in her ears, I thought her words would come back and all the other symptoms would just magically go away.

I enrolled her in an early intervention program so she could receive speech therapy. Within a few months, I went from thinking Sophia was catching up and had sensory issues to wondering if there was more to it. My dear friend told me about a website called Generation Rescue. She said they had a screening test on their website for autism spectrum disorders. I took the screening test and it indicated autism. It all made sense: the toe walking, staring at ceiling fans, teeth grinding, turning lights on and off, not able to point or talk. At twenty five months, the doctor came to our house and assessed Sophia using the ADOS. The diagnosis was moderate to severe autism. The doctor went over her recommendations with my husband and me. The primary therapies were

RDI (Relationship Development Intervention) and sensory integration. She also suggested we take Sophia to Dr. Berger. It was overwhelming. I thought autism was a disorder that affected boys.

I called Dr. Berger's office the day after she was diagnosed. He had a six month wait list. I told my husband we'd have to wait, and I will never forget what came out of his mouth next, "Fuck that! We are starting Sophia on the gluten and casein free diet now!" A few days later it was Mother's Day. My husband, Eben, gave me two books, "Louder than Words" by Jenny McCarthy and "The Kid-Friendly ADHD & Autism Cookbook" by Pamela J. Compart, M.D. and Dana Laake, R.D.H., M.S., L.D.N. I read Jenny's book and Eben read the cookbook.

The first four months after starting Sophia on the GFCF diet was like the movie "Ground Hog Day." We'd wake up, have breakfast, Eben would go to work, Sophia would watch Baby Einstein (which I know now was visual crack cocaine), the therapists would come to our house, and by mid-morning this weird rash would appear on her face but it would be gone by the time Eben got home. We observed enough improvements however that we stuck with the diet. Although we saw progress, it was an extremely isolating time for Sophia and me. She had so many challenges it was hard to go out in public. We had in-home therapy, Eben traveled a ton on business, there was no respite care and no one wanted to babysit.

In a roundabout way I found a local chiropractor/nutritionist. She had a few patients on the autism spectrum. She recommended an IgG test and when the results came back, it was an a-ha moment. Although Sophia was on a GFCF diet, the test showed she was allergic to eggs, almonds, peanuts, blackberries, raspberries and garlic. I'd been giving her eggs for breakfast, and all she'd been drinking was almond milk, and her favorite fruit was berries. We immediately eliminated those foods and per her suggestion, started Sophia on a probiotic. The first week, Sophia had flu-like symptoms and some pretty nasty bowel movements, but the changes were awesome! No more constipation! No more weird rashes and zoning out! No more teeth grinding!

During this time, I got a lot of advice from friends and Sophia's therapists. Hearing people say "autism is a marathon, not a sprint" really pissed me off. Then again, I was so angry at that time I ended up pro-jecting on a lot people that were only trying to help. I lost most of my friends and it was a strain on family, all of whom lived far away and did not understand what it was like to take care of a child that was aggressive, had no sense of danger, no language, and didn't want to be touched. Back then, the only way I could get eye contact with Sophia was if I roared like a lion.

Fortunately, I met the most dynamic mom. Her name was Kari, and she had two kids on the spectrum. She listened to everything I had to say, and very gently guided me to the Age of Autism website. Kari and AoA became my family. I'd talk with Kari every day. At first she was a mentor to me, but soon became my best friend. She guided me on the education process, local services and supports and most importantly, she listened. I honestly don't know what would have happened if she hadn't entered my life.

At three years of age, Sophia started preschool in the public school system in a blended program. I didn't want Sophia in a contained autism unit because I didn't want her to be around children that would teach her bad behaviors. She received the maximum amount of therapies in school and we continued our sprint with RDI, OT, horse and aqua thera-pies. It was the first break I'd had in over a year. I no longer felt like I was under house arrest! I met other moms at school and at horse therapy, and I started attending a support group.

Sophia was doing well with all her therapies but school was a big disappointment. When I received her progress report at the end of the school year, it was a wakeup call. Sophia wasn't going to make it in a blended class. A mom I'd met at horse therapy advised me to switch to a contained autism unit. She advised me to get all the help I could now, with the goal of going mainstream. It was very hard to admit that I'd been in denial. Sophia had the very same behaviors that I had not wanted her to be exposed to, and a year into diet changes, probiotics and a few supplements, Sophia was nowhere near recovered.

That summer, Sophia started neurofeedback. First she had a QEEG which showed that she had moderate autism. I cried on the way home from the doctor's office, not understanding how she could still be moderate when we'd done all those therapies. Eben told me not to worry; she'd get better with neurofeedback and LENS therapies. It was practically overnight that Sophia progressed. She started to point and request with a grunt. She became interested in characters on Sesame Street and in books. It was the beginning of connections. I remember watching Sesame Street with Sophia and we watched a skit and she laughed. It brought tears of joy to hear her laugh. RDI had taught us about co-regulation, shared experiences and joint attention. Easier said than done, but with neurofeedback, it was happening!

The new school year started and I made the rookie move of telling her new teacher all about neurofeedback. All Sophia's negative behaviors were then blamed on neurofeedback and the more sessions she had, we realized that it really was causing negative behaviors, making it hard for Sophia to learn at school. Eben and I met with the doctor and we decided to hold off on LENS until Thanksgiving break. It was a really bad time and the occasional poop smearing turned into a daily event. Eben and I couldn't figure out why this was happening, and sadly, although she was almost four years old, she was nowhere near ready to be potty trained. Eben and I were fighting a lot over what to do. Although Sophia had made progress, she had plateaued and we were losing hope.

I was in a funk, but continued to read Age of Autism every day. I especially liked Kim Stagliano, and she mentioned that she had a new book coming out called "All I Can Handle" and would have a book signing party at the National Autism Association conference in St. Petersburg Beach, Florida. That was only a few miles from where we lived. I asked Eben if we could go but he said that it wasn't in our budget. Then my brother-in-law came to the rescue and bought us tickets to the conference as an early Christmas gift!

The conference was a game changer. Not only did I meet my hero, Kim Stagliano, but Eben and I met like-minded parents from all over the country. We split up and saw as many presentations as we could so we didn't miss anything. We drove home talking over each other, so excited and full of hope! The last day of the conference, Eben attended a presentation on mast cells by Dr. Theoharis Theoharides (Dr. Theo), the Professor of Pharmacology, Internal Medicine and Biochemistry, and the Director of Molecular Immunopharmacology and Drug Discovery Laboratory at Tufts University School of Medicine. Afterwards, Eben approached me in the lobby and said, "This is it! Hurry! We need to get to their booth!" I couldn't remember the last time I'd seen Eben this excited. As we rushed to the booth, Eben said he could barely keep up during the presentation which took me aback. My uber husband? We got to the booth, which was already crowded. We bought a supplement called Neuroprotek that Dr. Theo had formulated, and picked up literature.

I was sad that the conference was over, but Eben and I were back on track. We started Sophia on Neuroprotek and Eben diligently researched mast cells and brain inflammation. Two weeks later, we left for a much needed vacation in the Bahamas. I was worried about Sophia's poop smearing but it wasn't going to stop us. The second day of our trip, I opened Sophia's pull up and found a perfect bowel movement. I yelled to Eben to get the camera. Yes, I took a picture. This was Sophia's first normal bowel movement since she regressed into autism! We couldn't believe it! Every day was yet another normal bowel movement. Then Sophia got her first tan. We live in Florida and Sophia could be in the sun without sun screen on and she would not get a sunburn or a tan. Neither of us fully understood the critical role of mast cells but it was obvious Neuroprotek was working. We celebrated Sophia's fourth birthday on our trip. We just knew this was going to be Sophia's break out year!

Once home, we started back up with neurofeedback. I was nervous, but Eben insisted, and he doesn't take no for an answer, especially when it comes to helping Sophia. Guess what? No side effects! Now, how could that be? Eben tried to explain it to me but it was way over my head. Finally he said, Neuroprotek penetrates the blood brain barrier and reduces inflammation. Okay but how do I explain this to my friends?

Over the next couple of months, Sophia was on a roll. I hadn't said anything to her teacher. In fact, I didn't even tell her Sophia had resumed neurofeedback. Sophia's eye contact significantly improved. Her teacher was beside herself with excitement. Sophia started to wave! She was trying to be social! She became both sympathetic and empathetic! She was able to use the PECS cards at school to communicate! Finally, after a couple of months, her teacher asked me what we were doing, so I came clean. She wanted to understand, so I emailed her some of Dr. Theo's research. Friends noticed too and I sent them the same information. No one had a clue what all this medical research meant, so I asked Eben to create a document called Mast Cells for Dummies which has since morphed into a parent-friendly website on mast cell activation.

Life was really good but there was one thing I wanted more than anything else in the world. It happened two months after starting Neuroprotek. My first kiss from Sophia! It was magical, and I still get choked up just thinking about it. Her kisses taught me gratitude. I was finally able to move away from all the anger I had in my heart and it felt wonderful.

The months flew by and before we knew it we were in Chicago at our first Autism One conference. Eben and I had been sharing Sophia's story with Dr. Theo and his team and it was good to reunite. Sophia had a blast in the child care provided by Son Rise. Eben primarily hung out at Mast Cell Master/Algonot booth and I attended lectures and met the most amazing moms on the planet, and we friended each other on Facebook so we could stay in touch. Some of those moms went on to create Thinking Moms' Revolution. It took us a couple of weeks to come down off our conference high.

In July, Sophia was doing so well that we were able to attend a birthday party. She had so much fun swimming and bouncing on the inflatable water slide. Oddly, the next day, Sophia was a different child. I thought she was having seizures and it scared the shit out of me. I took videos and sent them to her pediatrician, Dr. Berger, Dr. Theo, and her neurologist. Dr. Theo gave me Dr. Martha Hebert's number and told me to call her. At the time, I didn't know who she was but he thought she could help. She not only took my call, but reviewed the videos and asked what we'd done the day before. When I told her about the party she explained that a chlorinated pool can sometimes bring on tics and Tourette's. She then suggested that I contact a hospital in Boston. I did, and they asked me a lot of questions about recent illness and strep.

I called my friend Kari and told her I didn't understand why they were asking these questions. Kari asked if there were any other symptoms. I said "yes," and told her about the extreme OCD, frequent urination, major sensory issues, separation anxiety, loud vocalization and constant stimming. Kari said, "I wonder if it is PANDAS?" Ding! Ding! Ding! Thank you Kari!

I hung up, called the pediatrician and told him that I thought Sophia had PANDAS. He'd never heard of it but said to come in the next day. When we arrived, he'd researched PANDAS and did a rapid strep test. The results were negative, but he said that didn't mean anything and wrote a script for azithromycin. That summer was brutal, and I could write a book on the evils of PANDAS/PANS. Instead, I want to tell you that it was a collaborative effort, and thanks to Dr. Berger, Dr. Theo, Dr. Hebert, Sophia's pediatrician and Dr. Tanya Murphy she was diagnosed with PANS. I purposely didn't include her neurologist in this list. He ran the ASO test, MRI, and twenty-four VEEG and determined she didn't have PANDAS, and said she needed to be on an anti-psychotic drug. I told him "The only person that is going to take an anti-psychotic is me, so I don't kill you!" When we finally got to see Dr. Tanya Murphy, she told me I'd made the right decision not to put Sophia on an anti-psychotic drug because it makes PANS worse not better.

Getting Sophia back took time. The major symptoms were kept at bay with azithromycin and probiotics, but she'd lost all her fine motor skills. She couldn't even use utensils. When she returned to school her teacher and therapists were shocked. We had to rewrite her IEP goals. It was really fucked up. Sophia was on and off azithromycin for ten months. The good news was after about seven months of having to be held down and forced to swallow pills, she learned how to independently take them! The bad news was that without azithromycin, PANS would always come back.

During my PANS research, I found a website called Regarding Caroline. It had an alternative PANDAS protocol. Yes, there was a way to treat PANDAS without antibiotics! At Autism One, I attended lectures on these alternative protocols. I will never forget meeting Caroline's mom. She empowered me to keep on going.

After our first autism conference, Eben began volunteering at conferences, working the Mast Cell Master/Algonot booth. He has a way of talking to parents and doctors about mast cell activation and the benefits of Neuroprotek. That year, at Autism One, some of these doctors recommended we try Biocidin in place of azithromycin. Knock on wood, since starting Sophia on Biocidin she hasn't had a flare! Goodbye PANS!

Mother's Day always reminds me of Sophia's autism diagnosis. That year was no different, or so I thought. Eben and I had been working with Sophia on potty training. It didn't take long for Sophia to start urinating on the toilet but she wasn't able to get to the toilet in time to have a bowel movement. Eben spoke with Dr. Theo and together they decided to increase Sophia's Neuroprotek dosage. A few days after increasing Neuroprotek, Sophia had her first bowel movement on the toilet, on Mother's Day! We opened up a bottle of champagne we'd been saving for a special occasion and celebrated.

Now that Sophia was potty trained, private schools were an option. I found the perfect school for Sophia. They reviewed her IEP, FBA and met her, and it looked like she was a good fit. All the school needed was a progress report from her teacher. After they reviewed the report, they determined she would not be able to attend because they couldn't keep her safe. Sophia was a runner and they weren't equipped to handle runners. I was devastated, but it was for the best because Sophia attended a public school that year with an amazing teacher, aides, principal, therapists and behavior specialist. The school even advocated for a personal aide, and three months into the school year Ms. B. became Sophia's aide. A few months later, the school worked together and got her to stop running!

A mom I'd met at conferences started a Facebook post on Fridays called FUA (Fuck You Autism). She'd write about something great that her sons had done that week and then asked us to share our stories. At first, I'd post that Sophia didn't do x this week, but it didn't take long for me to catch on. Soon I was on a roll, and everything Sophia did, whether it be picking her nose, great fine motor skills, to shaking her head no, became a FUA accomplishment. It changed the way I thought about Sophia. Celebrating the positive and sharing with other parents is addictive and to this day is what keeps me going.

Time was flying by and it was conference time. I'd been looking forward to the National Autism Association conference because the keynote speaker was the one and only Eustacia Cutler. I'd read her book, "A Thorn in My Pocket," about raising her daughter, Temple Grandin, and couldn't wait to hear her present. Not only did I hear her and have her sign my book, I had the privilege of having dinner with Eustacia! She asked me to tell her about Sophia. She didn't like that Sophia was in a contained autism classroom. She went on to tell me about Temple's childhood and the wonderful Montessori school Temple had attended. She said it was there that Temple found her love of animals and learned to play. It sounded wonderful, but I explained that just didn't exist in Florida.

The last day of the conference, I went to the Speech Nutrients booth. I'd tried Speak supplement when it first came out, but Sophia didn't take pills then and wouldn't drink anything we tried to cut it with so I gave the bottle away. I completely forgot about it until I heard Dr. Sears's presentation at the conference and he mentioned Speak. Duh, she takes pills now! I was going to buy some, but the woman at the booth said, "Why not try it first?" and said "Open your bag." She gave me a month's supply of free samples.

A week into starting Speak, Sophia started to talk! We went to the same park we'd been going to for years and suddenly she walked over to the rock climbing wall and scaled it! Talk about FUA! Holy guacamole! Sophia had words and gross motor skills! I called the company that makes Speak. I had to understand and explain to, oh I don't know, everyone that came in contact with Sophia that knows her, why suddenly right before her sixth birthday she started talking! The vice president of the company, Speech Nutrients, told me that it just wasn't possible. She asked me what else we were doing. I told her we learned the hard way only to do one thing at a time. I then told her that perhaps the Neuroprotek we'd used for the past two years optimized the results of Speak. Who really knows why, but it worked! Sophia went from preverbal to verbal in a week! Did she instantly start talking like her peers? Hell no, but who really cares? She went from hurting me every day to saying no! The word "no" was music to my ears! Hearing "Mommy" even now, a year into Sophia talking just melts my heart.

In the meantime, I heard a rumor that our local Montessori school was starting an autism program. Could it be true? I called the school and scheduled a meeting. Yes, it was true, and they asked if I could share my resources. I remember sitting in the meeting sharing my resources and wishes. They said yes to everything, except converting their pool to a salt water system. I cried. Not because of the pool, but because they not only listened to me, but they said yes!

Sophia is now at that school and thriving! Ironically, the name of Sophia's school is the same as Temple Grandin's childhood school. To be honest, I never thought that Sophia would come this far in school. She is learning cursive, multiplication, has no need for a FBA and is reading! I post every gain on Facebook because it gives me strength, and I believe Sophia is a better person. FUA! and Never Give Up!

SPARTAN

My intent is to speak straight to your hearts, especially to the hearts of mothers with newly diagnosed children. I want you to know that I know how you're feeling right now. Lost, alone, and sad. I've been there. I can remember exactly what it felt like in July 2011, sitting across from the Naval Hospital physician being told these words: "Autism. New normal. Get him ABA therapy, occupational therapy, speech therapy." Not once was anything mentioned about the underlying medical symptoms of today's autism. When I actually questioned the doctor about my son's horrific constipation, I was told it was just "part of the autism" and was actually told that diet modification often times doesn't work, and other alternative treatments could be dangerous. At the time, we were stationed in Okinawa, Japan because my husband was a Marine. The first step in our journey was to return to the United States through a process called a tour conversion.

It took about six months for the tour conversion to go through, and it felt like an eternity. Once we were settled in our new home, I started my action plan. I refused to let this illness have my son. He was not neurodiverse; he was very sick. I was very fortunate to have spoken to a fellow military spouse who put me in contact with one of the best DAN! Doctors in Southern California. By this time, my son was two and a half years old, and I was more than eager to get the ball rolling. One of the first books I read while waiting for our appointment with our new physician was Dr. Kenneth Bock's book "Healing the New Childhood Epidemics." I had heard of Dr. Bock when I worked at a radiology facility in Kingston, NY. How ironic that I would end up needing his information ten years later. As I read each page of his book, I became more and more certain that my son's autism was treatable and it gave me a good idea what to expect at our first appointment with his new doctor.

It was almost one year after Connor's diagnosis that we had the first meeting with my son's new physician in June 2012. It ended up being more than I could have hoped for. I was treated with utmost respect and I was validated that indeed my son's underlying issues could be treated. We ran extensive blood, stool and urine analysis on him, and what they showed was both a relief and heartbreaking. My son had horrific gut damage, a depleted immune system, mitochondrial issues, vitamin D deficiency, and a high viral load.

After absorbing all of the results, I had renewed determination to get my child back. Almost one year later, we finally had a game plan in place. The first thing we addressed was healing Connor's damaged gut. With simple diet modifications, his digestion got better and his hand flapping decreased. After that, we started treating each ailment one by one and he continued to come back to us. It wasn't until almost one year of healing these issues that we then started to implement other therapies.

One of the biggest reasons I decided to actively write about my son is because I want you to know that you have choices, many choices, in regards to treatment for your child. Just because a doctor sits in front of you and tells you that your child was born this way — when you know different — does not mean you have to accept it. Seek out alternative treatments such as biomedical, homeopathy and chiropractic care. It may all seem daunting at first, or maybe too costly, but my question is: What is more important than your child's health? Instead of reading poems about Holland, I want you to research Bernard Rimland and exhaust every single resource available.

This year, the CDC just released their new autism numbers as one in 68 on the very same day my son was officially released from his IEP for special education. He has recovered. As I sat in front of the therapists and they signed off on my son's capability to stay on point with his peers, my first feeling was to rejoice, but it was quickly replaced by the sadness of those new numbers.

This has got to stop! It's up to us as mothers to protect our children. We are their biggest advocates. You can beat this; you can pull your child out of the throws of today's medical autism. We are here for you every single step of the way, and on the other side called recovery.

ORACLE

Oracle — *noun: Any person or thing serving as an agency of divine communication.* An oracle is someone who foretells the future; someone who has a deeper insight on what's to come than most people. Perfect! My friend TEX from TMR chose my nickname, and based on my experiences, it is totally me. While I am not a psychic or a medium myself, I do have vast knowledge of the subject matter, and have used it to help my child with autism heal. My book, *The Other Side of Autism* is a channeled book, where a medium and a spirit artist collaborated with me to help solve the autism puzzle. (www.theothersideofautism.com)

Now, don't roll your eyes and think that I am some airy-fairy freak. I actually was forced down the spiritual path and into the realm of mediumship as a way of healing grief after the sudden loss of my first husband nearly 20 years ago. After my now 15-year-old son was diagnosed with autism at age three, I learned a lot about healing him through this type of communication from my loved ones (and others) in spirit. In fact, prior to writing my book, I first learned that he was allergic to wheat during a session with a psychic medium. I had him tested, and indeed he was allergic to wheat, among many other things.

Backstory. My older son, Trevor, was born in 1998, at the beginning of the "autism epidemic." Now, when I say "autism," I mean regressive autism. The "not born with it" variety. It drives me insane that people can't figure out that there are different forms of what they are calling autism. I'm talking about sick children, not neurodiverse people with the same label. Not even remotely the same thing. This distinction needs to be made so we can treat the sick ones and love the rest.

My son was born 10 days late by natural childbirth, he had a perfect 10 on his APGAR at birth, and we were overjoyed to have a healthy baby (or so we thought). He was a blond-haired, blue-eyed beauty who walked and talked at nine months old, and met all of his developmental milestones early. I did everything to keep him healthy and happy, including naively vaccinating him. My husband's parents were Christian Scientists and did not vaccinate their three boys because of their religious beliefs (yes, they do exist). When the subject came up, I remember telling my husband that I thought it was "child abuse" not to vaccinate your children. I carry the burden of that choice, and feel like the Antichrist for my uneducated decision. Although my husband is from a non-vaccinating family, they understood that 99% of the rest of us did then, and the choice was ultimately mine. Ugh, if only... The pressure, fear, and threats from the medical community won me over.

When Trevor was between ages one and two, something changed. He stopped looking at the camera while I videotaped him; we jokingly called it the "Elmo Trance." He started walking on his tiptoes, started lining up his matchbox cars into elaborate patterns and got very upset if they didn't touch. His language that he was picking up suddenly stalled. He understood over 20 words at nine months and said "mama," "dada," "dog," "car," and "what's that?" He had 60 words at a year old. He pointed, played peek-a-boo, and was very physically strong and agile with great gross and fine motor skills. He fed himself with a fork at his first birthday party, then a year later, I was feeding him his birthday cake or he ate it with his hands. How do you lose the ability to hold utensils? He started pulling people to get what he wanted instead of talking. We had no clue what was happening.

He started limiting the foods he would eat to only wheat and dairy products. He was bottle fed (stupid me again), and was very colicky and had to switch formulas seven times in 15 months. I now know why he couldn't tolerate them, but I'll get to that later. He started waking up a lot at night, and wouldn't take a nap unless we drove him in the car. He was very sensitive to his environment, but so am I, so I didn't find that very concerning. He didn't like tags on his clothes (nor do I), he covered his ears at loud sounds (I sleep with a pillow over my head to block out sound), and he smelled things (I smell all food before I eat it). I also walked on my toes as a kid and nicknamed myself "Twinkletoes," so I could even reason that one away.

But then he began to do some really peculiar behaviors that I couldn't reason away: he wouldn't walk on grass with bare feet, he always had to carry toys or other objects in one or both hands, he looked at things really close to his eye and moved it back and forth, he made "hand puppets" with his fingers often looking at them out of the corner of his eye, he would freak out for no apparent reason and he started humming a lot. We went to a mommy and me gymnastics class and he just seemed more defiant than the other kids, he did not look at or listen to the instructor, and just wanted to do his own thing and run around and jump on the trampoline. I wanted him to be a gymnast, like me. It didn't take long to realize that it wasn't in the cards.

I was eight months pregnant with Trevor's younger brother, Damon, when Trevor went in for his three year check-up, and when his score on the Denver Prescreening Developmental Questionnaire that we filled out each time was worse than the previous visit, our pediatrician was concerned. I'll never forget the moment when I asked her what she thought was going on with my son. Before she could answer, I felt as if the room changed and I was alone in a tunnel and I heard the word "autism" in my head before she said it herself, and then the room returned to normal. I chalked it up to some strange pregnancy thing at the time. She referred us for an evaluation with a developmental specialist. On the infamous September 11, 2001, we had the evaluation which led to my son's first official diagnosis of autism. My world also imploded and crashed down around me. These were very dark days for me. Postpartum depression, newly diagnosed child, PTSD watching young widows grieve on TV, new baby, no sleep. Dark days…

More dark days were to come. Like most autism families, there were fights about money, therapies, depression, grief, listening to a screaming child for hours, stress, helplessness, blame, anger, and unhealthy coping strategies. Like many other autism families, my husband and I divorced. For three years. Fun fact…we got remarried! I do — part two. The grass is not greener on the other side, it's greener where you water it.

When my son was diagnosed, there was no Facebook, TACA, Generation Rescue, or TMR. There was no autism road map, so I had to create one for my son the best way I knew how. No one was really talking about diets, biomedical treatments, or any of the other things that are popular now in the autism community. Parents now truly have the best chance for recovering their children when they can start early. My son was five before I even started the diet with him. He had been suffering and still getting vaccinated for two more years after his diagnosis until I figured it out.

Trevor was evaluated by the school district as well at age three, and started in a developmental preschool program. They wouldn't even call it "autism" then, it was called "developmental delay" until he was six. So, he wasn't counted in the autism numbers. Once he started school, he was getting sick all the time from the other kids coming to school sick. I remember him having numerous ear infections back to back and put on all different antibiotics. We had been living in Southern California when both of my boys were born, and then when my younger son was seven months old, we moved to Nevada. Trevor started in another developmental preschool there. I remember the week we moved, Trevor got another ear infection, and we didn't have a pediatrician yet, so his old doctor phoned in another antibiotic prescription for him.

I read everything on the internet I could find about autism during every free moment, and voraciously read books on healing autism. My two early favorites were "Impossible Cure" from homeopath Amy Lansky and "Unraveling the Mystery of Autism and Pervasive Developmental Disorder" by Karyn Seroussi. Based on the later book, I began dabbling in the GF/CF diet, but it seemed too hard and he wouldn't eat anything I made. Mind you, I had to make it from scratch or order it online, because there weren't the options that there are today in the grocery store. I had briefly given up, until I had that reading with the psychic medium I mentioned earlier, who in no uncertain terms told me that wheat was making him sick, and I needed to strip it completely, and that he would get hungry and eat. And he did.

My son was five at this point. During this time that I decided to give the diet another whirl, a friend with a gluten allergy suggested that we started seeing her doctor, which we did. He was an Integrated Medicine Doctor, a former MD turned DO, who used homeopathy and herbal remedies. He used a non-invasive form of testing for food allergies, pathogens and toxins called an EAV, or Electroacupuncture According to Voll. It sounds like hocus-pocus, but I didn't trust that the people who got us into this mess were going to get us out.

I ended up doing the allergy testing on myself, my other son, and my mom as well. We started using allergy desensitization drops to hopefully get rid of our allergies. We also discovered through the EAV that Trevor had mercury, yeast, parasites, and clostridia difficile (from all the antibiotics). I did an Organic Acid Test, which confirmed many of these things (I was still unsure of the accuracy back then). We treated the metals, fungus, and pathogens with homeopathic detoxosodes. We also treated miasms and tried a constitutional homeopathic remedy. My son was getting better!

We eliminated all of the foods he was allergic to. I especially noticed when we took wheat out of his diet, it seemed like he felt pain for the first time in his life, and actually cried when he fell down. He used to wipe out and not even flinch. He said "too hot" when he put his foot in the bathtub. Things were happening.

I recently dug up the list of allergens that my son had at age five (I learned of more later on). Among them were: banana, beef, chocolate, corn, lettuce, milk, sugar cane, wheat, yeast, spelt, gluten, chlorine, red dye, yellow dye, formaldehyde, hydrocarbons, MSG, phenol, sodium nitrate, tobacco smoke, wood smoke, numerous molds and yeasts, cats, dogs, histamine, house dust mites, and numerous trees, grasses and weeds. My poor baby! Allergies affect people in different ways, causing multiple symptoms and can even affect the brain. They put stress on the body and prevent it from healing.

Being the impatient person that I am, I did not want to wait 12 –18 months to desensitize these allergens with the drops, and a friend had told me about our new doctor's old business partner, who did a quicker form of allergy elimination called NAET (Nambudripad's Allergy Elimination Technique). It involved muscle testing to find the allergens and then used acupuncture for adults or acupressure for children to instantly and permanently eliminate allergies. Count me in! We went to the new doctor for NAET. You can actually use the parent as a "surrogate" to do the muscle testing if the child is unable. This was a big treatment for him. I still didn't feed him the foods after they were eliminated, but it gave me some peace of mind in case he accidentally got something at school. I knew it worked on me. I was able to eat dairy again, never had to take allergy medicine again, and was able to be around a cat without having an asthma attack.

This was the start of my conversion to alternative medicine. After some real research and soul searching, I also stopped vaccinating both boys. My younger son was vaccinated until he was 15 months old and then I put a stop to it. Damon was very constipated, and I found out through our new doctor that he was allergic to milk, causing the constipation, in addition to many other things. He also had candida (both boys were born with thrush due to antibiotics I was given while pregnant), eczema, cradle cap (fungus), parasites, and mercury. We detoxed him as well with homeopathic detoxosodes.

His old pediatrician, whom I fired, tried to tell me that Damon had asthma, when he had bronchitis twice, and wanted to put him on steroids and a nebulizer. Damon wanted nothing to do with it, and he did not have asthma. He was sick with bronchitis two weeks before and again two weeks after a round of vaccines. I have no doubt that if I had continued to vaccinate Damon, I would have two "autistic" children. His brother saved him by teaching his mother what not to do anymore. Damon is a straight-A student and very talented.

As the next few years went by, I learned more and more and tried many different treatments and therapies for Trevor. He steadily regained skills every year, but he wasn't recovering as fast as I wanted him to. I kept searching and trying new things. I used homeopathy for all of our acute illnesses. If there is something that I feel is over my head, our doctor's program can pinpoint what virus or bacteria it is, and treats it with herbal and homeopathic remedies, not antibiotics, which do nothing for viruses anyway. The only time I would consider seeing a traditional Western Medicine doctor is in an emergency, like a broken bone or car accident. They are good for that.

When I did the sessions with the mediums for my book, I learned a lot about what happened to my son leading up to his decline, and also things that would help him get better. It wasn't just what was said via the spirit world, but who said it that was so remarkable. Without giving it all away, some of the things that were brought through in the sessions that were detrimental to my son were: my taking prescribed antibiotics and a painkiller (which was later recalled) during pregnancy for a respiratory infection, early cord clamping (depletes oxygen), the vaccines of course, especially the MMR (the rubella component is made from aborted fetal tissue), GMO food, wheat, pathogens and nuclear radiation. (The medium actually predicted Fukushima before it happened during our sessions!) It was made clear that there was brain damage done by vaccines and other factors. There is one other very big thing that I am purposely not going to mention here, you'll have to read the book to find out. Plus, I don't want to be put on a watch list. Oh wait, I probably already am. Let's just say that it also involves genetic engineering and pathogens.

Some of the things that were brought through that would help my son included: nutrition, especially eating non-GMO food. (I'm actually in the documentary "Genetic Roulette" after learning about this…long story), HBOT (Hyperbaric Oxygen Therapy, huge for him), alkaline water (we have a Kangen water machine), and much more. I was able to do 70 sessions of HBOT in the hard chamber, and he started waving to his friend at school and saying "Hi Austin." His mom called to tell me about it, and then they started doing HBOT. He also started buttoning his own shirts and putting on his own socks. Hello small motor skills! Each thing that was brought up to help my son, I tried, and he improved.

I believe that GMO's (Genetically Modified Organisms) in our food supply is a very under-rated causative factor for autism. There is a lot of new information coming out now, proving the connection. My son, born in 1998, was formula fed. GMO's were added into milk first, starting in 1996. Then corn, soy, cottonseed, sugar, and canola mainly. What is in baby formula? Milk ingredients, corn syrup, and soy. GMO's basically, unless it is organic. My son changed from formula to formula, tried soy, and cow's milk, and was intolerant of all of them. It was the GMO's. The built-in pesticides in GM corn are meant to rip open the stomachs of the insects that eat it. What do you think it is doing to a newborn with a compromised immune system? Leaky gut anyone? Other GM crops are "Roundup Ready" and engineered to withstand the herbicide Roundup (glyphosate). All the weeds die, but not the GM crop. Roundup has been linked to many health issues, including autism. Children's first foods are full of GMO's and wheat (another poison). I talk about it at length in my book, and Jeffrey Smith, who directed Genetic Roulette, has a lot of information on the connection between GMO's and autism on his website http://www.responsibletechnology.org.

In 2011, I also learned about Kerri Rivera and her protocol using MMS, now called CD, or chlorine dioxide. I became friends with Kerri, and we started her protocol, including the parasite protocol. My son made major improvements with this protocol, and it really showed in his behavior. His ATEC score dropped significantly and is now in the teens (depending on how I score him). Any number under ten is considered recovered. We did this for about two years, and I have seen so many dead parasites come out of my child, it's disgusting. And yes, I have the pictures to prove it. I am the pooparazzi. Kerri has helped well over 100 children who have lost their diagnosis, and thousands who have improved using her protocol. A few of the other moms in this book, as well as some of the original TMR's also used this protocol with different degrees of success. I met her at Autism One in 2012, we even sang Karaoke together, and am very proud to know her. She's obviously doing something right.

The most recent healing modality I've been using for my son involves the most advanced form of biofeedback, similar to the EAV that we used early on. It is called a Diacom, and it is Russian technology that they developed for and use in their space program to diagnose and treat the astronauts. Only a few practitioners in the U.S. have it. Using headphones, the computerized program "scans" your body, and compares the frequencies in your body against the frequencies of all pathogens, toxins, diseases, etc. and can even tell you what organs it is affecting. It can also reverse the frequencies, and treat the person, as well as make a water based remedy with the frequencies in it. It has been very enlightening and validating, to say the least.

During a recent session, we found an intestinal infection, and the pathogens that came up were the specific parasite species we had been treating for, along with Borrelia burgdorferi, the bacteria that causes Lyme disease (many children with an autism diagnosis have this), and Epstein Barr virus. Trevor was treated with the frequencies and later that night, and for the next few days, he had a red rash on his hands and feet. It was a viral detox, brought on by the energetic frequencies. Homeopathy is also energy medicine. So is Reiki and Reconnective Healing, which I also learned to do for my son. We also use essential oils and flower essences. Yes, I'm the one that's "out there." Our kids are exquisitely sensitive, and I find that these things work for him, and many others as well. There is more than one way to skin a cat. Frequencies can heal.

I recently requested copies of my kids' medical records from all of their past doctors from birth. I almost didn't want to look at them, especially Trevor's. Peeking into the past was a painful proposition. What stood out? Vaccinations every few months (34 total), numerous antibiotics for ear and respiratory infections including Cefalcor (in utero, as well as Darvocet, the recalled painkiller), 2 rounds of Amoxicillin, 2 rounds of Zithromax, 2 rounds of Augmentin, and Cefzil. There was projectile vomiting, and other medications including Mylicon drops for gas, Nystatin antifungal for thrush and later on Nystatin cream for a rash behind his knees. This was in the first three years of his life! I cried reading the doctor's notes.

Even through all of this, lots of the doctor's comments were on how well he was doing, how advanced he was, ahead of schedule…then it all went south. One startling thing I noticed in the records was that my younger son, whom I thought didn't have an MMR vaccine, actually did! Along with the DTaP the same day. I was mortified! These were his last vaccines. He was very sick two weeks later, just before I left the practice and ultimately turned to alternative medicine. I also noticed two Refusal to Vaccinate documents that I had signed! I was wising up!! Back in 2004. See, I am an Oracle…

So, where is my son today you ask? Is he recovered? The Holy Grail of autism. No, I cannot claim that. He is the best he's ever been. He's in a private school without an aide. He is verbal, but is limited. He can ask for what he wants to eat and do, but he won't ask me how my day was. He can read, write, do math, and type. We can take him anywhere now, and he loves going places. He is becoming more and more independent, trying to do everything himself. He is affectionate, and tells me he loves me, which is music to my ears. His laugh and giggles light up the room and everyone adores him. He is still recovering. There is no time limit on that. People recover from debilitating injuries and illness all the time. There has been a lot of damage done to these children at a critical time in their development, and it's not always an easy fix. From things this planet has never seen before, I might add. I will never give up trying to help him be the best version of himself, and for his body to be free of things that harm him.

What is the future that I see for our kids and for humanity at large? Even though it seems like an effort in futility right now to fight the powers that be, I do see a brighter future on the horizon. It will be the next generation. Their generation. The siblings. My generation is mostly a lost cause, unless they are personally affected, which is growing exponentially. And pretty much forget my parent's generation, unless they are autism grandparents, but even then…Try to convince someone to stop eating food that they have been eating their whole lives (that is now poison, and they're addicted to it). They won't, unless it directly affects them or a loved one, but even then… Gotta have that fast food, no time to cook.

Try to tell someone completely indoctrinated into the Medical Mafia that there is another way to heal. They won't listen; doctors know best. You're a "quack" if you look into other methods of healing, which were actually around for thousands of years before this messed up system of medicine hijacked ancient healing modalities.

"Science" proves it, don't you know? Selective science maybe, paid-for science, tobacco science. The studies exist that show what is happening to our kids, but when people don't have critical thinking skills anymore, and won't even read the other side, it makes everything that much more difficult. It is going to get worse before it gets better. It may seem like the modern-day David vs. Goliath, and it truly is. But truth will prevail, it always does. Tyranny can only go on for so long before the sleeping giants awaken.

And the people are waking up from their slumber, our kids are the catalyst to that. Because of our love for our children, and being the eye-witnesses to their regressions, we are tearing down the old, broken systems in medicine, government, food and education. We are exposing the corruption, and they are scared. We are owning our own power. There is power in numbers, and ours are growing.

Oftentimes, it is hard to see the forest for the trees. It is easy to be angry and unable to see the big picture. In hindsight and through in-sight, I can see the good that has come out of what happened to our son. If he didn't have "autism" we would still be eating and injecting poison, slowly doing who knows what to all of our bodies. We are literally human guinea pigs right now. Now, we only eat organic, non-GMO, gluten-free food. Yes, it's challenging, but it's worth it. We would still be taking pharmaceutical medicine, which merely serves as a Band-Aid, not getting to the root of illness. We have re-discovered ancient heal-ing modalities. We have cleaned up everything around us because of Trevor. Everything that we put in or on our bodies and in our home has changed. We are all planting seeds in others that we meet, and leading by example. Sharing their stories will prevent some of the lemmings from jumping off the cliff. Our children who were harmed are going to lead the charge, through us, to change the world for the better.

ROCKY

"Noah."

"NOO-AH."

"NOAH!!!"

I clap my hands in front of his face. My heart seems to stop beating. The room closes in on me as panic sets in. I've lost him again… My body tenses and I continue to watch and wait. Holding the phone in a vice-like grip, my knuckles begin to turn white. I suddenly remember my friend Diane is still on the other end. "What happened?" she asks. "I don't know, he just stares off and doesn't respond. It's like he's unconscious, but his eyes are still open," I explain. "How often does this happen?" "All the time, all day long."

Noah is back with me again, sitting in his highchair staring at Elmo on the TV singing the hotdog song, as he picks up a piece of waffle with his fingers and puts it in his mouth. I slowly exhale. I am able to breathe again.

The next morning is our 18 month wellness appointment. At 15 months, our local Regional Center diagnosed Noah with a Global Developmental Delay and a wide gait. And at 17 months, our occupational therapist added Sensory Processing Disorder and Hypotonia (low muscle tone). As a part of this diagnostic process, we would have to also rule out Apraxia, a disorder of motor planning that affects speech and movement. Dr. P. pops into the room a few minutes later "Hey guys! I will need you to fill out the MCHAT today." All trace of Dr. P's usual humor and pleasant demeanor begins to fade, replaced by a look of concern as he measures Noah's head. His head size has grown from the 25th percentile at 12 months to the 90th percentile at 18 months. Jason and I exchange nervous glances.

I complete the MCHAT and hand it to Dr. P. He scores it and frowns. He is from Israel, and until now I had always found his accent charming. But now, it is foreboding. "Hmm. Noah has failed the MCHAT. I am going to refer you to a neurologist to test for autism." Everyone becomes silent. Growing up in a large Italian family, I am accustomed to everyone talking loudly in an effort to be heard. I am not comfortable with silence. I hate the silence.

Later that day, I walk into Noah's nursery to wake him up from his nap and find him carefully walking a circular path in his crib, rhythmically humming. He no longer looks up at me as I approach him. Is this new? Or am I viewing my child differently now because I think he may have autism? He seems unaware of my presence. A feeling of emptiness envelopes my heart. "Noah… Noah… NOOAAH," I call to him. No response. "Why won't you look at me?" He focuses on his path. He methodically places one foot in front of the other, like a tightrope walker tuning out the world, intent on not falling into the abyss.

My despair increases as I fear I have lost a little more of him this day. His 2 words — "mama" and "dada" — are replaced by a strange, self-soothing sound. There is no babbling or baby talk. He is smacking the back of his head and jerking his head up and to the side. Is this autism? Does he even know I am here with him right now?

The next morning, I spend several hours with our ABA therapist in our living room asking Noah to sit down in his chair hoping he will make eye contact. The transitions into the gated play area for his sessions are unbearable for both of us. His therapist sits in front of him, blocking any chance of escape. I watch my son bravely struggle to overcome his fears caused by an oversensitive nervous system. Noah collapses to the floor. He wails, kicks, then grabs my legs, unable to enter the play area.

These meltdowns are excruciating and occur at every transition. I stand behind Noah and pick him up. He grabs a handful of my hair and yanks in desperation. His body goes rigid as I place him into the session and frantically peel his hands off of me. "Just pick him up and place him into the play area and leave him…ignore the behavior." As soon as he calms down, I am told to come back in. "Tell him to sit down." I am paralyzed by fear. I cannot do it. I am afraid to tell my son to sit down because I know it will trigger another meltdown. And again from the therapist, "You need to remove the emotion. Ignore his behaviors." Just like my son is relearning basic skills that he has lost, I am relearning how to parent my child.

With each session my heart breaks a little more. I witness Noah's fears growing and his tolerance for the world around him diminishing. It becomes more debilitating for him each day. Noah prefers to stare at the spinning wheels on his toy car. To walk his path. To repeatedly throw his toys out of the play area. We are instructed to use behavior momentum, which involves reinforcing positive behaviors and holding back all reinforcement for unwanted behaviors. It does not work. It is unmitigated torture, both to observe in therapy and to attempt on our own. His meltdowns continue to escalate. We are doing the prescribed 20 hours of therapy each week — why are Noah's behaviors getting worse?

"Autism" is clouding everyone's judgment. No one is considering Noah's "health" as a contributing factor. Our pediatrician explained to us that "Treatment should be based on evidentiary studies" meaning the research would need to show evidence that there is a medical cause to autism. There is no evidence. I countered him, "Yes, but we know this is happening to my son RIGHT NOW…and we do not have time to wait. I need to help my son now."

There is chronic diarrhea and nutritional malabsorption caused by candida and clostridia overgrowth in his gut. Eczema. Drool. Food Allergies. Seizures. Poor Methylation. Mitochondrial Dysfunction. Cerebral Folate Deficiency. Kryptopyrrole, a B6 and Zinc deficiency that causes symptoms similar to schizophrenia. High Oxalates, causing lethargy bordering on hypothyroidism. Low Sulfate. High Nagalase.

Reflux. Noah will eventually be diagnosed with all these conditions. The medical studies are beginning to confirm these health issues in subsets of kids with autism. Unfortunately, our pediatrician was not current on the latest research. Noah was suffering from severe abdominal pain. His nervous system was badly damaged. If the medical community is not looking deeper at the cause of his behaviors, how are the ABA providers supposed to know to take physical pain into consideration? No one is looking or thinking beyond the behaviors. No one seems to be thinking at all. Is it productive to force Noah to work through his pain? Are we doing more damage in the process? I know something is very wrong with my son beyond the "autism."

Following our ABA session, I feed Noah lunch and then drive him 30 minutes to an OT appointment with Tim. I sigh as I look at the pond between the parking lot and Tim's office. It is a good distance with many small stone steps to navigate. I have to carefully maneuver those steps while carrying a resisting and agitated 18-month old Noah who is unable to sit upright in his stroller. We do not yet know that Noah has mitochondrial dysfunction which on a bad day will cause him to have low energy and stamina. Noah can no longer walk from the car to Tim's office. He is unbearably heavy and slips out of my arms, which are beginning to grow numb. He hates to be touched or picked up, making the trek from the car to the office much more difficult.

And, as if to push the limits of my sanity, Noah picks this moment to unload number two. At first, I think I am okay because, yup, I am a prepared mommy and I double diapered him today. Unfortunate for both of us, 2 diapers is no match for this load. It is massive and explosive and leaks through both diapers, onto his clothing and onto me. By the time I arrive at Tim's office, there is diarrhea all over me and Noah. I feel like I am going to lose it. "Shit! Shit! SHIT!" I hate my life. "Oh God. And I am sick again?" My cold has turned into bronchitis, I have the chills and I am coughing from deep down in my chest and so very, very tired.

I make it to Tim's office and run past the receptionist, already 10 minutes late. I head straight to the back room to the changing table. I brace myself as I do my best to gently lay Noah down. He refuses. "No. No!

NO!!! You've got to be kidding me. Please, please, let me change your diaper." Noah fights me like his life depends on it. He cries, screams, pulls my hair, punches and kicks me — anything to avoid being laid down in that position. What the hell? How is he so strong? Shit is everywhere — literally. Why are you doing this to me? YOU ARE GOING TO MISS YOUR THERAPY. Please, PLEASE, stop fighting me! PLEASE!!! Oh God, I can't think straight, my head feels foggy. Why won't you let me change your diaper?

Noah suffered from severe vestibular dysfunction. The feeling of being at the top of a roller coaster the moment you are about to plunge down-ward. Noah was experiencing this all the time, which also made sitting upright in his car seat and his stroller terrifying for him.

Completely spent, shit smeared on my clothing and in my hair, I carry Noah into Tim's office. Tim looks at me with a deep level of compassion as I hand Noah over to him as if he is the anchor in our makeshift relay team and he takes over for me, for at least an hour. Noah cries the entire time. He is unable to sit in the swing, touch the shaving cream or find the floor in front of his feet as Tim walks with him, giving him joint com-pression. In addition to vestibular dysfunction, Noah also has tactile dysfunction (oversensitivity to touch) and proprioceptive dysfunction (lack of body awareness). For Noah, sensory integration dysfunction triggers excessive emotional reactions. Leaning against the wall in the large therapy room, I let myself slide slowly to the floor. I am emotionally depleted, torn between the urge to end Noah's session, unable to bear his cries, and the urge to postpone the inevitable battle of getting Noah organized and back across the pond and into his car seat. At this point, it just seems like more than I can bear. I just want to lie down, close my eyes, and have someone else take over. For today at least.

Jason and I are silent the next afternoon as we sit in the waiting room for our appointment with Dr. N., the neurologist. Fortunately, there is a train table to keep Noah entertained while we wait. Noah is obsessed with trains. We are alone with our thoughts. We are eventually led back to Dr. N.'s office, where he asks us various questions and tests Noah. Nothing can prepare you for what comes next, even if you already sus-pect it. "Your son has autism." Just like that.

"I don't believe it. Why is it autism? Why not Sensory Processing Disorder?" Dr. N. smiles and replies, "Guys, this is a good thing. It's autism. Now you know." No bedside manner. I hate him. I need someone to direct my rage and it may as well be him. Looking back, I am grateful that this Neurologist was direct with us. And he was right; someone had to be. But, at that moment, future warrior mom continued to argue with him as he insists Noah's autism must be genetic. "But, no one in our family has anything like this." Dr. N. tears out a sheet of paper from his notebook and writes out a "prescription" for 25 hours of therapy per week that includes ABA, Speech, OT and PT. "Oh, and some of my clients have had success with the GFCF diet, but there is no evidence to back it up. And document the staring spells. They could be seizures, but I don't like to do EEGs unnecessarily. And schedule a follow-up appointment in six months." It would take us three years, two DAN! Doctors, a nutritionist and a second neurologist to get what were in fact seizures under control.

I am devastated and cannot stop crying. For my son and for my family. When Noah was born, I had the usual hopes and dreams for Noah. But autism had suddenly taken these hopes and dreams hostage. Now I wonder if he would ever talk, go to a regular school, be able to make friends. I resolve to give my son his childhood and ultimately, his life back. I keep asking questions, knowing deep inside that there are answers different than what we have been told. There has to be. That night I make a promise to Noah that I will never give up on him. I cannot sleep and am googling for information late into the night.

I sit in on Noah's next session with Tim, taking notes as we discuss everything that has transpired over the past few days. Tim mentions that he is working on a study that looks at the growing number of children with sensory issues in areas of high fungal rates, suggesting that mold may be a consideration. Tim also loans me his copy of "Children with Starving Brains" by Jaquelyn McCandless. After the session, he writes out a list of labs and biomarkers to bring to our doctor.

Jason hires a mold inspector to come to our house the next day. The inspector opens a small panel in the wall of Noah's nursery and discovers a large amount of black mold. Samples reveal a high level of aspergillus. We later learn that our landlord had had shoddy plumbing work done shortly before our tenancy began. Our first DAN! Doctor will test for mycotoxins in Noah's urine and finds a high amount of ochratoxin, a biotoxin derived from aspergillus and penicillin.

Later that evening, as we sit down to discuss the possibility that mold may be contributing to Noah's developmental delays and health issues, I feel like the room is closing in on me. What the hell? We chose this house! It was our responsibility to ensure a safe environment for Noah. If we had been more careful, our son would be fine. We were responsible and wanted desperately to fix it. Was it possible to do so?

Over the ensuing days, between finding a new place to live and shuttling Noah to and from various therapy appointments, I begin to wonder — could the vaccinations also be contributing to Noah's condition? Through conversations with Tim, I begin to realize that perhaps there is not one single contributing factor, but rather a combination of exposure to biotoxins (mold) and subjecting a weakened immune system to multiple strains of live viruses (vaccinations). Was Noah's body overburdened with environmental toxins?

I call Dr. B., a DAN! Doctor, and schedule our first appointment at the California Integrative Hyperbaric Center in Irvine. At that first visit, I meet David Kartzinel in the front office and he gives me the 411 on biomedical treatment and talks to me about vaccines and environmental toxins. I feel at home and am overcome by emotion. David hands me a TACA card that says "My child's behavior may be disturbing to you. My child is not spoiled or misbehaving. My child has autism." On the back: "Autism is a devastating biological and neurological disorder that can affect individuals in different areas" listing the five areas: communication, social, behavior, sensory, and medical. As I read it, tears roll down my face, realizing that these TACA folks are describing my son. For the first time since starting down this path in search of answers, I feel as though someone got it just right — someone is seeing the whole picture, the whole child. This is when it hits me like a ton of bricks how significantly our medical community — the people I trusted to fix this

— have let me down. Autism is not genetic. Noah's autism is caused by toxins in his environment that are poisoning him, destroying his health. I take the card with me as I am called back to Dr. B.'s office. This is the first true step to recovery, and I will never look back.

It is Thanksgiving week 2013. It is the three-year anniversary of our diagnosis. I am driving with a 4-1/2 year-old Noah in the back seat. It is a beautiful day. My parents are on their way to our house to join us for the holiday. This will be our first "paleo" Thanksgiving so that everyone can enjoy a meal together as a family. I feel healthy and energized. I stop at a light and use the opportunity to look at Noah in the rear-view mirror. He is a truly beautiful child. I am momentarily mesmerized and think at that moment that he is absolutely perfect. I take the moment to ask, "Noah, what are you most thankful for this Thanksgiving?" He brushes aside a strand of his long blond hair and looks up at me with his steel-blue eyes. "You mommy. I am thankful for you." As tears fill my eyes, I turn my attention back to the road. Our journey of healing is not over. But I know that we are heading the right way.

Lioness

"If you were to hear bad news, would you want to hear it now or after you got some rest?" I was still in my post-natal, epidural induced haze when my husband asked me this, so I did not "get" what he was telling me. I told him that I probably would want to hear the news before the nap, and it was then that he told me they thought my newborn daughter had Down syndrome. The thought briefly crossed my mind that he was joking, but I knew that this was something he wouldn't joke about.

You see, we had checked for this with a genetic counselor during an ultrasound in my 20th week of pregnancy. It was the BIG thing that we were worried about. We had one "soft" marker for it, a calcium deposit on her heart. Then the counselor looked for her nasal bone. Apparently, the shortening or complete lack of it, and I don't remember which, was a huge marker for DS, and we waited ten long agonizing minutes to find out if she had one.

My poor husband, being a true Sicilian and the only boy in a large family, wanted a boy of his own. Now he was discovering that not only was he having a girl, but he might also be having a child with Down syndrome. We both just desperately wanted to find a nasal bone, and she finally allowed us to see it. Relieved, we went home with the comfort that our chance of having a child with Down syndrome was one in 145, not much. So we continued with this pregnancy basking in the joy of having a healthy, "normal" baby on the way.

I continued to work at the local pet store and was planning to work until the middle of November, giving me another four weeks to get ready for the baby. But I started to get very uncomfortable and left work earlier than intended. A few days later, I "sprung a leak" and the midwife induced me. At 11:19 pm, November 2004, my sweet baby Mina was born, a little over three weeks early.

Mina was in the hospital NICU for six days, and she was hardly ever in my arms. I was having a hard time nursing due to all of the stress and the separation from her. She had been given IV antibiotics, and even as a newborn, it took three nurses to hold her to do this. I think about this now and laugh because they had said that her "floppiness" among other things lead them to believe that she had DS. Even my sister-in-law remarked with astonishment that she couldn't be that weak and floppy if it took that many nurses to hold her down. Now I know what they were talking about, but at that time, I was really confused.

As many NICU moms know, there is always a flurry around the unit, and my child was one of those cooped up in what my husband has affectionately called the "baby spa," otherwise known as the bili lights for jaundice. Finally after six days of lights, CAT scans, IV antibiotics and monitoring, they said she was ready to leave. We took our new family member home in an emotional blur. We were not even ready to have this baby yet, no furniture put together or anything. And on top of it, we had to take on something we had not been prepared for. We were bringing home a child with a disability, THE disability we feared most.

When I worked at the pet store, I had seen groups of older kids and adults with cognitive disabilities come in with their group home support and teachers. I always felt uncomfortable around these people. I feel ashamed to say this now. It was more like I felt like my boundaries were being invaded physically, and so I think that is what made me so upset about having a child with DS. That coupled with the fact that my mother so impressed upon us that intelligence was extremely important, more so than looks. At least that was what I picked up from her, she would never had expressed that verbally. She even worked with people with disabilities as a nurse's aide, and she would have a glow in her eyes when she talked about the people she cared for. But somehow, I picked up that in order to be worthwhile, I had to be the smartest, or at least extremely intelligent. So here I am with a child who belonged to "that" group of people, and I wondered if I would ever be able to bond with her. My husband, God bless him, said to me, "Honey, if you can bond with a hamster, you can bond with her." That was all it took, and I knew then that I could let that thought go.

Time passed, and the fears started to melt away. Mina was such a cute baby, such a joy! We had therapists come into the home through Early Intervention, and they worked with her. We just spent time getting to know our little girl and watched her blossom. Others used to comment on how bright her eyes were, how she seemed to be such a bright, smart little thing. Meanwhile, my husband found internet forums for me to join, so I made sure to do that. It was so nice to be connected to others who "got it."

One of my sisters and sisters-in-law also found out about multivitamins for DS specifically, so with my Dad's help, I bought some. I figured that with time, the therapies, and with these vitamins, that my daughter would become one of those "superstars" of DS that we heard about. She would be almost neurotypical, I was sure of it. I didn't want to accept the idea of her ending up as a bagger for a grocery store (I cringe at having even felt this way). She could do so much more.

When I brought her home, I tried to get her to nurse, but I wasn't producing much, and she was falling asleep at the breast. So after consulting a lactation specialist and failing miserably at our "assignment" to pump ten times and feed ten times each day for a couple of days, we decided to formula feed. This was a hard decision for me because each decision to not do the optimum for my child was a decision to not have her succeed in my eyes. And other than perhaps a little bit of reflux, she did fine. She suffered from constipation, though, and we were recommended to use Miralax daily to combat that problem. Over the period of a year or so, we were able to introduce baby foods to her, oatmeal cereal, and some pureed meats. She was progressing well in terms of motor development and rolled all over the floor, and she wasn't a picky eater. She finally smiled and laughed, and that was so fun to see.

With the speech therapist, we eventually got her to begin to chew some of the puffs and other mashable toddler foods as well. She loved Goldfish crackers and Cheerios. Those were her favorites! The problem area for her was sleep. She would wake up crying at night, and she would take half hour naps. She began waking up for hours at end in the middle of the night. We had a sleep study done, but we couldn't get the electrodes placed on her head. We did determine that there was no apnea, so that was good, but there were no real answers to her sleep issues.

Something I did notice was that she did not seem to develop like the other children on the forums and she also didn't play with toys. I was told over and over by the moms that the children all developed at their own pace and in their own time. But this just didn't sit well with me, so one day, I decided to Google "child with Down syndrome doesn't play with toys." Nothing popped up for Down syndrome. However a slew of articles came up for autism. So I decided to look at the diagnostic criteria, and what I saw shocked me. My daughter fit most of the traits of an autistic child! I made sure to tell my husband, and then I consulted with all of her therapists. They all basically decided that she was too social to have autism, however our developmental therapist agreed to contact our service coordinator to let her know our concerns.

We ended up having what was called a Medical Diagnostic Evaluation done, which involved a psychologist, developmental pediatrician, and one other specialist. They interacted with Mina for three hours or so, and after doing so, told me that she was in fact too social to have autism, so her issues were chalked up to the delays of Down syndrome. We went home thinking that it was just a matter of time before she would develop these skills. I returned to my forums determined to see what others did to help their children learn to play, and I was told many different things. Unfortunately, I had done all of these things and nothing was working. During this same period, we decided to have another child, and we figured that having a sibling would be great for Mina too. So we went ahead with trying to conceive and succeeded. I got pregnant with my youngest and gave birth to her in the fall of 2008.

During the infancy of my youngest, I found myself withdrawing more and more from the Down syndrome forums. It was too depressing seeing the difference between my child and the others. Mina was still not developing, and she just seemed so reactive to any change in her environment. Every time we tried to take her somewhere and away from watching Barney, she would melt down. She refused most touch, and the light just seemed to have left her eyes. She hated getting her hair or body washed, and she only wanted to watch TV and eat copious amounts of crackers and Cheerios. Meanwhile, my second child had issues sleeping, and I had to hold her during her naps. So, during those times, I began to read while she slept in my lap.

I don't remember why, but I decided to read Jenny McCarthy's book, "Healing and Preventing Autism." I was dumbfounded to see that so many kids with autism had the same issues as my Mina had, and I wondered if perhaps some of these things that worked for autism would help her. I also started to think that the evaluation that she had had was incorrect, so I looked up the DSM IV and realized that Mina fit all of the diagnostic criteria for autism. I relayed my suspicions to our pediatrician, to her school social worker and psychologist and to her therapists at Easter Seals.

The school psychologist said that after putting on her "autism" lenses, she began to see Mina's behaviors in a new light and noted what she discovered. The OT at Easter Seals recommended to present Mina to the Medical Advisory Board that met once a month at the center. We had to make three videos, one for each therapy session, and then present the video to a board of physicians of different specialties and see what they recommended to us.

It was at this time that I began to supplement some probiotics and Vitamin D. I also visited the nutritionist at Easter Seals who recommended a high dose multivitamin for malnourished children. Within a week of dosing Mina with the Vitamin D, her therapists were talking about her eye contact and how it had improved. This was exciting for me, and I knew I was on to something. The day before the MAB, we went to see a neurologist. After about 30 minutes of observing Mina jerking around and asking me questions, he said that she was, in fact, autistic. I felt an overwhelming sense of relief, but I wanted to be sure, so I waited to see what the MAB would have to say. The day came, and after it was over, the OT told me that after her three minute long video of Mina during her OT session, the developmental pediatrician said, "Before we go any further, you DO realize this child has a secondary diagnosis of autism." A-Ha! I KNEW it! I felt vindicated. Finally! Answers and a direction to go in.

I began reading more about autism and also had started giving Mina her multivitamin and continued the other things. Mina's teacher, who had gone on maternity leave, came back and asked me who this new child was! I noticed it too. It was like the world suddenly existed and she was seeing it for the first time. She was malnourished. I decided that the treating physical aspects of autism was really the way to go and not therapies, so I took the money that would be going towards more therapy and directed it to her health.

We had a consult with Judy Converse, a dietician and nutritionist with an autistic child herself, and we began the conversion to a gluten and casein free diet. All Mina ate was gluten and casein filled Gerber baby food, Cheerios, and Goldfish. This was going to be interesting. But after a little bit of sweat and cursing my existence, I was able to do it, and three days or so after removing the last bit of casein and gluten, she got a really high fever. I read about this in Judy's book. Mina's body had stopped fighting food and was finally fighting "bugs!" After this fever was gone, she was smiling and laughing. Laughing! My daughter was laughing…and happy! And after a few months, she had lost about 12 pounds, pounds that she really needed to lose as she was getting heavy. I was really, really excited. And then I was really, really angry.

My daughter lost valuable time that she could have had to heal. She might be chewing by now. We wasted time hearing that her big belly was just low tone. She wore an abdominal binder to support her back and gut. I know now that that bloating is from bacteria or yeast as it only gets bigger at the end of the day after she has eaten. How uncomfortable that must have been. She should not have been fed crackers and cheese. It just made her sicker. Before she went gluten and casein free (and now grain free), she had extremely low IgA levels in her stool test results. After testing again a couple of years later, they returned to the normal range.

She has been alert and is off of the multivitamins now because she is eating nutrient dense food. I could have started earlier, and I cannot get that time back. I warn parents now to push for an evaluation if they suspect that their child with Down syndrome also has autism (one study has suggested that 18.2 % of the DS population has autism.) I tell them to trust their guts and to follow any and all information to get the resources they need to help their kids. I wish I could go back in time and do so for myself. I have apologized to Mina for not getting a second opinion, for not doing more sooner, and I am still working on forgiving myself and the professionals who should have known.

Since the diagnosis, we have tried supplements, dietary changes, and now homeopathy. Each has brought gains, and Mina is one of those kids who responds slowly and steadily. She is not an overnight responder as many children with "just" autism are. She, like many other children with Down syndrome, take more time to heal, and I have found that they respond similarly to Mina, slowly but without spurts. She still doesn't talk, but she has gained sounds without losing them, has become engaged with her environment and also handles changes in routine a little bit more easily. One of the best things to happen is that she cares that we exist. She has even cuddled, and that is HUGE for us! Just to be able to get a giggle or a snuggle out of her is priceless.

At this stage in the game, we are using homeopathy to help heal her, and we have seen increases in cognition and flexibility. She is also a "Lovey Dovey" girl these days and looks for her parents and sister, grabbing our faces in affection. I look forward to more changes after returning from SonRise Start Up soon to address any attitude issues that impede our relationship with her. I have a feeling that this will create a whole new chapter in our lives.

Meanwhile, I am taking more time for myself and am trying to create a more loving and positive attitude in my home. The effects are astounding, and I wish I had let go of the stress sooner in the journey. I will follow what I think God is telling me to do, and then let go for the sake of Mina, for the sake of my family. I have a feeling that healing Mina will result in the healing of our family and ourselves. What started as a nightmare has become a blessing to my family. Would I have chosen this for us? No way! But God is using it to bring us to Him and to heal us all.

Some of you may be wondering what I think caused my daughter's autism. I have thought about it a lot. There is a much higher incidence of autism in the Down syndrome population than in the general population. Estimates run from 5 – 8.2 % of the population depending upon the source. (http://www.ncbi.nlm.nih.gov/pubmed/2035732). Some experts in the Down syndrome community have speculated that there is a genetic causation of the autism in Down syndrome. Some of us that are in the unique position of having a child with the dual diagnosis have other thoughts.

Personally, I think that people with Down syndrome have mitochondrial dysfunction. In the news, we all saw the Hannah Poling vaccine injury case in which she unknowingly suffered from mitochondrial dysfunction. It was ruled that this dysfunction was triggered by her vaccines, causing her to descend into autism. In Down syndrome, not only are there physical differences like smaller nasal passageways and ear canals, but there are also physiological differences as well. One difference is the insufficient production of glutathione which is necessary for "taking out the trash," and detoxing heavy metals. There are other issues as well, like an increase in diabetes and leukemia, and one can go to this site to read more (http://einstein-syndrome.com/). So as a mom with a dually diagnosed child, the following study finding immune system genomes in common in Rett syndrome, Down syndrome, and autism was no surprise to me. (http://www.ncbi.nlm.nih.gov/pubmed/21130877).

A lot of the choices I made as a parent clearly compromised my daughter, though I didn't know it at the time. I fully vaccinated her up until a certain age, even when a close family member expressed concern about vaccines and autism. But I did it anyway because the doctors all said that children with DS need to have all of the vaccines available because of their weak immune systems. I gave her Miralax to ease the constipation, a standard medication that is used by almost all children with Down syndrome. Mind you, this drug is on the FDA watch list for neuropsychiatric events now under the name of polyethylene glycol. If you look at laxative labels, this drug is everywhere. I formula fed her, gave her a high gluten and dairy diet (celiac and sinus issues are high in Down syndrome), had a Terbutaline shot after I fell at work during the pregnancy and had Pitocin, an epidural, and antibiotics during and after her birth. She also took antibiotics every time she had a sinus infection… all of these things contributed to her autism. I almost laugh when I hear people claiming that parents of kids with autism just want someone to blame, because the reality is ultimately that I gave her autism. I made the poor choices that brought her to this place. So now I have had to do what I can to reverse the damage I caused by those choices.

As far as what I think needs to be done to reverse the downward spiral of our kids' health, it amounts to this: A massive overhaul of our environment, the food supply, the drug and chemical companies, and shutting down nuclear power. Our children's genes are being mutated and bodies destroyed by massive amounts of radiation. Then we feed them pseudo food which is constantly being altered in the name of profit and supposed humanitarianism. Our children are sent to school as soon as possible and not given a proper childhood while parents are stressed out trying to feed their families. It is a whole societal overthrow that needs to happen.

It starts with the choices we make as parents, and we can use this autism epidemic to wake people up. It is happening. I hear elderly people talk about skipping the doctor and taking Echinacea and vitamin c when they are sick. My own grandmother stopped getting the flu shot as she got sick every time she had one. Once she stopped, she stopped getting sick. We need to stand up as a people and demand change. We need to start to go back to "the good old days" of clean food, clean water, and community. We need to stop working so much and play more. Our kids' lives depend upon it.

JUICY FRUIT

When I got pregnant, I already knew that I wanted to delay vaccinations, see a midwife, breastfeed, never do daycare, and on and on because we had been trying for so long that I'd already been lurking on the natural parenting boards. I knew we wanted to at the very least delay vaccines, not circumcise if we had a boy, and not throw tons of antibiotics at our baby. I was prepared. So, we had a midwife. I had exactly one ultrasound, and it was just a quickie to find the heartbeat at about 10 weeks. I had no flu shot, no Rhogam, and no amniocentesis. We were prepared.

Dominic ended up being a hospital transfer with a vaginal birth (the attending doctor had C-section paperwork done and waiting, and I'm sure he was irritated that he only got to bill for a vaginal birth) because I just got too tired after 40+ hours of labor to push him out at home. I needed a bit of a break. So there was an epidural, and I am pretty sure some antibiotics in my IV, but I'm fuzzy on that part. We found a pediatrician willing to hold off (with a lecture of course) on vaccines until he was two and then only give one at a time, spaced out at least by a month. I breastfed until he turned three.

Dominic was amazing! He was developing perfectly on schedule, and I compared notes with my fellow mommies at playdates all the time. He had friends. He was talking up a storm, climbing, laughing and labeling. Such a little miracle. Life was full of potential.

But there was also yeast, so much yeast. He developed the worst diaper rash I'd ever seen. We were using cloth diapers, so we changed our laundry routine, stripped them, did naked time, and even tried disposables. The only thing that got rid of the rash was potty training, which he did at age two. What no one told me was that cracked and bleeding on the outside means cracked and bleeding on the inside. And cracked and bleeding in the gut means leaky gut syndrome, and a crashing immune system. The doctor once even suggested straight corn starch on his rash. I looked it up when we got home and realized that starch feeds yeast.

He was in the throes of the yeast rashes when he turned two, and the doctor said it was time to start vaccinating per our agreement. So we started. We did one at a time, and midway through that year he got his first (and only) MMR shot. I didn't notice anything right away as far as developmental changes, but the following February when he turned three, we attempted to start him in a Montessori preschool. He had tremendous separation anxiety. Then he brought the flu home from preschool which knocked the whole family on our backs for two weeks. After a solid week of a high fever, Dominic stopped speaking clearly and started babbling. And a few weeks later the babbling stopped. In a matter of a month our talking, happy, interactive three-year-old regressed before our very eyes.

Six years later, I can tell you what happened. The measles component of the MMR he had received seven months before had stayed dormant in the speech center of his brain while I breastfed him. (Presumably my immunity held it off, even though I was also vaccinated for measles instead of having them naturally). I weaned him about a week before he started preschool. The flu virus he caught there sent a cytokine storm into his brain which activated the measles virus cells. They then destroyed the developing myelin sheathing in his brain. It took a number of years of testing and backtracking to get to this point and it's not something we'll ever prove. But we know.

We went to the pediatrician...who ordered speech and occupational therapies. We got a brain MRI and a Sedated ABR (auditory brainstem response – hearing test). We had our first IEP and got some early intervention. We found nothing. The audiologist was the first one who said the "A" word. He said "You might need to look at autism." I said "but he doesn't fit the diagnostic criteria, he didn't regress until after his third birthday." We rode the denial train right out of there.

The OT we were seeing ended up suggesting to us that we should consider the gluten-free diet. By this point, I had made an appointment with a Defeat Autism Now! Doctor and had our pediatrician get us into the best pediatric neurologist in town. We saw the neurologist a week before the DAN! Doctor, and I will never forget what he did. He wrote these words on a prescription pad "Autistic Regression Syndrome." He didn't even say the words or look us in the eye. He said that this was something neurologists were seeing a lot of now and they didn't know why. And he sent us out with just that one slip of paper. He gave us no resources, direction, or support suggestions. We came home after that appointment and both of us just sobbed.

The next week, we saw the DAN! Doctor, and left with $1000 worth of tests to do, supplements to start, and a very restrictive gluten, casein and soy free diet that I had no idea how I was going to pull off. We had no hope. I read a book about parents who fought to get their kids the help they needed that week. I read it cover to cover, and sobbed my eyes out. That book put steel in my spine. If those families could do it, so could we.

When we told our pediatrician about the DAN! Doctor, his eyes rolled so far back in his head he resembled a Las Vegas slot machine. And he told us that gluten-free diets didn't do anything, not even for Celiac disease; that the only thing we could maybe try was ABA therapy and we couldn't afford it anyway (those were his words). We never went back to him.

The GFCFSF diet that the DAN! Doctor put Dominic on was a miracle. The first week it was like watching a dark cloud lift over our son's eyes and we started to see him again. His ATEC score was 92. I learned how to do stool and urine collections, and we held our screaming four-year-old down for what seemed like countless vials of blood. And then the DAN! Doctor fine-tuned. Every time we visited, we spent a ton of money. Some things were good — the diet, EFA's, probiotics. Some things were really bad — Chelation was horrible — in three doses of oral DMPS we lost every gain we'd made since starting the DAN! protocol and then some. I learned that DAN! Doctors would give you generally whatever you asked for. He was at that time one of the few DAN! Doctors in the country who still took health insurance, so I figured we were getting a bargain.

I started spending my lunch hour reading studies, taking notes, stalking the internet — looking for that next thing that would help Dominic and writing it down so I could tell the DAN! Doctor to prescribe it. Oh, and I started blogging so I could keep a history of what we tried and how it worked. By the next summer, we had raised enough money to start ABA therapy, and I bullied our health insurance company into reimbursing us for it. We did ABA 15 hours a week for 3 ½ years. It had its ups and downs, but mostly was good. It was an in-center program that was local to us and I'm glad we did it. We learned a lot of techniques to help our son and I really believe the support and tools the regular meetings gave us saved our sanity. But we never stopped trying to find our answer. We did all the supplement fads that came through, and we constantly fought yeast.

In 2012 we started seeing an amazing Cranial Sacral Chiropractor in Colorado Springs who had decided that she wanted to heal autism. We have seen her weekly since then, and she can stop a yeast rage in five minutes. It was and is amazing to see my formerly completely combative child crawl in her lap and place her hands on his head. Every time, it floors me.

Dominic turned seven and was still getting ABA therapy, and I was still digging for the latest and greatest intervention. His ATEC was down to around 25 with almost all the points that were left in the Speech category. He still was not communicating in more than one to two word phrases and it was so exhausting and demoralizing. I just wanted to be able to have a conversation with my son.

I caught wind of a new treatment, coming from another autism mom in Mexico who had apparently had a ton of success recovering children in South America. There was an online petition against her, of all things. She presented at the Autism One conference that year. I didn't get to go to that conference, but I watched the recording as soon as it went on-line. Then I found a group of people she was working with in the US and started her protocol. I watched in wonder, as these moms and dads talked about the improvements their children were making. Every day, someone had a moment to celebrate — and the community of parents celebrated right along with them. I watched for about a month, and then did the protocol on myself for about a month. I wanted to be sure that it was safe, that I wasn't going to hurt my son.

I talked to our chiropractor, I talked to our family practitioner, and I made sure that I had everyone on board to support us before we started on Dominic. Right around that time, our DAN! Doctor also decided to stop taking insurance. So we stopped seeing him and started using our primary care D.O. to monitor Dominic's progress. That healing protocol, now published in the book "Healing the Symptoms known as Autism" by Kerri Rivera, has gotten Dominic's ATEC down to an eight in the two years since that we've been doing it. An ATEC under 10 means you have lost the diagnosis of autism. Turns out he had parasites as well as yeast and biofilm and bacteria and heavy metals and we were just feeding all those pathogens with the supplementation regime from our DAN! Doctor. That was a hard pill for us to swallow, but we were doing the best we knew how to do at that time.

We are still fine tuning, and we still play the one step forward, two steps back game, but the changes in our son are astonishing. I have hope again for his future. I can see the light at the end of the tunnel. I will be forever grateful to all the parents doing the CD protocol, but especially to Kerri Rivera for having the bravery to share what she was using to help her child improve. Every kid is different, but if we don't share what we're doing that works — we might never hear about the thing that might recover our child.

What I have found in the last two years of doing this protocol is that the autism community is fragmented. There are a lot of people who truly believe that our children aren't sick — they believe our kids are just quirky and we shouldn't be trying to fix them. I cannot wrap my head around this attitude because I know Dominic was fine and then he wasn't. I believe in my heart that if we had vaccinated him on schedule, he would have just never developed. We had such a clear regression because he had the opportunity to develop while we waited to vaccinate. I know my child wasn't born with autism.

In these last few years, I've found the most amazing community of autism warrior sisters. I have met my best friends doing this healing work on my child. Autism moms have backbones of steel and hearts of gold. We take care of our own. I am so honored to have been asked to tell our story for this collection — because it is in the telling of our stories that we help prevent what happened to our children from happening to other children.

COUGAR

Recovery is possible! We are designed to heal, and will heal if given the opportunity. Don't let anyone tell you otherwise. The underlying causes disease, including the symptoms know as autism, are a result of toxicity, an acidic body, and lack of oxygen to the cells. All of these things can be addressed and reversed, leaving "autism" behind. My son is living proof that there is hope.

My son's journey into and out of autism began over ten years ago when my husband and I found out I was pregnant. We were thrilled! The nursery was perfect. The baby shower was perfect. I felt great throughout the nine months of pregnancy. Our baby boy was developing normally. At the time, I considered us healthy eaters. We were eating a vegetarian diet with some fish. Fish is known to be a source of mercury, and we don't eat it now, nor did I eat any seafood with my next three pregnancies. Other than the fish I ate when pregnant, I had no other source of mercury. I had no cavities or fillings of any kind, and did not get a Rhogam shot which does contain injected mercury. Overall, the pregnancy was easy and enjoyable.

My son was born in September of 2003 via an uneventful, routine C-Section. My son had normal APGAR scores, good hearing, and normal reflexes. He was a healthy, beautiful, bright blue-eyed, strawberry blonde boy. On the day of his birth, Christopher was given an injection of synthetic Vitamin K and a Hep B vaccination. We had not researched either of these injections but were doing the norm with a hospital birth. After those injections, our son became jaundiced. We were clueless as to the reason for the jaundice and accepted the explanation of the hospital's pediatrician. I now know that jaundice is a clear indicator that the liver is over-taxed.

Who decided that all babies need a large injection of synthetic Vitamin K? Why are we injecting every child with Hep B that affects less than one percent of our population? The two at-risk groups for contracting Hep B are adult, promiscuous, homosexual males and IV drug users that share needles. A day old baby fits neither of these two categories. Why was my son injected with two things that we were not fully informed about by those administering the injections?

Our first night home with Christopher was bittersweet. Sweet because we had this wonderful little person who was now a part of our family, bitter because he had feeding issues. The frenulum under his tongue was connected all the way to the tip. None of the lactation consultants had noticed this because he latched well. He would latch, but was unable to extract milk. The first night at home he screamed from hunger almost the entire night while we "finger-fed" him formula. I was in pain, and the finger feeding was ridiculous! The next day, he went from a breast fed baby to a formula fed baby. We were 'healthy' eaters and I had just finished a super baby food book that listed healthy ways to feed a baby. This book promoted soy, and since we didn't do dairy, Christopher began soy formula.

I was not informed that soy formula is basically poison. It's especially bad for boys, because of its estrogen mimicking properties. Ninety-eight percent of soy is genetically modified, so when the soy fields are sprayed with poisonous pesticides, it's the only thing that remains. This formula made my son chronically constipated. This was discussed with his pediatrician, who told us to add corn syrup to every bottle. I'll never forget the appointment with her, in which we waited for a half hour to see her for less than eight minutes of her time. She commented "how cute," noticed his tongue tie, to which she said that we "just needed to watch it" and recommended corn syrup for the constipation, and ended with, "the nurse will be in with his vaccines." Christopher was only weeks old, and was eating poisonous soy formula, with added corn syrup from a Dr. Brown's BPA filled plastic bottle that I had dipped in boiling tap water to sterilize. All of this was the backdrop for his vaccine injury.

I could write an entire book on vaccines because of the last eight years of research I've done and my personal experience with a vaccine-injured child. I could tell you how and why they do not provide immunity, the history of them all the way back to Edward Jenner, the thousands of other parents that I've either read or talked to about their experience with vaccines, and how their children were also harmed, and some whose babies died after just one vaccine. For now, I'll just give you my favorite vaccine quote as food for thought:

"What the promoters of vaccination fail to realize is that the respiratory tract of all mammals contain secretory IgA within the respiratory tract mucosa. By passing this mucosa aspect of the immune system directly injecting organism leads to a corruption of the immune system. As a result, pathogenic viruses or bacteria cannot be eliminated by the immune system and remain in the body where they further grow and/or mutate as the individual is exposed to ever more antigens and toxins in the environment. This is especially true with viruses grouped under the term "stealth adapted"... The mechanism by which the immune system is corrupted when you understand the two poles of the immune system (the cellular and the humoral mechanism) have reciprocal relationship. Thus when one is stimulated the other is inhibited. Since vaccines activate the B cells to secrete antibody, the T-Cells are subsequently suppressed. This suppression of the cell mediated response is a key factor in the development of cancer and life threatening infections...."

Rebecca Corley MD, VIDS
(vaccine induced diseases) expert

How did vaccination affect Christopher? His gut was a mess from all the soy and corn syrup. That was the underlying factor for why he couldn't detox all the known neurotoxins in the vaccines he received. He had high pitched screaming, a sign of neurological damage, with both hands up by his ears after each vaccine. The pediatrician was completely clueless about this and never even considered this to be a sign of a vaccine reaction. We ended up leaving the pediatrician's practice because a light bulb had finally gone off. We were questioning why we were giving Christopher all that corn syrup that we wouldn't eat ourselves.

We started slowly waking up. We went to a new pediatrician who did not agree with the corn syrup method. This pediatrician appeared to be more informed. We were still vaxing on schedule and Christopher still had the high pitched screaming each time. Somewhere before the nine month "well baby" visit, someone at work had planted a seed in my husband's mind that maybe all these vaccines weren't so great. We asked the new pediatrician about it and he assured us that he had read everything and that our worries were unfounded. He talked us into keeping on schedule, a decision we will forever regret. Christopher screamed after that nine month set of vaccines for forty minutes until he passed out. The next day, he projectile-vomited his soy formula across the living room. He wasn't the same after that well visit.

Christopher started having OCD type behaviors, where he would repeat the same motion over and over. He lost eye contact. He started staring into space for hours while twisting his wrists and ankles. Some family members would comment that he was "so well-behaved" but he was in a fog. He stopped responding to his name. He did not develop language typically. He had no comprehension of what was said to him. He did not interact socially with other children and he had daily meltdowns over nothing. He always had to hold something and would freak out if it was dropped, even if the object was given back to him. His stool was never normal. He went from constipation to liquid orange stool that smelled like alcohol. In many ways, this was not the same happy, attentive, alert baby we once had.

All parents have special memories of their children's major life events, the first birthday, their first day of preschool, etc. This is what I remember from Christopher's early years. At his first birthday, he was in a fog. He sat in his high chair with the little cake made just for him and stared into space. One of his grandmothers kept calling his name, and put his hand in the cake. We wanted him to dig into the cake on his own like one-year-olds are supposed to do. That never happened nor did it happen at his second birthday. He was unaware of the gifts right in front of him and didn't tear them open at his first birthday, first Christmas or his second birthday.

I remember taking him to the park when he was twenty-six months old with his cousins, their friends and my sister-n-law. All the other kids were interacting, having fun. Christopher was walking on the sidewalk that went around the perimeter of the park, staring at the ground directly in front of him, not responding to his name. I spent the entire day following behind him so that he didn't wander off. When we left, I had to pick him up and carry him to the car while he kicked and screamed. He screamed from the moment I lifted him until he finally passed out in the car seat, a half hour later. Christopher was in a fog almost always. He was often completely unaware of his surroundings.

Christopher would be happy in his little fog, and then some random thing would happen that sent him into meltdown mode. Meltdown mode is not your typical kid tantrum. These meltdowns are over absurd things and they can last up to an hour or even longer. Our family made a trip to Target once and Christopher wasn't holding anything in his hands, so he fixated on a blue bottle of carpet spray. We were not there to purchase carpet spray so we left without it. My husband ended up carrying Christopher out to the car under his arm, while he screamed and kicked. Our little guy just didn't understand what was going on. We stopped at a drug store on the way home, bought a blue bottle of carpet cleaner, and the meltdown stopped. My husband was taking out the trash one day, and Christopher didn't understand. So he had a forty-five minute meltdown. There was no amount of consoling that would stop this type of behavior. This was not normal.

Another memory etched in my mind is of Christopher having a seizure. A family member had hugged him with some kind of tanning cream on her skin. He broke out in an immediate red, swollen rash. The Pediatrician was called and told us to give Benadryl which caused a seizure. Christopher was unable to focus on us and ended up with his eyes rolling back in his head. He has had that type of seizure happen once, but he's had several absence seizures. During an absence seizure, the person is stuck. It's like the body freezes for a minute or two before they snap out of it. With all that being said, there were good memories even during the bad times. Christopher had always been a tender-hearted, loving boy!

At twenty-one months old, Christopher was still having feeding issues. Part of that was sensory related, where he had an aversion to the textures of certain foods. However, the tongue tie was still a problem. He couldn't fully move his tongue. An ENT put him to sleep to clip his tongue. "The tongue tie was so thick," the ENT told me, "that's why you couldn't breast feed." Christopher was not yet three at the time of this surgery, so our state Early Steps Program sent an Occupational Therapist to our home to work with him on eating. At this point, we knew something wasn't "right" with Christopher, but because he was our first child, we weren't sure exactly what. The OT eventually became a friend and told us that on the first day that she met Christopher, she knew he had autism.

At twenty-eight months, per the OT's recommendation, we had Christopher evaluated by a person from the state. I will never forget that day. The testing was done at our home. My son had such poor motor skills that he couldn't even jump. It never occurred to him to climb the steps to his bunk bed, nor to slide down the other side. He had no comprehension of what this lady was saying to him. She asked, "Christopher, can you hand me the blue ball?" The ball was right beside him on the floor, and he just stared blankly at her. She repeated the question three or four times, finally handing him the ball, to which he robotically said, "blue ball."

He was declared developmentally delayed and scored around a nine-month-old level, almost across the board. It was at nine months that he had had that horrific vaccine reaction. When a child is declared "delayed" or "autistic" or anything related, the parent is a crying mess, like I was, but the people doing the evaluating are not there for comfort. With so many children having a learning and/or developmental delay, they must become numb to it all. The day Christopher was declared delayed, I got a "you'll be okay" as the person was walking out.

When most of the crying was over, it was time to devise a plan of action. The state had officially declared him delayed, so he was now eligible for more services from our state's Early Intervention Program, starting at age three from the school system. Without getting to the root cause of the neurological damage, all the help was not enough. The speech therapy and Special Ed instruction provided through any state is very limited. Christopher got one half hour speech therapy session with a group at a local school. In addition, a Special Ed teacher came to work with him at our home for a half hour, three days a week, which was quickly reduced to two days a week. This was back in 2006 – 2008. One can only imagine how limited state sponsored interventions are today with one in six children now diagnosed with a learning, behavioral, or developmental delay.

Rather than pay out-of-pocket for extra therapy, we chose to pay out-of-pocket for biomedical intervention. Our first stop, a local DAN! Doctor. We waited six months to get an appointment. We spent approximately three thousand dollars on that visit. This included a fee for the appointment, tests that were ordered, a blood analysis on a microscope, a truckload of supplements, and our first batch of compounded B12 injections. This was just the beginning of Christopher's journey to recovery and the expense. We have currently spent the equivalent of a college education on him, and he's worth every penny. We were fortunate to have very supportive family members to which we are forever grateful! The day of our initial appointment, my husband's aunt slipped us one thousand dollars. My in-laws have paid for countless supplements, my parents have purchased many other things we needed, all without question! We spent more per month on food and supplements than our mortgage. We were fortunate to be able to afford the biomedical treatments that Christopher needed to recover.

The test results were back in a few weeks, and here is what we saw: mercury, aluminum (both vaccine ingredients) and lead off the charts, a horrible bacterial infection in his gut, and yeast everywhere. His blood analysis on the microscope showed his red blood cells to be deflated in the middle, more kidney shaped than round, and clumped together. Behind the clumped blood cells were small white strings, which the doctor said was undigested food. On the undigested food was yeast that looked like cotton candy. The doctor commented that most of the autistic kids she sees have this condition.

Based on the results, we did the following biomedical interventions: daily MB12 injections from a compounding pharmacy for two years, then B12 nasal spray after that, 105 CaEDTA chelation IVs, we removed all wheat, dairy, and soy from our diets, HBOT, infrared sauna, and a spreadsheet of daily supplements. The spreadsheet was empowering, and with each check, we knew that Christopher would recover. For the chelation IVs, my husband took off work every Thursday morning and we drove to the doctor's office as a family. The DAN! Doctor and her staff became close friends and would ask us to speak to parents who were there for the first time.

I cried a lot during that season. For the most part, the autistic kids in our country are hidden. At school, the majority are in their own class-rooms. Many of the parents can't go out to a restaurant or out shopping with them. It was very sobering to see what these DAN! Doctors do. I remember meeting a Mom with beautiful two and a half year old twin girls. One was talking and playing with my daughter, while the other twin stared blankly into space. The mom told me that their Pediatrician had vaccinated one girl twice with MMR and the other got no MMR. I've heard this same account of vaccine reaction causing autism a thousand times. But every week hearing these accounts still made me cry.

Christopher's progress on his biomedical protocol was slow and steady. When we removed the soy, wheat, and dairy, his fog lifted. He started looking directly at us rather than out of the corner of his eye. As we removed the metals from his body, he started to engage us more, and started losing his sensory issues. He would now eat solid food, rather than just applesauce, yogurt, and other soft foods. He stopped labeling things, "cup, book, mommy," and started echolalia. Echolalia is when the child knows they should respond to what was said or asked of them, but doesn't know what to say, so they repeat the last thing said to them, or just the repetition of familiar words or phrases.

We had Christopher in a three day a week preschool program. When I picked him up in the afternoon, I would ask, "What did you do today?" to which he would respond in a robotic voice, "Did you paint a green frog?" I would say, "Did you paint a green frog?" to which he would again say, "Did you paint a green frog?" This went on for months. He wasn't painting a green frog every week for months. This is all he knew to say. Then one day, I was in the kitchen while our children were at the table playing with Play-Doh. Christopher looked at me and said, "Mommy, can you squeeze the Play-Doh?" I burst into happy tears. Christopher was almost four, and that was the first time he addressed me as Mommy. Progress!

After every sixth chelation IV, we collected Christopher's urine for eight hours and sent it to a lab for analysis. This showed what metals were pulled out of his body at that time. He had mercury across the page for months, as well as aluminum and lead. The more those metals came out, the more typical Christopher became.

He was born in September, so we had him repeat the four-year-old pre-school class. He had the same teacher both years. In that second year, she told us that she was so happy to see him really enjoying school and playing with the other children. It was completely the opposite of the first year, where I was told Christopher seemed younger than the other students. The year he was five, he really made a lot of progress. Looking back, chelation was huge for him!

Christopher officially lost his autism diagnosis at age six, testing out of speech and Special Ed. All his OCD behaviors were gone, his melt-downs stopped, and his motor skills were greatly improved. He was now a social kid who laughed at things that were actually funny. He had friends. Girls at school liked him. He was still somewhat of a literal thinker, and would get frustrated easily with his siblings. For example, he would tell me, "Susan is lying," to which I would explain that she wasn't lying; she was just a two-year-old. Because of these behaviors, we began homeopathy.

We wouldn't necessarily do the same things again with Christopher if we had to do it all over again. We would have not injected him with known neurotoxins and carcinogens for the illusion of "protection" from disease (vaccination). We also would have skipped the soy formula and BPA bottles. But even if we had done those things again, and were starting over with bio-med, we would have done some things different-ly. There are other, less invasive, cheaper ways to chelate metals beside IVs. We would have never used an antibiotic or anti-fungal medication. When we started this journey of recovery, we were in panic mode. We were following the DAN! Doctor's recommendations to the letter. Now that we are eight years into this, we are much more confident in making health decisions for our family. After Christopher, we had three more children, two girls and another boy. We never once thought that any of them would have autism. They are not vaccinated, and never had soy for-mula or corn syrup. They are all healthy, happy, neuro-typical children.

When Christopher was seven, we did a year of sequential homeopathy. Homeopathy was an excellent way to help Christopher's immune system get rid of injected viruses and bacteria. With sequential homeopathy, we did a timeline of life events from birth to present day. This timeline in-cluded all vaccines, antibiotics, anti-fungals, and even all those chelation IVs. Once the timeline was established, we started at present-day and worked backwards, clearing these out of the body. Christopher stopped being aggressively frustrated with his siblings after we cleared the Hep B vaccine. He also stopped having bad dreams during this time.

I have since read that homeopathy is not great for chelating metals because there is no chelator for the metals to bind to in order to exit the body. Some may disagree, but the thought is that because there is no chelator, homeopathy just re-distributes the metals. Christopher de-veloped an oxalate issue that got progressively worse as we did this year of homeopathy. To clarify, I am not against homeopathy. It may be that our choice of practitioners wasn't the best.

So now we had this beautiful, funny, typical boy, a brown belt in karate, with a fantastic, sarcastic sense of humor, who had an oxalate issue. Oxalate crystals are composed of oxalic acid that is combining with calcium or heavy metals. Christopher's body was producing these oxalate crystals for a reason, a protective reason. Kidney stones are seventy-eight to ninety percent oxalic acid. Christopher doesn't have kidney stones, but has enough oxalate crystals in his urine to indicate that his liver is producing them. This could be caused by a few things, one of which is lead in the liver. For Christopher, the oxalate crystals were in his bloodstream and depositing in the soft tissue around his eyes. His eyes were red, swollen, and painful most of the time. He was miserable.

Lots of foods also contain oxalates, and eating these makes the symptoms worse. For two and a half years, we were forced to put him on a low oxalate diet. Sweet potatoes, nuts, summer squash, spinach, green beans, pinto beans, most fruits and berries were all out. I cried for two days when I realized that Christopher needed to be on the low oxalate diet. And it didn't even seem like it was helping! I started him on Andrew Cutler's low-dose, oral chelation protocol, added all the recommended herbs and supplements for oxalate issues, and started giving him a remedy made from his own crystals. Nothing was helping.

I then heard about and researched alkaline Kangen water. I am happy to say, after eight days on the Kangen water, Christopher's eyes were back to normal. Oxalate crystals won't be formed in an alkaline body. Christopher's body was acidic and toxic. The oral chelation was taking care of the remaining heavy metals, and the Kangen water was removing metabolic waste, yeast, and other "floaters" in the cells. We were kicking this oxalic acid to the curb!

Parents to be, or parents of babies and young children, I encourage you to research. Find out for yourself what has happened to a generation of children. Ask questions until you feel a logical answer has been given and then ask more. Above all, trust your instincts. You are the God-appointed steward of your child; not the pediatrician, not your relatives. Your parental instinct trumps any expert. Expert opinions and even current day science is subject to change. If you don't feel comfortable with your pediatrician's recommendations, don't do them! If we had just paused and done our own research, not only about vaccines, but about formula, corn syrup, antibiotics, and anti-fungals, we could have saved money, blood, sweat, and plenty of tears. Please, trust your instincts! I encourage all parents of newly diagnosed children to never give up. Your child's body wants to heal. It's designed to heal. Recovery is possible! My Christopher is living proof!!

Co-Pilot

"Nothing can resist the human will that will stake even its existence on its stated purpose."

~Benjamin Disraeli

Standing in my kitchen I feel tugging on the back of my shirt. I turn around to see my five-year-old daughter, Emily, holding a Talk About Curing Autism magnet that says, "Autism is Treatable. Recovery is Happening." She asks me, "What does this say?" So I tell her. She looks down at the magnet and appears to be satisfied with the answer so I go back preparing dinner. She investigates further, "Mommy, what is autism?" I try my best to explain what autism is and she tries to process my answer. I am delicate in my words. Such a sterile label for something so difficult. Nearly forbidden and spoken in hushed tones; always kept remote from Emily's name. Her next question was nothing I was prepared for...."Mommy, do I have autism?" I freeze.

How do I answer that? I thought it would be awhile before we had this conversation. I always pictured her being a teenager when these questions came up and I have played out in my mind what questions she might have. And I was ok with that because she would be old enough to understand. We would have closure. The battle would be done. But here was my five-year-old standing at my side wanting answers now. Why was it so hard to give her an answer?

Truth is, I have spent more time thinking about when would be a good time to talk about what she has been through and not enough time thinking about what I would say to her. Anytime the thought enters my mind it is quickly replaced with feelings of guilt. How do I tell her what happened to her? Will she blame me? Will she remember how hard we fought to help? I start thinking about the last five years, and wonder how much she remembers.

Emily was born very early on a Wednesday morning. We are a military family and at the time we were stationed in a small town in Oklahoma. I remember hearing the pelting rain and howling wind of the storm outside. But the moment she was born I only felt peace in that room. I looked at her and saw a happy, healthy baby. I thought there was no way anything could go wrong. Life was so perfect. She was perfect.

For the first two months everything was great. We did everything we were told. As first time parents, who were we to question our pediatrician? Doctor's orders, right? That was until a family member gave us some information on vaccines. We were very confused. I had never had any reason to question vaccines. I was indoctrinated as a child that immunizations were important. As a parent, I was conditioned to do the same.

During my daughter's two month check-up, we asked questions about vaccines and their safety. Naively we figured our pediatrician would be able to give us the pros and cons of vaccinating and would support our decision. Instead he retorted and scolded us. So much for informed consent. By the end of the appointment, he had me convinced that my child would die of a disease if I didn't vaccinate. So I relented and Emily received the DTaP and Hep B vaccines that day. A few hours later she was cranky and had a fever, but by the next morning, those symptoms disappeared and she suddenly had reflux. We expressed our concerns to her doctor, but he spouted the CDC's dogma. He coldly declared our daughter fine.

So a few months went by, and we went back in for more vaccines. At around seven months of age, it seemed like Emily had become weaker and she was not sleeping well. Through the next several months Emily continued to meet all her milestones. She loved to talk and learned new words quickly. She loved books and interacted with others. Her giggle and smile were enough to make anyone's day.

Military life demanded another move so we began seeing a new pediatrician. At 19 months, we went in to get her the last DTaP and flu shot. Things were never the same after that; our daughter plateaued. I made an appointment and expressed my concerns. Again, I was bullied and made to feel like a complete idiot. But this time I wasn't going to let anyone convince us to continue vaccinating our daughter. After a lengthy discussion, my husband and I decided to stop vaccinating Emily. We were too late. In the weeks following Emily's 19 month shots her stomach became very distended, and a few weeks after that she was in the hospital for complications from the flu. While there, she received IV antibiotics. A few months later she got cellulitis (a bacterial skin infection). We still have no idea what caused it, but she was once again hospitalized and given IV antibiotics.

During this time, my husband was gone on his first deployment so it was just Emily and I. Emily had never been very sick, so being hospitalized twice within a few months was puzzling. And it got worse. It seemed that every month there was something new that I noticed. I could not find answers, and my research raised more questions. Emily struggled with constipation for several weeks and then would switch to diarrhea. I made an appointment with her pediatrician. I was assured my daughter was merely struggling with her daddy being deployed. I left with a useless referral to a child psychologist. Absurd. I stood my ground and demanded a referral to a gastroenterologist. It took a few visits, going in and making our case, but finally we had our referral. The gastroenterologist took some x-rays and performed a barium enema. The tests showed she was constipated, but everything else looked normal. They cleaned her out, but after a brief reprieve the symptoms returned. I was worried but sought comfort in the test results. I continued to make excuses and find explanations for the things I was seeing. Then my wakeup call came.

At two years old, I enrolled Emily into a play-and-music class. I watched the other kids running around having fun and trying the activities and couldn't help but compare them to Emily. She stood close to my side with a look of panic and hands placed over her ears. She was so anxious that it took two months before she started trying some of the activities. When she did, I noticed she just couldn't do what the other kids were doing. She also showed no interest in the other kids; they seemed invisible to her. We eventually stopped going to the class as Emily began having anxiety anytime we left the house. She spent most of the day crying and screaming unable to communicate beyond the screams and pointing. When Emily wasn't screaming, she acted like a drunk. She would walk into walls, randomly fall over, and laugh hysterically for no reason.

Again, I found myself in the doctor's office airing my fears. I expected to leave with no answers, but that day was different. The pediatrician finally heard my concerns and referred her to be evaluated. I felt a bit relieved but also puzzled. I wanted answers but I was also hoping to hear that my kid was ok, even though I knew she wasn't. I questioned the doctor as to what she felt was wrong. The answer was something I never thought I'd hear. "I want Emily to be evaluated for autism." Autism? That can't be. My world froze as I tried to process what I had just heard.

I looked down at my daughter who was sitting on the floor anxiously pinching her neck. She had dark circles under her eyes and a look of pain on her face. Her stomach was huge and I watched as she made uncomfortable swallows as she tried to keep the reflux down. My child was in physical pain. She was born happy and healthy and then something changed. It didn't make sense. I began to wonder if the behavior and health concerns were connected. But her doctor assured me they weren't and would not offer any help for the pain. She felt that the physical symptoms I noticed were of no concern. This bothered me. My child was visibly not well but I was being told that she was fine.

I came home that day feeling so depressed. I sat at my computer for several hours reading about autism and trying to convince myself that Emily did not have that. But the more I read the more I knew it was true. Two months later she received a diagnosis of PDD-NOS. She was also delayed in fine motor, gross motor and speech. She was very weak and had low muscle tone. Emily needed speech, occupational, physical, and feeding therapy.

When asked what things would look like in the long run, the doctor replied by telling us that she would never function as a normal adult and there was not much hope in changing that. No hope? This couldn't be the answer. I knew it wasn't. There is always, always hope. I wanted more for Emily. She deserved better. I knew I had to fight for her. I was motivated to find answers and prove all of her doctors wrong.

At least I would not be fighting alone. My husband returned from his redeployment. I needed reinforcements. We turned to my husband's aunt who had been through the same thing with her child. She pointed us in the right direction and we started biomed. We owe everything to her and would not be where we are today if it was not for her help.

In addition to the help from our aunt, we got connected with TACA and found a lot of helpful resources. Within a few weeks after Emily's diagnosis we headed to our first DAN! appointment. It was the first time I actually felt like we were getting somewhere. Within a few weeks we had answers to so many of our concerns. We started with diet and added probiotics, melatonin, and vitamin B-12 injections. After one week, some of the fog had lifted. The changes were noticeable, and we knew we were on the right track. Emily was talking more and was jubilant. It was major progress. But I could tell she was still having stomach problems. Again, my husband's aunt came to the rescue and recommended a GI specialist in Texas who she was sure could help us. So we made the trip to Texas and boy, was she right. After having Emily scoped, results showed her intestines were a total mess. It was hard to hear but we had more answers. We had more work to do.

Over the next several months we worked with both our DAN! Doctor and the GI specialist. The changes were amazing. Emily began communicating better and the echolalia was gone. She began showing major improvements in physical therapy and conquering huge milestones we thought might never come. Reflux was finally gone and for the first time Emily began eating meat. She had been on pureed food for the last year because she was too uncomfortable to eat regular food and did not have the strength to use utensils.

Emily continued to make giant leaps towards recovery. Her therapists were amazed as she met goal after goal and became more confident and less anxious. The transformation was amazing. I cried tears of joy with every victory, whether big or small. Every milestone was worth celebrating.

We were on to something and despite seeing improvements, we still had a lot more questions. I wasn't ready to settle for "good enough." We had opened the door to recovery and now that we knew it was possible, there was no looking back. I wanted answers to everything. We were still seeing a lot of progress but with every leap forward, we would fall a few steps back. New things would pop up and we would once again find ourselves confused and full of new questions.

When Emily was four years old she got sick with a bad stomach flu, and for the first time in a long time we found ourselves in the hospital. She got through it, but shortly after that we began seeing bloating, stomach pain, sleeping problems, and some other odd symptoms. I found myself feeling exhausted and in need of some inspiration to get out of this temporary setback.

Around that time, my husband bought me an amazing book, The Thinking Moms' Revolution. I read the book several times, feeling renewed hope. I was so inspired listening to the stories of moms who had been through the same thing and continued to fight for their kids. I knew I had to do the same. So we headed back to our DAN! Doctor and got the answers we needed, and a few weeks later Emily was doing better than ever.

Today, Emily is five years old and has lost her diagnosis. She is anxiety free, reflux is gone, communication is great, sensory problems have dissipated, and her physical strength has greatly improved. She is very happy and loves to socialize with others. We still deal with stomach problems from time to time but I hold on to the hope that one day she will be permanently pain free. We have come so far from where she was a few years ago, proving that anything is possible.

In survival training, the military teaches that a person can live three weeks without food, three days without water, three hours without shelter, three minutes without air, and only three seconds without hope. We never lost hope and we kept fighting. There have been so many ups and downs in our journey to recovery. Looking back, it's hard not to feel guilt and sadness over what happened. But for the most part, I find myself feeling stronger than ever. I feel proud of my daughter. She should feel proud of herself. But the question still stands: Do I tell my daughter she has autism?

Emily is still standing in front of me, waiting for an answer. I can't put it off any longer. I choose my words carefully as to not cause too much confusion or frustration. "Emily, you were born very healthy and so happy. Then you got sick. So mommy and daddy worked really hard to help you and you worked really hard to get stronger. Do you remember any of that?" She nods her head yes. I point back at the magnet to the word, recovery. "Recovery is happening!" I tell her in an excited voice. "Recovery means you are getting better and feeling healthy again. It means autism is gone. Do you feel better Emily?" She thinks about it and pulls up her shirt to show me her belly. "Mommy, my tummy feels better. I feel happy." I smile at her. "That's all that matters Emily. Recovery is all that matters." It's at that moment that the guilt over what happened is gone. Recovering her from this is all that matters. It's what we put our strength and energy into every day, and every day we are stronger for it. Does my daughter have autism? No, I can honestly tell her, she does not. Autism is gone. Recovery is happening!

SPARK

"I don't see autism," the doctor said after Jackie's re-evaluation. "She is social and makes great eye contact. She is speech delayed and seems to have some developmental gaps. We can keep the diagnosis on paper for now so that she continues to get the services that she needs, because she still needs them." We are almost there, I thought. Almost! Many of the symptoms that are known as autism have disappeared. It isn't because she never had what they label as autism, it is because of all the hard work we have done to heal those symptoms.

We chose to be proactive in her healing and recovery. Just six months before this evaluation, Jackie was waking up in the night screaming in pain and fear. She wanted us to hold her, but when we would try she would scream even louder and push us away. We didn't know what to do and didn't know what was taking over our little girl. She would run around in circles all day long and flap her arms. We would scream her name and she wouldn't look at us or respond. She didn't make eye contact. It was as if it would cause her pain to look us in the eyes. She had some words, but mostly she would point at what she wanted and melt down when we couldn't figure it out.

Jackie was diagnosed with Autism Spectrum Disorder just after her 3rd birthday. I knew before then that it was probably the diagnosis she would receive. I had been searching and reading everything I could about the symptoms she was having for almost a year before her diagnosis. Jackie is my third child, and I knew what she was experiencing and that how she was developing was not normal. Although I had concerns at her 2nd year "well child" visit, she wasn't delayed. Everything was developing as it should be, I was told. I had her checked again six months later and yes, now she was delayed. We got a referral and started speech and occupational therapy immediately. Her speech development at that point just stopped as if she was stuck. I then obtained a referral to a developmental doctor and he gave the diagnosis. Autism. I left there with three prescriptions to try out and was told to come back in two months to see how she was doing.

I left feeling confused and angry that the only thing to do was to try and drug my child. I didn't blindly trust in giving medications to children and thought there had to be something else that could be done. I only encountered one other family who were going through the same thing as we were, and they were as lost as we were. Nobody could tell me what to do when she had a meltdown. Some folks said to try to avoid any situation that might cause a meltdown, and others said she would just have to learn to deal with life's situations and that we had to take her out because she had to learn to be out in society. That was easy for others to say, as they weren't trying to handle her while handling three other kids and never knowing when it would happen or why. I was stuck in panic mode going anywhere with her, but I was not giving up. I was going to try to stay strong and keep positive.

On top of all the emotional stress she was going through, she was also very sick. She projectile vomited as a baby and was late sitting up and walking. Weak stomach muscles couldn't push her stools out. We did a hearing test to make sure the reason she wasn't talking and responding to her name wasn't because of hearing loss. None of the doctors ever mentioned that all her ear infections and vomiting could be from a food allergy or intolerance.

It wasn't until my sister recommended I talk to a woman she knew from La Leche League that I found out she might have a dairy allergy. I never thought to question keeping her on the vaccine schedule even when she was constantly sick and on antibiotics. I didn't know that those antibiotics were further damaging her gut. I didn't know a lot of things and neither did the doctors who were treating her.

I wanted answers! My research continued and upon my searching I came across groups of people on Facebook and Yahoo that were using alternative methods for healing and were getting results. For the first time, I was learning that there were all different paths to healing our children. I was getting the hope that I was searching and yearning for. I was learning all kinds of fascinating things. The first thing I wanted to do was to try and eliminate foods that could be causing Jackie to be sick.

A friend recommended a book by Julie Matthews called "Nourishing Hope for Autism." I learned that gluten and dairy must be removed from the diet especially if there were gastrointestinal issues. To this day I have yet to meet a child with autism who hasn't had some type of GI issue. I have heard that they do exist, but I have never encountered one. They are rare indeed! Even when there aren't evident gut problems, there are usually other issues that are not being pinned down to food intolerances. For instance, removing the foods also stopped my daughter's unusual meltdowns. The kind that none of the doctors, therapists or specialists could tell me how to handle or control.

It was a long, hard road to get gluten and dairy out of her diet, but boy am I glad that I did! Jackie stopped waking up in the night screaming and was now sleeping through the night. She was making eye contact and responding to her name. She was no longer having bouts of diarrhea. The meltdowns started slowing down and then stopped altogether. Yes, all this happened just from removing dairy and gluten from her diet. But, I knew I had to do more and I wanted to do more.

She was now trying to talk in sentences but we couldn't understand anything she was saying. Her speech therapist said it was because she had apraxia. I knew there were many paths that I could take, but I did not feel comfortable giving supplements and doing treatments without the guidance of a professional. In my area, I had the choice of a MAPS doctor or a naturopath that treated all types of childhood illnesses. The naturopath felt like the way to go (and was much more affordable), so I called up and made an appointment.

You know the feeling when you walk in somewhere and it just feels right? I sat down with her, we started talking and didn't stop for two hours. I left there with such a different feeling than when I had seen the developmental doctor that was supposed to be the specialist in my area for autism. I felt so empowered and full of hope. I was getting answers as to why food was causing her issues. I was given the chance to do tests to see what was in her stools and immediately start on a good quality probiotic. Once her tests came back and we found dangerous bacteria and yeast I was given the opportunity to treat her with a very powerful yet natural herb.

She also told me about a private school that she had done many workshops with for kids on the spectrum. Jackie was in special education through the county and attended public school for just a short time. That system was a failure for us. I made an appointment to take a tour of the school our naturopath recommended. When I sat down and talked with the director it felt right. She told me how she started the school, after becoming frustrated while searching for schools for her own children. They had programs like brain gym, yoga and oral motor exercises daily in the classroom. There were monthly meetings tracking their progress and they kept a very detailed chart of the child's progress and challenges. They immediately called for an IEP meeting after Jackie started and added services to her plan.

We still have a ways to go to total recovery, but healing continues steadily and she has lost her autism diagnosis! She still has apraxia and that is what we are working on recovering from now. We are still doing a GF/CF diet but have also removed soy and GMO's. We only eat 100% grass-fed beef and pasture-raised chicken and eggs, and nitrate free bacon, sausage and lunch meat. We try to keep sugar and processed food to a minimum. I make probiotic drinks like kefir water and root beer. All beauty and cleaning supplies we use must be organic and free of allergens. We are doing energetic healing Quantum Biofeedback (SCIO) and starting on essential oils. We take cod liver oil, magnesium and probiotics daily.

As Jackie healed, I started her protocol for myself and my family when I realized that we all had many of the same issues. I soon found out that my health issues were directly related to hers. After Jackie was born and I first noticed her having unusual health issues, mine started as well. I was vomiting, had unusual rashes appearing on my legs, constantly having diarrhea. I was losing weight without even trying. I had a well-respected homeopath tell me that the only cases of autism that she had come across that weren't caused by vaccine damage were when the mom had taken antibiotics during pregnancy.

I later learned of a certain class of antibiotics that were poisoning many people who took them. They are called fluoroquinolone antibiotics that include antibiotics like Cipro and Levaquin to name a few. There is now a black box warning on this class, but they are still being prescribed frequently. Amongst many symptoms these can cause are leaky gut and candida overgrowth. These are what I was given for a sinus infection while pregnant. I have never been the same since. They don't always cause an immediate reaction but people can start to notice problems even months after taking them. It is what we call getting floxed, and almost all now have major gut issues, candida overgrowth, depression and neuropathy. This is why I believe Jackie had such a destroyed gut at birth. She was poisoned in the womb and then the poisoning continued. I did an IgG test and reacted strongly to dairy. I removed dairy from my diet, and I no longer had the sinus and upper respiratory infections that plagued me since I was a child.

Since Jackie had such a damaged gut at birth she was always spitting up and hated to be on her tummy. I didn't realize what an impact not having her do tummy time would have. Not having her learn to be on her tummy caused her to crawl and walk late. She skipped over important milestones. Tummy time is critical to brain development. We are exploring different programs to help balance her brain and build those pathways that were lost during her very early years.

I know there are people who think that all of the things that moms like me do are quackery. Most of us are under the guidance of a professional, and we only give supplements based on concrete testing. We have seen our kids directly improve as a result, and it isn't just growing out of it or a coincidence. When mainstream doctors start to realize how powerful food is and how dangerous toxins are, more of us moms will learn to trust them again.

Today, Jackie's main problem is that her brain has motor planning problems using her lips, jaw, and tongue needed for speech. She knows what she wants to say, but her brain has a hard time coordinating her muscle movements to say it. She is receptive to everything, but has a difficult time expressing. The awesome school that she attends is working hard with her doing oral motor exercises and she is becoming more intelligible every day. Right now her apraxia is our biggest hurdle, but she will overcome it.

I would love to see more schools adopt the policy that Jackie's school has. They only eat the food that the parent of the child sends in. They also do not use any chemicals to clean the campus. The words of the director were that she just doesn't know how those chemicals are affecting developing brains. I completely agree and am so thankful that I don't have to worry about her being exposed to all those toxins while away from me. They still have holiday parties and special occasions and you know what? They don't miss out on any fun. We do not need to have parties filled with sugar, dyes and who knows what else on a weekly basis in schools.

While I did not see an immediate regression in my daughter like so many that I know with children on the spectrum, I do believe that vaccines did affect her in a negative way. I believe that they affect all of our children to some degree. I am not asking you to take my word for it; I am simply asking you to do your own research. Do not just blindly believe what all the mainstream doctors are telling you. Many of them haven't done any research into vaccines or autism at all. I know this because I know many nurses and doctors who saw the negative effects and decided to do more research. I know now that my daughter should not have continued to receive vaccines while she was constantly sick and on antibiotics.

A good book to read up on all the effects is "Vaccine Safety Manual" by Neil Z. Miller, with a foreword by Russell Blaylock, MD. I know that my children and I are greatly affected by toxins and that we have trouble detoxing. I also know when a child is vaccine damaged, it is very difficult for the parents to get justice. The vaccine court is not a court that was built on justice. The vaccine makers have blanket immunity. They have protection and cannot be sued if one of their vaccines injures a child. To read about this you can go to http://www.nvic.org. You can ask to read the inserts of the vaccines before given. To find the inserts online you can go to http://www.immunize.org. The vaccines not only contain live viruses, but also highly toxic substances such as aluminum and formaldehyde. What is the cumulative effect of these toxins that are being injected through the blood stream and not through our mucous membranes like we naturally receive viruses and invaders?

As so many have said before me, what works for my child may not work for yours. I am by no means saying every child will recover like mine has, but I do believe no matter what the condition of the child that there is hope and they should be given that chance. I have hope that this book and all of our stories will reach out and help others to the path of healing. Keep hope alive as your child is worth it. Don't be afraid to think way outside of the box as that is usually where we find the most useful tools in healing. I didn't accept that my daughter was going to need medication to function in life. I don't accept that she will have a permanent speech impairment. I am choosing to be a positive force for her. I know that is something we all must do for our children.

Our children feel our energy, and the positivity in our minds and hearts affect them for the better. There are so many negative things that happen on this journey but I have pledged to stay positive and be a light for my daughter and all children. When she no longer needs me to fight this hard for her, I will always be a part of this community. I am ready to fight for all our kids and keep hope alive for all involved. This is my life long journey. When I have extra money, I give it to moms who I know are in need. Sometimes the most valuable thing is just talking to a mom who needs someone to listen so she can let it all out. My goal is to keep the spark alive and be a positive force in this community. We will support each other so we never burn out, and can continue this battle with strength, united as one.

ShamROCK

In writing my chapter, I have had to reflect on the darker side of my life, and my family's life, over the last eight years. It has been hard to face, let alone to even think of writing it down for all to read. But in the midst of those dark days, there have also been incredible times of joy, and I must not forget those. Our two beautiful daughters were born, we stuck together as a family, and we came out of the dark and into the light together.

Our son, S. was diagnosed with autism the day before his fifth birthday. He is now almost eight. I'm not going dwell on that day. I knew it was coming. You see, it took us three years of searching in the dark to get to that point. You must wonder how he wasn't diagnosed at 12 or 18 months, like the media tells you is now possible. The reason is because he wasn't autistic at 12 or 18 months. It happened over time. S. was one of the one in 42 boys that developed "regressive autism," or autism that takes over the child's mind and body in a matter of months and years and the parents have no clue what the hell is going on. Some of our Thinker friends will call it "iatrogenic autism" (a medical disorder caused by a physician). I'm not totally sure if this is the case for S. but if it looks, walks and talks like a duck then…quack quack.

So how do I tell his story? How do I explain to friends and family, many of whom have no idea about what was going on? I doubt they could begin to understand the stress on our home life, living under a kind of intimidation of our child, every minute of every day. I don't think I am in a place to tell it all in great detail right now. I want S's story to be one of hope and triumph and not one of despair, fear and grief. I want it to be one I can tell him when he's older and he'll say, "Mom, you're crazy. What was all the fuss about? I'm fine."

We have had S. in some kind of therapy since he was two years old and it wasn't until we discovered biomedical protocols when he was six that we saw the most improvement. The last two years of that part of our journey have been the most rewarding and also the most distressing.

The process of grieving started all over again. We had to research the reasons for his symptoms and come to the realization that we had been lied to by doctors we trusted. Or perhaps they genuinely didn't know this part of their job, but in my opinion that's equally as abhorrent.

My son's autism stemmed from a toxic overload of his immune system. I believe that there were many things that lead to my son to be so toxic, that perhaps it began with my own health, my nauseating pregnancy and his traumatic birth. However, we now know that a single trigger event most likely tipped his toxic barrel over and we have been cleaning up the mess ever since. That trigger, on an already loaded gun, was five shots in one day at 12 months old. Within hours he had a reaction (per the manufacturer's package inserts) and within days he was hospitalized and had surgery to remove an infection walled off in his lymph nodes.

It was a pretty extreme reaction but at the time it was not called that. It was called a chance happening, a mystery. They told me it was a teething reaction, that he was getting his molars! And I believed those doctors. Somehow, after a week in the hospital with my baby boy, I walked out with a sense of relief that it wasn't the vaccines that put him in there, because that would have been too much for me to understand. I believed in the vaccine theory of herd immunity and I didn't want that belief shattered. I was extremely passionate about that stance, and I wouldn't listen to any argument against it. I had that "What to Expect" book memorized. I wanted to do what everyone else did: obey the rules.

I don't like to assign that event with this lofty accolade of triggering my son's decline because it starts the wrong conversation. There is an entire media machine out there debunking everything I have to say on that issue so I am not going to explain it, except to say that it happened and no one can deny it. I leave the difficult task of vaccine advocacy in the capable hands of the Canary Party, Age of Autism and Safeminds. In my view, the wrong conversation for me begins with "vaccines cause autism." I think it should begin with "autism is a medical condition and vaccines play a key role in harming our children's natural immunity and contribute to their overall toxic burden." Actually, I think removing the label "autism" altogether would be a better start. Wipe the board clean. Call it what it is. Our kids are sick, mine was sick, that's it. We know it, they know it and no one's doing anything about it, except the parents and a few brave advocates and doctors.

Let me point out that my children have all been fully vaccinated. My son had 43 doses by the time he went into his Special Education self-contained kindergarten class. That's right, I continued to vaccinate him after he fell ill at 12 months. Why? Well the doctors did such a great job of allaying my fears that this was just a mystery and a coincidence. And to be honest, I was happy with that because I so wanted to believe that this wasn't my fault. I didn't want to blame myself for not taking better care of him when he first got sick — was I giving him enough Tylenol for the fever? Oh yeah, Tylenol. I was told recently by a prominent scientist that Tylenol stops sulphation dead. I know now what the process of sulphation means to the human body, so that sort of information is shattering to me, and makes me feel ill with guilt and regret.

I didn't want to be blamed for his decline. How selfish of me to think of myself, I know, but I was afraid to admit fault. Defending vaccines was part of that. I felt guilty for never asking questions and not doing my own research. At that time, I didn't know what a package insert was. In fact, my pediatrician had a policy of only seeing patients if they followed the recommended vaccine schedule. I wanted to believe that it couldn't be the vaccines, that it must be something else. That's a tough thing to deal with when you are in denial that your child is showing signs of autism. You start to ask yourself, "What did I do to him? What did I do wrong when I was pregnant? Why did this happen to my son?"

Let's imagine that my son's vaccine reaction did not trigger his decline. I am still left with the fact that he had an adverse reaction within hours of receiving those shots. A reaction so severe as to hospitalize him for a week, resulting in surgery. I feel like he should get the vaccine injury equivalent of the Purple Heart! Why? Well he took one for the team, statistically. My kid got sick…so yours didn't. It's almost catchy.

So, how did we begin to get him back? That's what everyone wants to know but won't ask openly. I get wide eyed stares when I start that conversation. Sideways nodding, silence, no questions. It's very interesting to me. But I used to be them, so I give them all a pass. One day they will remember our conversation and will say, "OMG, that crazy autism mom was right all along." I don't want to be right. I only want the truth to come out.

It wasn't until he was six that we finally stumbled across the answers we were looking for. It is a tale of coincidence, belief, divine intervention, cosmic alliances, and whatever else you want to call it. But we finally found a way to get him back from the clutches of what they still call autism.

At this time, I was going to lots of talks on autism and thought I was getting the latest and greatest information, but I hadn't found the magic potion yet. Then I heard a lecture by a doctor who treated kids with autism and ADHD via brain integration technique (BIT). It was right up my alley; non-invasive, not too crazy and I wouldn't have to change his food. You see, at this point, I had never looked into the gluten and casein free diets because I had chosen to listen to the sources of information that dismissed them. It was just way too much work and I was exhausted and spent at this point. My son's autism was manifesting as severe OCD and tantrums. I had very little left to give to challenging myself even more. Even my own pediatrician said it was just anecdotal hearsay so we couldn't rely on it. Good, because getting him to do anything was so hard, changing food was not on my list of priorities. I had no clue.

The talk had me riveted. Holy Hell, you mean the brain can do what now?? I needed to get an appointment with this doctor! Time was not on our side and I needed to figure this out. This doctor was a naturo-pathic doctor and slowly (remember, I was a tough nut to crack on this holistic stuff) she began to peel away at the onion that was my child and his symptoms. It was distressing to me to learn how ignorant I was about food and how it related to the body, about GMO food, sugar, corn syrup, gluten, casein, the biology of the human body and the gut-brain connection. And boy was ignorance bliss.

Our new doc was able to tell me, just by observing him, what he needed to calm him down. At this point his symptoms were "reduced" to: severe sensory behavior (rolling on the floor, bending over chairs on his tummy), no peer interaction or reciprocal play, and angry outbursts. He had more language, but his behavior was still very unpredictable and aggressive. I was worried for the future. She sent us home with a diet plan, supplements and a recommendation to read Dr. Bock's book. Within days things just got better and easier. Cue choirs of angels singing.

Right away, I started to do some research and found what I now know to be closer to the truth than I have ever known before. My son could be healed naturally. I felt late to the party. Why hadn't anyone ever told me this before?? I used to believe that if there was a "cure" I would hear about it on CNN. I was glued to that channel for years. I never heard that he could have medical testing done to find out what was going on and why he was behaving the way he did. He had intestinal yeast?? I felt like I'd been living under a dark rock, an incredibly noisy and stressful rock, but a dark rock nonetheless. What I was about to learn sent me into a tailspin of research, reading and hope.

We started by adding the supplements he needed to calm his neuro-chemistry, reduce inflammation and control the yeast in his intestines. Then slowly I started to change his food. The first thing to go was dairy and we noticed an immediate change, and I mean immediate. He started talking more and he was engaged and less angry. We had so much hope, I was hooked. This autism bitch wasn't going to ruin my family! I was fired up! I was taking back my child and God help anyone who got in my way! I get it now, and if anyone tries to talk to me about awareness and blue lights again, I might lose my mind.

As my awakening continued, I joined Facebook groups for support and information (those mamas know their stuff) and for the first time, I felt a call to action for my child like I had never known before. Then I came across a post for FUA (Fuck You Autism) Friday in a group called The Thinking Moms' Revolution. What? You can say that about autism on Facebook? What? It was not negative, it was a rally cry. These ladies were saying this in public, supporting each other, defying the odds, cheering each other on in their kids' recovery. I was so overwhelmed.

The first blog I read that first Friday was by Goddess and the title was "Ignorant Bitch." I cried and cried while reading that as I felt I had finally found a home with women (and one man) who were fighters and Thinkers and who weren't going to take it anymore. Getting their kids and our kids better was all they cared about. I will be forever grateful to my Facebook friend who sent me over there that day.

In the last 18 months since I clicked 'like' on TMR's page (there were only 2,000 of us back then), things have changed for our family in the most amazing way. My husband got on board after reading Dr. Bock's book and never really questioned my judgment on my son's healing. He understood that there was more to this thing than genetics. It was extremely important for me to have him support me and thank God he did. I needed that support. My daughters were getting to know their brother for the first time and could play with him now, something they hadn't known before. We were getting healthier as a family and we were healing.

This journey has also meant a lot of change for me personally. I found myself finally waking up and finding purpose in my life. I began researching and learning all I could about biomedical protocols, natural healing methods and alternative therapies. It all just made so much sense. I was glued to books and the computer for a solid six months. But I must admit it has been difficult. At first I was distraught at the realization that I closed my mind to this for so long. There were some brave moms who tried to tell me about diet and supplements in the past, but I wasn't ready. They knew that. But as soon as I was, I called upon them for help. They were there without judgment. I think we all find the right answers when we are ready and thank God that those moms planted the seed in my mind early on so I could go back to it later. Those are tough lessons to learn. But I am thankful to have met the many women that I have, to teach me how to navigate these times. My passion has sometimes caused me to be impulsive but that's the learning curve I am on. It is very steep and fraught with challenges.

Today, I often find myself reflecting on my life "before I knew" and I can't quite recall what I was thinking! I wasn't, that's obvious, but I do this to understand what it was that kept me from seeing the truth so I can have compassion for others who do not yet see it. We all know that there is nothing on this Earth more important to parents than their children's welfare. It invokes a kind of visceral passion and defensive instinct that we cannot interfere with. We need to be mindful of that sacred bond and not judge or feel entitled to have an opinion about it. We should show kindness and allow peace to flow.

I do have to ask myself, though, why is it so easy for everyone else to turn away from this and not want to understand this epidemic as a threat to their children or their future grandchildren? Perhaps they don't believe it and perhaps they don't think it will happen to their kids. They might think that just because they are aware of it, that's enough. "It can't happen to our kids. We have lit everything up blue — the Empire State Building, the Eiffel Tower and the Sydney Harbor Bridge. It can't happen to us because of all the awareness. Surely that's enough?" Well it isn't. Awareness isn't prevention. Awareness isn't treatment. Awareness isn't hope.

Not long after my awakening and before TMR, I joined another group of smart women whose plan it is to change the world, and when you interact with minds like that, it tends to start more wheels turning than you knew you had. So yes, now my mind rarely stops thinking. And being part of Team TMR has only enhanced that. Our new way of thinking is empowering and gives us hope. This empowerment will change the course of history for our children. We are seeing leaders in this fight whose primary job is raising their kids, many of them with at least one child with ASD, but they are showing us what it means to be brave.

There are mothers who used to be in the boardrooms on Wall Street, now on the boards of their own non-profits so that they can fight this thing head on with all they have left. They don't get paid; they just have our kids in their hearts. I have also met many fearless doctors who refuse to be silent and fight for our kids to get the medical treatment they need and deserve. There will be a great reward for them one day and I will be there in the crowd cheering them on.

I truly believe that passion and hope are intrinsically linked. My job is now clear — recovering my son. I finally have hope and it can't be taken away. S. has recovered so much that he no longer meets the criteria for an ASD diagnosis. He scores 10 on the ATEC scoring system which means he does not have autism. This is not an official get out of jail free card, but it is indicative of how far we have come. At four years old he scored 112. We still have work to do, but he is no longer a severe case.

S. is learning how to interact with his peers. He is learning about the world around him with a new curiosity, more typical of a five or six year old. He loves to ride his bike, goes to the movies and plays "Avengers" with his sisters. He has a few friends at school. He asks questions now like "How do you say 'how are you?' in French, Mommy?" He can write roman numerals from one to one hundred, and he taught himself! Just today, he looked into my eyes and said, "Wow Mom! I see myself in your eyes!" He was seeing his reflection, but I was seeing much more. What he said was beautiful and meaningful on a level he will never understand, except for the day when his child says the same to him. We now have a child that is present, engaged, trusting, nurtured and loving. He's not my tortured soul anymore, he IS my soul. I can finally see myself in his eyes. What a beautiful thing.

Let me finish with a story that is often used in the special needs community to console parents when they are first thrown into this unknown and scary place. It is called "Welcome to Holland" and it is written by Emily Perl Kingsley. You can read it here: http://www.our-kids.org/archives/Holland.html. The story generally describes a scenario where someone has planned a trip to Italy, and has done all the research and is excited for the trip, but gets off the plane in Holland instead. And while they wanted to go to Italy, they learn to appreciate Holland and its tulips instead. Her point is that if you spend all your time upset that you didn't get to go to Italy, you will miss out on all the wonderful things about Holland.

When I first heard it, I cried because I was grieving and it was comforting. It still comforts many people today. But right now I'm going to call bullshit on this essay for many reasons. I think the people of Holland would be pretty pissed to know that their country was being thought of as a dumping ground for pissed off special needs tourists from America who really wanted to go to Italy for the pasta and wine. It also assumes that all families of special needs kids are going to accept this change of plan and calmly soldier on…in Holland!

Using this analogy to explain what it's like in my community right now… I'm with the pissed off tourists who want to go to Italy. You see, when you learn the language in Holland, spend some time there, see all the sights and smoke some pot, you're kind of done with it. We have to move on to where we were supposed to go. We can read and learn and reinvent the plan. We find out that there are trains and busses out of Holland and if there aren't any available, we can walk. One foot in front of the other will eventually get you out. I have to do this for my husband and my daughters. Our family won't be broken by this. We're going to Italy and we will tell every person we meet along the way how we are doing it so they can follow or find their own way. If they can't walk, we will carry them.

That's the journey I want for my family. It's very hard, but what's harder is living with what they call "autism." So whatever the world says about our approach to healing our child from autism (that disorder for which there is no known cause or cure), I say "The world is not flat, smoking does cause cancer, and Holland is not Italy." FUA!

ROGUE ZEBRA

"Absence of evidence is not evidence of absence."

Like the curiosity of a zebra's stripes — black with white stripes or white with black stripes — I often wonder if we are a spectrum family with additional medical issues or a complex medical family with autism-like tendencies of older child and concerns for his sibling. Our diagnostic expedition started with a stroke....

"Negotiator" was a reality check into parenting. He had clear likes and dislikes — he liked being held and the tighter the swaddle, the better he slept. Dad would become proficient and Negotiator would sleep through the night. He disliked tummy time, rolling in one direction, right arm tucked. His milestones after six months came on the late side of "typical" range. At his nine month well-check, I mentioned Negotiator's one-sided tendencies — had been dragging his right foot when he cruised furniture. Then there was his preference for using left hand. Nurse Practitioners' interest grew, "How often is the hand preference, 50%, 25%?" My heart sank. Hesitantly, I said, "90%, <clearing my throat>. 90% of the time, when we hand him something he initiates with left." The clues were so clear and obvious, now that we were looking at the whole picture.

Neurologist met with us as a family, discussed family history of "southpaws" and ordered an MRI. Negotiator was sedated and a head

MRI was done at 11 months. Diagnosis was suspected Periventricular Leukomalacia (PVL or ventricle stroke) or delayed myelination in left parietal lobe — dismissed as "too vague, we won't ever know what happened." He ended this appointment with phrases "one time event," "you probably don't even need to tell extended family" and "he might walk with a slight limp." We trusted his words to be able to live without the fear of what's next. Trusted ourselves, having done what was expected by listening to ob/gyn, pediatrician and now neurologist.

18 months later, "Crash" arrived. Crash was a sleepy, quiet dispositioned babe with porcelain skin and a head full of dark hair. Crash achieved her milestones — she simply had a poor quality to her skills. She rolled one direction, proficiently. She wobbled her petite head, yet hated being on her back. She earned her strong tummy-time core, sitting at six months. She babbled and smiled at the slightest prompt. Her arms and hands couldn't hold a bottle until half empty. At five months, her legs couldn't hold her own body weight when supported. Even later, she would try and try to rock back and forth like pre-crawl or pull to a stand, only to get frustrated with effort and cry for a toy. We had concerns and weren't going to miss the signs again. Our pediatrician acknowledged our concerns, and ordered an MRI of her head — the results were normal.

Crash started PT at seven months for a "short episode of care, three to six months." Her core was strong, but her arms and legs were unsteady. Supporting our observations and PT's concerns, our pediatrician ordered an MRI of her lumbar spine — results normal. She continued PT for another six month episode of care. Now 11 months old, Crash could pull up, her right foot planted, knee bent and leg pushing up while other leg tried to sneak in support; time elapsed was seven minutes. We continued for another three months. Crash was discharged from PT, stepping independently for short distances at 16 months old. Crash did not have a brain injury or lower spine injury to explain her hypotonia and gross motor delays.

Around two-and-a-half-years-old, Negotiator began screaming between 60 – 90 minutes after being laid to sleep. He'd be alert, but not awake and responsive. Neurologist said night terrors. And we listened, again trusting his judgment. After 18 months and a broken collarbone from falling out of bed, we had a second opinion who agreed. When the screaming started occurring at nap time as well, our pediatrician said to get a third opinion, at an international-renowned clinic.

They did a full week of testing with few answers, but did confirm seizures and started a medication. The medication helped his seizures and nighttime wakings, but behaviors and emotional tantrums increased tenfold. Six months since the first visit, I figured life could not get worse than where we were: Stroke + seizures + ADHD + speech delays + four-year-old's tantrums of epic potential…and Crash with her own developing issues. We already had full-time sensory processing, behavioral and rehab therapies, plus home routines that included specific fine motor or gross motor skills. These were not helping anymore. ASD of whatever label the psych decided that month, was winning.

I had my own sensory processing meltdown, deciding Negotiator & Crash were going gluten-free for six months. Cold Turkey. Crash didn't eat much table food yet, still preferring scheduled pre-digested formula in a bottle, at two years old. Suspect food went into the freezer or pantry. Milk and cheese were THE favorite of Negotiator. We cut off dairy/casein two months into GF trial. The peak of withdrawals occurred at the holidays that year. Life went from crazy days to living in each chaotic moment, focused on the unknown recovery possibility. Six months of Gluten Free/Casein Free gave us enough evidence to continue. He had no seizures in six months — yes, still on meds but no breakthrough seizures. Improved emotions, more communication, more engaged activities out of his comfort zone.

We planned a trial of adding gluten again for 1 week, not telling therapists. But it only took 3 days for the hand flapping stims and behavior extremes to return; his OT asked what we had changed. Future diet challenges, over the years, reproduced his complex partial seizures and emotional extremes.

Our initial success with GFCF, led to additional biomed protocols with guidance from warrior moms who blazed the trail. Learning the signs of Candida, then treating with OLE and probiotics. Food journals. Poop journals. Tracking activity and behaviors. Checking developmental progress on AAP & CDC charts. Learning lifestyle tweaks for phenols, oxalates and other micronutrient food groups I'd never the considered the existence of before 2005. Eliminating phthalates, chemicals and cross reactive foods. We were solving problems one or two at a time with lasting results.

Negotiator was stimming less, working for behavior rewards more. Crash stopped vomiting, finally. We turned that corner in 2009 and had no major changes to baseline for three years, when kids' issues began to shift back toward more medical symptoms. Skills plateaued for both, but they were thriving and excelling in virtual school setting, where we could work at their pace, without distractions, illnesses or bullies.

In 2011, Negotiator started a compounded mitochondrial cocktail, Crash didn't tolerate her custom supplement cocktail. In 2012, we survived flu season needing only IV fluid support, without long term hospitalization or regression of skills. Puberty also hit both kids, despite the three year difference in age. In 2013, new symptoms continued to appear — central apnea requiring bipap nightly and weaker respiratory muscles requiring HFCWO added to daily nebulizer protocol. Fatigue continued to progress; currently both use powered wheelchairs for community distances. These are more medical treatments than any child should bear, but far fewer than other Mighty Mito Fighters routinely have for their daily living care.

In those same eight years, we have seen dozens of medical specialists, locally and across the country. Negotiator's stroke led to night terrors and seizures, after which his muscle weakness and fatigue would not improve. Crash was holding her own — a phrase I'd often use to describe her lack of progress. Their constellation of signs and symptoms — stroke, seizures, ADHD, hyper mobility, muscle weakness, growth delays, sleeping 10 – 12 hours, nutritional deficiency, Asperger's, verbal & oral apraxia, delays in gross/fine motor, receptive/expressive language delays, and social deficits — represent many possibilities, if the doctor excluded one or two symptoms.

Each new specialist added their perspective, some offered testing for a specific group of possibilities — Rett syndrome, congenital myasthenia gravis, spinal muscle atrophy, congenital myopathy, thyroid diseases, mitochondrial disease, fatty acid oxidation disorders, urea cycle disorders, osteogenesis imperfecta, Ehlers-Danlos, deconditioning (of muscles), few years of being "undiagnosed" and recently Charcot-Marie-Tooth possibility. All of these lead back to clinical mitochondrial disease until another disease is proven.

Results would come back as abnormal but non-diagnostic — EEG, EMG, frozen muscle and skin biopsy, fresh muscle and skin biopsy, mtDNA & nDNA genome tests, MRI with MRS; or a rare negative/normal — chromosome tests, complete metabolic panel and other blood/urine lab tests. A buccal swab screening test came back confirming mito dysfunction at 90+% deficiency — "Crash was significantly low, Negotiator was more extensively diminished." We have labs, physical history and genetic findings to clinically support a probable mito diagnosis. Science is still unraveling DNA to make our diagnosis solid.

There is a Someecards meme that states "A special needs Mom's research is better than FBI" That's me. I have no plans to be a doctor or other medical professional but I do have a vested interest in my kids' health and wellness. Partly because of the early oversights and partly out of genuine curiosity, I still spend my late nights reading. I often read back through the extensive 3-ring binders of clinic notes and ask questions — and explore a new tangent. Maybe the doctors missed something — since food choices clearly improved outcome — new tangent, more ideas. I review clinic notes, looking for any new information about a mutation found six years ago — a lifetime in genetic research. I found really awesome medical websites to help me fit our puzzle pieces together. I was gaining a greater understanding, that all of our kids' symptoms were metabolically driven. I narrowed my focus on metabolic processes — how protein, fats and carbs are used, broken down, or stored; and mitochondrial disease — how food is converted to energy.

My knowledge, our diagnostic expedition and non-pharma successes sets us up for suspicious doctors. You know the ones. They've had a one hour lecture on mitochondria and genetics in four years of medical school. The proud confident doctor, who can see your red flags without gathering a 10-year history; who surely knows more from books or lectures that haven't been updated in the last five years; who observes for clues, never talking to patient directly and completely ignores parental insights. His/her perception is parents are doing this "diet" because it's simply a trendy fad or easy and fun lifestyle. Heck, even the child's diagnosis is an attention seeking behavior.

Obviously, we would choose eight years of rehabilitation therapies, so our child could achieve age level skills, only to lose those gains with the next viral illness. Clearly, we could be content with having the slowest runner, the struggling reader, or the student who can't write more than their name. Understandably, we would choose special complex "diets" that exclude our children from family gatherings, school events, and virtually every major public facility. Who wouldn't? Please.

The reality is we make these choices and the sacrifices so our children thrive, and expect to do more despite what the poorly informed medical community has done to them. We didn't have children just to survive in mediocrity. Our children's bodies are failing them. We are competing in a race against time. They don't have the energy to live day to day like other kids, so how can they do more?

Mitochondrial dysfunction causes their behavioral, social, physical and cognitive difficulties. We continue to need specialist support — so we chose a virtual mito doctor, who created a practice for mito patients with them in mind. She understands the travel limitations, the effort travel takes and expenses involved. She understands the frustration of waiting for science to catch up, the vagueness of labs and varied presentations within a family. She communicates that understanding. She validates that the buccal swabs support our kids' symptoms and historically quirky labs. She is not as familiar with biomed, natural alternatives, or other related topics. She is willing to support a probable mitochondrial disease, until a different diagnosis if and when is discovered. She shows the support by listening and giving precise answers, even when she can't predict the outcome. She easily adapts her answers to your understanding — novice or late night reader. She gives us peace of mind and confidence to continue this journey, guiding our direction while enabling us to THINK as parents, not solely medical advocates.

Unlike zebras, who are born with their stripes, Negotiator and Crash were not born with Mitochondrial Dysfunction, Autism or any inherited diagnosis. Medical students are taught to diagnose by idiom, "When you hear hoof beats, think horses, not zebras." Same for people or non-thinkers. People see the white stripes, but not the black stripes or the skin underneath. People see the illusion of the able bodied healthy looking kids. People miss the reality, kids fighting to live longer. Our expedition continues, seeking the distinction between the mimicry of the zebra's white stripes and the zebra's true black stripes. Optimistically, their recovery will outlast my lifetime. Negotiator and Crash will recognize the power in themselves to make choices and consider the consequences of those choices. Negotiator and Crash will think for themselves as children of The Thinking Mom's Revolution.

REBEL

My story begins June 16, 1998. My family and I had recently returned home in April, after living as expats for 3 1/2 years in the UK. It was time to take my two-year-old daughter to her well child visit. As a Mom who was seriously interested in the best health care for her children, I dutifully brought my daughter to a pediatrician in Germantown MD, whom I had carefully interviewed and subsequently selected. At the time, I had no reason to mistrust doctors.

The only odd thing I remember about this appointment was that I had to sign a paper prior to my daughter being given her annual vaccines. I remember questioning the nurse as to why I had to sign my name before the DTaP and the Hib were administered. She said, "Oh, it is something we do now." In hindsight, this was a red flag. You generally do not sign for something unless there is a reason. Liability comes to mind. Of course I was given the normal instructions "If she runs a fever, give her Tylenol." They say this to you very nonchalant, like it is perfectly normal.

In the evening, my daughter ran a very high fever. I remember her crying and in my middle of the night stupor, took her to bed with me. I did not take her temperature but I was shocked how hot she felt. I dutifully gave her Tylenol which I now know put her deeper into autism. Her fever came down and I thought no more of it. I found out several years later while researching that Tylenol lowers glutathione levels, giving the body less ability to fight toxic insults of the vaccines.

It was customary for my family to attend the fireworks display each Independence Day. I noted that this time instead of enjoying the excitement of the fireworks, my toddler screamed the entire time. As a young mother, I thought this was odd. My daughter had attended fireworks displays before in the UK and had never had a problem with them.

As time went on, my daughter became known in the family as our love bug. She always wanted hugs and of course we all obliged her. She also was petrified of elevators and escalators which at times became a real inconvenience. How do you shop in a fancy mall without doing that? I can also recall a time when we were at West Point burying my father-in-law and my daughter again refused to go in the elevator. At the time, as a parent I thought, why is my child so out of sync? The grandparents looked at this behavior and blamed me. "You are not disciplining her enough," I often heard.

Then around the age of five, my daughter was doing a writing exercise with her cousin, who was a year behind her, under the instruction of her grandmother who had special education background. My mother-in law noticed my daughter was behind in her fine motor skills. She could not keep up with her cousin. My mother-in-law mentioned her concern to me that day, but I brushed it off. Who wants to think about their child being behind? We all think our children are smart and they are! Still very much in the dark as to what had happened to my daughter, she received the required vaccines prior to kindergarten. By this time, we had also made another move to the state of Florida.

When my daughter reached second grade, she was still struggling to tie her shoes and ride her bike. She also still wanted to be carried. It was very difficult to transition her to different activities. Eating as a family was almost impossible. The food was always too hot, if she did come to the table. School was beginning to become a nightmare. My daughter was begging me to homeschool her. The complaints were coming in again from her teachers…lack of focus during instruction and seatwork time, hard time staying on task, spending too much time visiting with her classmates at her table, difficulty listening and following directions, was not putting in her best effort, and did not manage her time. It was common for a short period of time for the schools to perform a Connor's Rating Scale for students who were inattentive to the instruction at hand. My daughter scored in the 100th percentile on the ADHD index!

I will never forget the next doctor's visit. I armed myself with her schoolwork and records to ensure that the pediatrician could get a clear understanding of the cognitive difficulties my daughter was encountering in school. My husband also accompanied me to this visit. The doctor never looked at my daughter's school work or records. She spent very little time and just handed us a psychotropic drug called Strattera and sent us on our way. A pill for every ill, right? I left feeling very disillusioned, but I went along with it. After all, trust your doctor right? Maybe a pill would fix all of this? Perhaps there was some improvement in school for the next six months, but it could also been attributed to placing her in a charter school with a laid back teacher. The medication stopped working after six months. It also affected her appetite, and caused my daughter to lose weight she did not need to lose.

From there it was drugs, drugs, and more drugs. This is how a typical morning went in my house. I would literally have to drag my daughter out of bed. She would get dressed as long as it was not cold in her room. If it was cold, she would not leave her bed. When she made her way downstairs, she would lay on the couch and sleep. Breakfast consisted of a breakfast bar or dry cereal on the way to school if she was not sleeping. Once we got to school it was another fight to get her out of the car. I remember how the drugs would cause her to talk nonstop. This was very scary to watch. I also remember looking at her dilated pupils. Now, in hindsight I ask myself, "What are we doing to these kids?"

Math tutoring began in fourth grade. We would arrive early in the morning when I could get her out of bed. Passing the FCAT, a required state test in Florida, had alluded her since third grade. I remember her fifth grade teacher told me they had to rub her back to keep her on task. I tried several times over the years to get her an IEP, but I was unsuccessful. I was told because she was a B student she did not qualify. She was too smart. Her doctor wrote a letter indicating that my daughter should never be given timed tests. The letter was ignored by the school.

She did her best in school in fifth grade when she was chosen to perform in "Miracle on 34ᵗʰ Street" with the Orlando Reparatory Company. This involved performing four shows a week during school and on weekends for six weeks. The school principal was very much against this and I had to get the school attorney involved to make this happen. I marvel now at how we were able to pull this off despite all she was going through.

There have been many a-ha moments on this journey. The last day of 5th grade I heard these words from her teacher, "Your daughter is not in the classroom." I knew she was physically there, so I made a decision right then and there that I was going to have her cognitively tested before she entered sixth grade and she would have an IEP in place prior to starting middle school.

The summer before 6ᵗʰ grade we began what is called a neuropsychological exam. My daughter was not the most cooperative. There were times when we were scheduled to test and I could not get her to cooperate, or we would get there and Dr. H. could not get her to focus on the testing. We were able to finish the testing with help from a female intern.

During this time, my oldest daughter was also working with a neuropsychologist because she had received a diagnosis of ADD the summer of her junior year of high school. It turned out this neuropsychologist, Dr. G., actually trained Dr. H. After Dr. H. completed the testing he gave my daughter the diagnoses of Oppositional Defiant Disorder, Depression and ADHD. One of the recommendations on the report included the Interactive Metronome, which is what my older daughter was doing at the time. This involves movements that cross the mid-line with hands and feet to the beat of the metronome. So my next stop was back to Dr. G. to see if the Interactive Metronome would be an appropriate therapy for my youngest daughter. I was sitting in Dr. G.'s office having handed him the neuropsychological results to see if my daughter could benefit from Interactive Metronome Therapy. He walked out of his office with the report in his hand, shaking his head and told me the diagnosis from Dr. H. was not right. He said my daughter had autism. He is clear that she does not have Asperger's. She has Pervasive Developmental Disorder Not-Otherwise-Specified. From my limited knowledge of autism, I knew it was not a positive diagnosis.

Without wanting to lose any hope I asked him if Interactive Metronome Therapy could help my daughter. The look on his face said it all. I could try, he said. Dr. G. said he would be contacting Dr. H. about changing the report to the correct diagnosis. The whole time my daughter was laying on my lap appearing completely out of it. Dr. G. gave us referrals for life skills, social skills, and for a vision processing specialist. I left there stunned but determined to beat this autism and determined to find out what caused autism and how this happened. My life as an independent researcher and an avid reader began.

Our next appointment involved an evaluation by an Occupational Therapist. At this appointment I learned more. My daughter had low muscle tone and muscle strength. She also had significant deficits in bilateral integration, upper limb coordination, balance skills, auditory, proprioceptive, and vestibular deficits. Some of this was starting to make sense: how she holds her pencil, her difficulty in riding a bike, her fear of riding escalators and elevators, why she never runs, and why she could not hear me if there was any background noise.

It came time for my daughter's IEP meeting. I was prepared with an advocate, my husband, my daughter's picture, my daughter's school reports going all the way back to kindergarten, and most importantly, information stating the law from wrightslaw.com. When you enter these meetings you will find yourself very outnumbered. I think this is done on purpose, to intimidate. Fortunately, I had a good relationship with the school counselor because he knew my middle daughter who was in the gifted program. At one point in the meeting it looked like they were leaning to putting my daughter in a school where they warehouse these kinds of kids but once I began stating the law in regard to limited strength, vitality, or alertness, including a heightened alertness to environmental stimuli which resulted in limited alertness with respect to the educational environment, the whole mood changed. I heard the words "other health impairment" and I knew I had won! The advocate

I had hired leaned over to see what I was reading. I still highly recommend having an advocate at your initial meeting because you are too emotionally involved in the outcome and you need someone there that is not personally involved should the discussion turn adversarial.

In the state of Florida, once you have an IEP you are eligible for a McKay Scholarship which enables you to attend any approved private school on their list. We chose a Montessori School. I liked how everyone worked at their own pace. I also knew the owner, and felt my daughter would be taught in a way where she would learn. While we were there, the school did a screening for speech and language. My daughter's screening indicated she had language deficits and needed further testing. We followed through and paid out of pocket again to find out she had language deficits which mimicked a traumatic brain injury. She never had a traumatic brain injury, unless you count what the vaccines did.

For the next two years, my daughter would attend three more schools. It was during puberty that violence came into play. You never knew when she would go off, with another meltdown soon to follow. I found myself in a constant state of Post-Traumatic Stress Disorder. Thankfully, she was able to hold it together in school. While my daughter was in middle school, a hair analysis test for heavy metal toxicity was given to me by a doctor we were seeing from the College of Vision Development. The results of this test gave me my next a-ha moment.

The testing results revealed my daughter was very high in copper, magnesium, and manganese. My holistic pediatrician referred me to a DAN! Doctor who he was shadowing at the time. I was told by the DAN! Doctor to begin Epsom salt baths every day for one week. He also prescribed liposomal glutathione to begin the following week. Within days of the start of the Epsom salt baths I knew we were on our way to healing because of the calming effect I was witnessing. I am particularly proud of an accomplishment involving this DAN! Doctor. I was the first mom in his practice to win my insurance case with Aetna and receive full coverage of care! Becoming a researcher extraordinaire paid off!

Chronic fatigue remains a constant symptom in my daughter's life. In high school it became so debilitating that at one point my daughter would come home from high school and sleep for five hours. As an original member of the Autism-Mito task force out of Boston, mitochondrial disorder was also on my radar screen.

In July 2011, I made the decision to buy a water ionizer that produces Kangen water for my daughter. My daughter went from sleeping five hours after school to one hour, and she had her best school year ever in regard to attendance! Unfortunately, this came to an end the following year because her classroom teachers discouraged the students from using bathroom passes and offered extra credit in its place, which my daughter sorely needed. When you drink the thinnest water on the planet you have to go when nature calls!

Where are we in our journey to wellness? I feel like we are still climbing the hill. My daughter recently agreed to visit a holistic doctor who uses electro dermal screening by measuring the frequencies in the organs. She then matches her findings up with over 500 different kinds of remedies. I found out what "autism" is in my daughter. Autism, in my daughter, is mercury, toxoplasmosis, h pylori, parasites, compromised liver, leaky gut, and hypoglycemia. We came home with an overwhelming array of supplements, tinctures, and a soak. Following this protocol may have lasted two weeks. It also did not help that my husband thought this was hocus pocus and has openly stated so in front of my daughter.

In the last few months my daughter has embraced the gluten-free/casein-free diet. Currently at age 17, she suffers from severe anxiety where she can no longer attend school while it is in session, and going to the movies is currently a challenge for her. Chronic fatigue is still present. She is unwilling at this time to take supplements consistently or participate in detoxing. My daughter is currently seeing a licensed clinical social worker at my husband's insistence. It is my belief that mercury toxicity is playing a huge role with her anxiety and chronic fatigue.

Her strength lies in the right side of her brain, where she is extremely high functioning. Most days you will find her rehearsing for her next leading role and taking online classes. My daughter has perfect pitch, plays the piano by ear, has a passion for musical theater, and a keen eye for photography.

I will leave you thinking about what I believe today is the truth about vaccines. Vaccines inflame our brains, delete our DNA, cause microflora dysfunction, lower our immune system, reduce oxygen and blood flow, lower our frequency, and compromise our primary reflexes which relate to the functioning of the left and right side of our body and brain. I cannot help but believe that "autism" is intentional. "Autism" does not reflect the greatness that our Creator intended for us to be. In Psalms 139:14 it says "I praise you because I am fearfully and wonderfully made; your works are wonderful, I know that full well." I will not stop recovering my daughter until she reaches that greatness that God intended not only for her, but for us all.

Sunflower

Whenyou become a parent for the first time, you have so many hopes and aspirations for your child. You research potential names and their meanings. You start thinking about the theme for their nursery, the paint color, cribs, rockers, mobiles, and toys. You read Consumer Reports and do exhaustive online research to find the safety rankings of the best strollers, car seats and baby carriers. You anticipate the time when they can start participating in sports, music, theater, and other creative activities. Where are the best schools, and where might they go to college? You are looking toward the far horizon with hope and confidence.

Our first son was born in 2005 and was a pure joy to our entire family. Then our second son, Ryan, was born 18 months later in 2006, and we had all the proud expectations of parents of two boys. The future was bright. We had happy, healthy babies.

During the early years in your child's life, you are expected to attend well baby visits. I loved the opportunity to weigh them and have their height and weight checked against the growth charts. It was exciting to see the forecast of their eventual size at adulthood. At that time, we had no reason to question the medical protocol. There was no discussion of how many vaccines were being administered to our children. We were neither provided an information sheet prior to vaccination (known as a VIS sheet) nor given the opportunity for "written and informed consent," as is required by law. When we brought forth reasonable and natural questions, the doctor and staff were always very vague in their answers and in a hurry to administer them as soon as possible. We were told firmly, "no shots, no school," and felt pressure to comply. Well, we now know that "NS-NS" is simply NOT true! (http://www.Vaxtruth.org).

My intuition told me that something about this process and the behavior of the medical staff was wrong. Why the resistance when we ask thoughtful questions? We were not trying to cause trouble; we just wanted to know what was going on. As informed parents, shouldn't we strive to learn everything we can about the health care of our children? Our plan was to raise the boys at home, and I intended to be a full-time, stay-at-home mom. So why in the world would the boys need a hepatitis B vaccination when they would never be exposed to either intravenous drug use or illicit sexual activity (the primary risk factors for hepatitis B)? I remember at one point, it was too painful for me to watch as one of my sons was strapped down and injected in his legs and arms at once.

According to Dr. Joseph M. Mercola, DO (licensed physician and surgeon), "Your doctor is legally obligated to provide you with the CDC Vaccine Information Statement (VIS) sheet and discuss the potential symptoms of side effects of the vaccination(s) you or your child receive BEFORE vaccination takes place. If someone giving a vaccine does not do this, it is a violation of federal law." Furthermore, the National Childhood Vaccine Injury Act of 1986 also requires doctors and other vaccine providers to:

a) Keep a permanent record of all vaccines given, including the manufacturer's name and lot number;

b) Write down serious health problems, hospitalizations, injuries and deaths that occur after vaccination in the patient's permanent medical record; and

c) File an official report of all serious health problems, hospitalizations, injuries and deaths following vaccination to the federal Vaccine Adverse Events Reporting System (VAERS).

If a vaccine provider fails to INFORM, RECORD or REPORT, they have violated federal law. As Mary Holland, JD, co-author of *Vaccine Epidemic*, says, "If a person can't decide what substances are injected in their blood stream, then we don't live in a free society." (http://www. tropicaltraditions.com/vaccine-epidemic.htm)

Once the boys were given their vaccines, we started to notice weird and unusual things. Our older son would cry and cry all night, and my husband would have to spend hours holding him, walking through the house, comforting and soothing him. We observed delays in his speech development along with emerging sensory issues. He constantly sought our elbow pressure on his eyes and wanted his head squeezed. We learned later that this is a sign of brain inflammation.

When the pediatric staff quizzed us regarding deficiencies in the boys' developmental milestones, we were directed to the state's Early Steps system for evaluation, where we were introduced to speech, occupational and behavioral therapy intervention. Fortunately, as time went on, our older son showed improvement. Not so much with Ryan, who is the primary focus of this chapter.

On April 15, 2009 we were told that Ryan had autism, mild to moderate, more on the mild side. In December 2010, I was invited to an open house for a Christmas gathering. A friend said that most of her mentors would be there. I was on the edge of my seat, listening to one mom's story about her autistic son. She advised me to get my sons' vaccination records immediately. When I called in the records request, the pediatrician's staff was very vague and even stated that they do not reveal the manufacturer and lot number of the vaccines. They called me later and said they thought the records had been lost. Then they claimed they had been sent to long-term storage. It was obvious that they were engaging in delay tactics in order to stall access to our own healthcare information.

We learned later, through an unnamed source, that the doctor had been reluctant to give us the records because he was afraid that he was in trouble. His concern was not for us, but for himself and his own possible jeopardy. Our source encouraged him to cooperate and to give us what we asked for. We eventually received a package of medical record copies, but with the essential information missing. I was in tears when I saw them. Not only were there no parent signatures or initials, but the manufacturer and lot number were clearly whited out for each vaccination. This is information to which we are entitled, and it is clear that the pediatrician went to great effort to obfuscate the data trail and to hinder our ability to seek legal recourse. Do doctors really do this? You betcha!

We set ourselves on a course of discovery, to investigate every possibility of cause and effect, in a maximum effort to understand the full scope of the problem and figure out what to do about it. We were referred to a genetic specialist in 2008 and 2009 who determined, through testing, that there were no genetic traits linking either of our sons to an inherited cause of their delays. In our case, genetics were not the root cause of the onset of autism.

We contacted the Centers for Disease Control (CDC), whose representative confirmed that our pediatrician violated federal law by not giving us any pamphlets on the vaccines our boys were receiving. Nor were we ever given any descriptive data about the components in the vaccinations and their associated risks, or the opportunity to consent to or decline the immunizations administered to either of our sons. Information was clearly withheld from us.

When I finally connected the dots in December 2010, another pediatrician pointed out to us that our younger son had received shots that were not even required for school. Hepatitis A was administered, and the rotavirus vaccine (Rotateq) was received twice. He stated, "I never give those vaccines." It is painful to recall the many sleepless nights that our boys would cry all night, while we paced the floors with them immediately after they received multiple vaccinations. There were many long middle-of-the-night car rides to try to help them fall asleep, as their little brains struggled with the effects of inflammation. There were many episodes of projectile vomiting, frequent periods of long blank stares as Ryan suffered with silent seizures, and many spiked fevers, for which we were told to give liquid Tylenol. The painful experience of continuous diarrhea was a daily certainty. The mainstream doctors we saw later would neither give us any useful direction, nor give us any hope; they merely prescribed an endless and ever-changing array of psychotropic pharmaceuticals as they appeared to be simply guessing at answers to problems they didn't understand.

I also recall being advised to have a flu shot while pregnant with Ryan, which I later found out contained 25 mg of mercury. I also had old dental fillings of mercury amalgam. I remember seeing our MAPS (Medical Associates Pediatric Specialists) practitioner in November 2012, and he said, "Open your mouth . . . mercury, mercury, mercury!" There is a real problem when you have all that mercury leaching into your body for all those years. These are factors contributing to a child's pre-disposition for adverse reactions to vaccines. Our MAPS practitioner wanted to check our boys for MTHFR. I had never heard of it but discovered our youngest was positive for one of the markers, negative for the other. With certain ingredients in the vaccines, it *can* trigger autism he explained.

We do have one area of mystery that might somehow be an underlying factor. However, we will probably never be able to know if this was an actual contributor to the boy's issues. My husband had completed a full military career. Upon initial entry to boot camp, he received multiple vaccines, as did all his peers. They made him so sick that he landed in the hospital for a week. The remaining question is…could all these invasive compounds somehow, many years later, been passed through to our children? It's a very appropriate question and exposes an area needing a great amount of continuing research and scrutiny. Side effects can kill you and can really disrupt your DNA.

My husband and I are completely devoted to our boys, but we never imagined how challenging parenting would become once we had children. We deliberately chose to not have amniocentesis performed in order to prevent any chance of harm to our babies in utero. The consulting physician was primarily focused on determining any presence of Down syndrome. Never were we warned about autism and the possible causes thereof.

A healthcare provider should always interview the parents to discuss the risks and benefits. In 2010, we had the privilege of meeting a

well-respected pediatrician who spoke about vaccines causing neurological damage, especially if given in multiple amounts at a young age.
This doctor takes a more holistic approach to health care and interviews
parents to find out their family's medical history prior to any vaccinations.
This is an incredible display of care, responsibility and due diligence. It
requires a bit more work and time.

In November 2012, the Congressional Oversight and Government
Reform Full Committee Hearing, "1 in 88 Children: A Look into the
Federal Response to the Rising Rates of Autism" was conducted with
the stated goal to . . . get a clearer picture on what is being done, what
questions still need to be answered and what needs exist for those children,
adults and families who live with an Autism Spectrum Disorder." Many
families were elated to finally hear the questions voiced for which we
had waited so long:

1) Has a study ever been conducted comparing unvaccinated and
vaccinated children?

Answer: NO.

2) Has there ever been a study of the effects of multiple vaccinations?

Answer: NO.

However . . . we discovered hope. A friend shared that she was attending the National Autism Association Conference (NAA) in November
2011. That got my attention. We attended the conference, a life-changing
experience for our family. We met many autism families who all told
similar stories of vaccine injury. But for the first time, I heard lecturers
saying we could recover our children and there was hope. I learned
about biomedical intervention, homeopathy, hyperbaric oxygen therapy,
infrared saunas, diet, nutrition and supplements, and how all these processes can help our children to recover their lives.

One of the sessions was a Q & A panel with some of the top physicians
in the autism recovery field. They broke out the detail of the related conditions generally described as "autism":

a. encephalology, (brain inflammation)
b. gastrointestinal inflammation
c. microflora dysfunction

    d. oxidative stress

    e. heavy metal toxicity

    f. gluten and casein intolerance, and other food allergies

In May 2012, I went to Chicago to attend the Autism One Conference, a global forum with attendees from around the world and doctors who are on the front lines of autism recovery presenting information. It was refreshing to be able to speak to them about vaccine damage. God forbid you bring it up to a mainstream physician. The image of an ostrich with his head in the sand comes to mind.

We had started Ryan on a gluten-free/casein-free diet in November 2011. This was initiated following direct and personal advice given to us from THE preeminent world expert in gastroenterology and its connection to autism. Those of you who have been at this for a while can probably figure out who I am referring to. Ryan finally had a firm bowel movement for the first time in his life! We soon noticed his speech improving slightly, and he was eating better. For those unsure of the diet, or that think it's too hard or too expensive to maintain, we highly encourage you to try it! We only wish that we had known these processes years ago. What happened to our boys, particularly our younger son, is no longer unusual. It's happening every day. Our children are being robbed of their childhood. It's a horrible and tragic event that never should have happened in the first place.

Meeting so many wonderful families through the conferences and hearing the lectures lit a fire in me, and I made a promise to my younger son that I would turn this around. I often struggle with guilt for not knowing any better then and for allowing this to happen when it all could have been easily avoided. My revelation turned into resolution. I imagine myself as a battleship, bringing out the big guns to help our little boy.

Through this journey, I was grateful to discover the Thinking Moms' Revolution. When I read their daily blogs, I was blown away by them! They were so completely relatable. Two of the Thinking Moms, Goddess and Poppy, were always there for support and help as we ventured in new areas and asked advice about doctors, nutritionists and interventions.

I am also grateful for Rebel and Barracuda of Team TMR. Rebel told me one of the best things she ever did for her daughter was to give her Kangen alkaline water. I was intrigued. As we had samples of the water, I noticed immediate changes in my son's speech and potty behavior. I met Barracuda at the National Autism Association Conference in 2011. She and her husband were very knowledgeable and told me to be sure to hear a particular doctor in the morning. He was brilliant!

The most helpful things for healing my son were implementing a gluten free/casein free diet, alkaline ionized water, biomedical intervention, homeopathy, cranial sacral therapy, chiropractic care, hyperbaric oxygen therapy, neurofeedback, essential oils, and various therapies over many years including speech therapy, occupational therapy, physical therapy, and behavior therapy.

Ryan has mastered riding a bike now, but we still use training wheels. We must hold his hand in public at all times. He will often flop down in a store due to low muscle tone. Our family has been given so many angels on this journey, and I thank God for them. Our speech therapist, who worked with Ryan in 2008, accompanied me to our appointment the day he was diagnosed. Our occupational therapist was truly another angel in our life, working so hard to help in so many ways. I learned a whole new language with terms such as brushing, vestibular, and proprioceptive. They used weights, jumped on trampolines, bounced him and rolled him on huge exercise balls to give him the input his body was seeking for calming and regulation.

Ryan is not recovered yet, but he has made huge strides in every way! Ryan's speech has blossomed recently. He is teaching himself Spanish from a children's DVD series we bought him. He can accomplish basic math problems in addition. He is speaking in more complete sentences and asking questions. He is not stuck, we see him recovering every day. Ryan is a very loving little boy, always happy. He loves his family, and we are grateful to my in-laws who have supported us tremendously on this journey. I also turn to prayer every day for our little boy and his daily path of recovery. My promise to our little boy is to make what was wrong, right. He will inspire and surprise everyone with his achievements.

My TMR nickname, Sunflower, is in honor of my late mother who passed away in 2008. Sunflowers were her favorite flower. Sunflowers are a fiery flower. They stand strong in the sunlight and are always reaching upward. Sunflowers represent kindness, love and strength. My Mother was a very strong, kind, selfless person. I am who I am because of her.

Another mom told me that, while what happened to our children was wrong, it was all in God's plan and purpose. She cited Romans 8:28: "And we know that in all things God works for the good of those that love Him who have been called according to His purpose." I truly feel that God has put people in our life for a reason. As the saying goes, "People are put in your life as either a lesson or a blessin'." I'll never forget my dear friend sharing her story with me while attending the Autism One Conference in Chicago 2012. "I used to hold a lot of anger," she said, "but I need to channel that anger into recovery." I reflect on that and my faith to see us through.

When given the opportunity, I share our story. I help educate parents and encourage them to contact the good doctors who ask questions and take a more holistic approach. I reflect on Philippians 4:13: "I can do everything through Him who gives me strength." I am now a source of guidance and encouragement to other families. Recovery is possible, and we are determined to stop at nothing less. One of the many reasons I share the Thinking Moms' Revolution book and website with so many families is to offer them hope, the hope I've found. I am taking our experience and using it to help others make informed choices, something we were never given.

QUEEN B

We've been on this autism journey for eight years; it's hard to know where to begin when telling our story. I really want to share all of the events that we know led to her autism diagnosis, but it would end up being more of a book than a chapter. A very long book full of heartbreak, fear, anguish, deceit, lies…the list could go on and on. Although it was important to experience the bad medical advice that led us to the real truth of what happened to our daughter on some level, I could have done without that part and skipped right to the section of healing. And once that understanding really sunk in, the damage that had been done at the hands of a mainstream medical system whose job it was to protect her, well, you don't come out on the other end of that type of realization as the same person.

When I meet parents that have a child newly diagnosed with autism, ADHD, ODD, seizures, I automatically assume the mother hen role with them. Although I may come off as overbearing, what I'm really trying to do is to save them from all of the mistakes I made. I want to be able to shove eight years of ups and downs on this journey and my "do not do" list in one sentence. The passing of time is difficult to deal with when it comes to autism. I know, I know. It is a marathon. But as much as I hate to face it, the clock is ticking. I am sprinting as fast as I can to find the answers we need to lead her to recovery because childhood only lasts so long and I want her to be able to enjoy some of it.

It was a squelching July morning in the summer of 2005, and I was making day care plans for my four-year-old son so I could take my daughter Lily to her daily three hour long therapy. She needed to go to therapy. After being diagnosed with moderate to severe autism at 25 months, I needed to take her there to feel like I was doing something to help her because I truly felt helpless. I was desperately trying to connect with my daughter and understand why she was upset all of the time.

Per usual, I was running around the house like a crazy person while my son entertained himself by watching TV and Lily sat in the corner of the room and stared at her toy elephant. She was completely disconnected from the world at almost three years old and had zero expressive or receptive language. While I was upstairs, I heard the door slam and remembered that I had not closed the outside garage door earlier in the morning when I had taken out the garbage. I left the door up because I knew we would be leaving later that morning to go to therapy. I wasn't in a panic yet because she had never attempted to open a door or even go outside. She really didn't initiate any type of activity. Our biggest concern at the time was always trying to engage her in the world around her and it never occurred to me that I would need to protect her from it.

As I came into the family room, I saw my son in the same spot I left him but she was gone. I scanned the room and saw that the door to the laundry room was open and the door that leads to the garage from the laundry room was closed. I questioned my four-year-old about where she went, like it was his responsibility to keep track of her that day. I'm convinced this day will also be etched in his mind forever and we should probably start the therapy fund now.

Standing in the driveway, I scanned the neighborhood. It became very apparent that she had been gone several minutes before the door slammed. Panic set in. I threw my son in the van and I had no cell phone because it was dead and I had no charger for the car at the time.

To say I was an incoherent mess is probably one of the biggest understatements ever made. I still remember my son begging me, "Stop screaming Mommy! You're hurting my ears!" In those moments as a parent, you know what the right thing to do is. I should have remained calm and collected for my son. However, the fear and anxiety had taken over and all my good parenting sense from all of the books I'd read, which I thought helped make me such a great parent, went out the window. All I could think about was that our house sat a quarter mile east of the DuPage River.

I still imagine how I looked that day in our usually quiet neighborhood at 10:30am driving around screaming a scream that would rival any horror movie scream. A scream that I knew deep down she wouldn't even respond to if she did hear me. At that point, she didn't respond to anything really and was nonverbal. And of course knowing this added even more to my panic. I stopped the first car I encountered and begged the stranger to help me look for my daughter and call the police for me. More screaming and praying ensued as I continued to drive around our neighborhood which consists of four blocks. I wanted everyone to wake up from their suburban slumber in more ways than one. This was not how our daughter's story, our family's story was supposed to turn out. We couldn't be the only ones who had gone through this? How could people be drinking coffee and watching Oprah while this was happening?

When I came across the man who called the police again as he was also looking for her, 12 police units had been deployed to find her. The visual of what that meant…this wasn't just a harmless little "my child got away from me for a second" incident. The crazy set in for me and yep, the even uglier cry began. If you can't get crazy when your child has gone missing, when can you be? I stopped another neighbor that I really didn't know to ask about Lily. He had seen a little girl by Lily's description in the street a few houses down and it appeared she was playing with an older child. I wanted to tell him that my daughter doesn't play and doesn't really know anyone else exists. But there was no time for that now.

I drove slowly, continuing to scream and cry her name and people were starting to come out of their houses to see what the commotion was about. As I drove down the same block again, another officer stopped me to assure me that an entire fleet of police cars was scanning our village, I noticed another police car pull up to a home along the river. Within a few minutes, it was over. They had found her. I guess my obvious distress was enough for them to realize that I wasn't a neglectful parent that was letting my child roam the neighborhood unsupervised. As my son and I were led to the home, it occurred to me that this was a house I passed by every day but I didn't really know who lived inside. It looked like we were about to meet under some interesting circumstances.

The officer informed me that the owner had called the police and brought her inside because she saw her playing in the street and running in circles. That's when I knew for sure we had found her. I relayed to her that she was developmentally delayed and non-verbal…in my panic I still couldn't even say she was diagnosed with autism at the time. It was so obvious to everyone…why did I also need to say that ugly word that had taken so much from my daughter and my family already?

My little runaway was playing in their toy box and didn't even realize I was there. As we were leaving, the neighbor then told me she actually heard me screaming for her after she had brought her inside. She heard me. Don't get me wrong, I thank God for this woman every single day. However, I always wondered why she didn't wait outside especially when she heard a mother desperately screaming for her child. Was it a little zinger she wanted to throw my way? A way for me to "pay" for my neglect? Looking back, I really can't blame her. She had no idea about our situation and I wasn't about to have a sit down with her at that point. I would like to say that we were lifelong friends after this incident but I cannot. I would see her in passing but we never spoke again.

Lily started fading away in May 2004 when she was around nine months old. I can't give an exact day or time. That period of our lives was such a blur and the sequence of events that led up to her fading away seems so similar to what other parents experience with their children. She had thrush issues as a baby, problems regulating her temperature after her first dose of the Hep B vaccine. After she received her fourth dose of the Hep B vaccine at nine months old, the constant state of sickness began. The ear infections and sinus infections started to run together as well as the constant dosing of one antibiotic after another. Each time the infections would come back, stronger and harder to kill.

The second time we noticed a pronounced regression was after her flu vaccine at 16 months old. Even though she was sick so often, the pediatrician did not once recommend delaying her vaccines. By 25 months old, we had seen a developmental psychologist who slapped her with an autism diagnosis. As devastating as it was to hear that diagnosis, the complete lack of help or guidance provided to us by this psychologist was bewildering. All she could recommend was that we start ABA for her right away and gave us information about an intensive behavioral program offered through early intervention. That was it.

When I asked about her theory on diet and the link between vaccines and autism, she sat there with complete confidence and said vaccines had nothing to do with autism and that special diets did not help children at all. I wasn't so confident in her answer. Even early on in the journey, call it common sense or my mommy instinct, how could a doctor be so sure about what doesn't work when they didn't even understand why she had regressed into autism in the first place?

Do not be afraid to question your child's pediatrician about vaccines or medications they are prescribing. I was always rule follower and looked to the pediatrician as an authority figure. It never once occurred to me to read the package insert for the vaccines they were administering, or to consider how many more vaccines they were giving my child compared to the schedule I had received as a child, or to consider the toxic ingredients they contained. If they take offense to your questioning, run away as fast as you can!

There are more and more doctors out there that get it, so don't waste your time with doctors that don't. We learned this lesson the hard way. When we requested Lily's medical records from our previous pediatrician, they gave us a hard time. I wanted to say, "Ummm...your practice injected my child with neurotoxin after neurotoxin in the form of vaccines. I think you can take five minutes to make the damn copies!"

As difficult as it was to read page by page it became clear to us much too late that she was having a reaction to almost every set of vaccinations from nine months old and beyond. We now know that based on her medical records, she was displaying definite signs of encephalopathy which is listed right on package insert of almost every vaccine as a possible adverse reaction. We followed the rules and listened to the pediatrician, vaccinating her according to the CDC vaccination schedule, but now that she had an autism diagnosis that same doctor had no answers for us. The next time a doctor tells you that they know better than you about your child; ask them if they are the ones that will have to live with the consequences of the decisions made. We all know the answer to that question.

Do not underestimate the power of sequencing therapy versus interventions. When Lily was first diagnosed, we were told by the developmental psychologist (that I now want to punch in the face) that behavioral therapy was the only intervention that would help her. The day we left her office, I spent hours pouring over therapy after therapy that would be the best fit for our child. And there are many phenomenal therapies and therapists out there. We discovered Floortime, ABA, Discrete Trial, RDI…And these were all fantastic interventions, but they would have been better applied after we addressed the fact that the source of her autism was medical. We went the therapy-only route for almost two years. What we should have been focusing on first was the medical component of her autism. When your child is in a state of constant pain and discomfort due to gastrointestinal distress and inflammation, ABA drills and play-based therapy don't address the root of the problem.

Do not ever give up. I had actually started hearing about how dietary changes could make improvements in children like mine and had the opportunity to attend a movie that explained the changes in detail when she was only two. I asked the director of the therapy center she was attending at the time if she thought I should attend and she went on to remind me that dietary interventions weren't helpful and it would be a waste of time. And I listened to that BS.

Thank God I had started to do my research and read Karyn Seroussi's book, "Unraveling the Mystery of Autism and Pervasive Developmental Disorder." Dietary intervention not only made sense, it was one of the least invasive interventions we could do to help our child. I've learned that when treating autism, as with anything else, if you don't understand the reason why you are doing the protocol you are doing, it's pretty likely you aren't going to stick it out. There are no Cliff Notes here.

When we started the gluten free/casein free/soy free diet, she was four years old, and we noticed an almost immediate improvement in awareness. At around the same time, we began to try biomedical interventions with the help of a DAN! Doctor. Over the next three years, we tried anti-fungal, anti-viral, and biofilm strategies with slight improvements here and there. Thousands of dollars later, we learned she was a biomedical non-responder.

During the course of biomedical treatment, between the ages of five and seven-and-a-half years old, she would go through periods where she would scream for hours on end. And. I. Mean. Hours. The screaming was awful! At almost six years old, she started pulling out her hair, in clumps. She almost looked like a child that had been through chemotherapy because she had completely pulled out a good portion of her hair on the top of her head. We took her to the pediatrician, ENT, dermatologist, and they all really wanted to help and get to the source of what was causing the pain, until they heard the autism diagnosis. An appointment with each new specialist went something like this: the minute they heard the "A" word, they suddenly went from an expert in their specialty to having less knowledge than I did on how to help and would send me on my way. There was never a real curiosity on their part as to what could be causing the pain. They had their theories; it was behavior, sinuses, migraines. The ENT even suggested a CAT scan which we followed through with. It revealed zip.

We tried acupuncture, cranial sacral therapy and lymphatic massage. Our lives were in a constant state of survival mode and I didn't know how much longer I could watch my child suffer and not know how to help her. It's hard to even begin to explain the pain I felt as I watched her scream in pain for hours and had no clue how to help. The despair put quite the damper on the entire family dynamic. We had no idea what each day would bring.

On the days that I sent her to school, I was always waiting for the phone to ring because they were always asking me to pick her up. I had no idea how to help my daughter on so many levels, how could I expect her teachers to be able to do it? I truly felt helpless and that we had exhausted all of our options. Part of me wanted to take her to Chicago to one of the top Children's hospitals and just ask them, what is wrong with my child? I had grown so accustomed to receiving bad medical advice on what all of these doctors considered to be the mystery of autism that I just couldn't go there anymore. I was desperate, she was in pain and our family was on the verge of falling apart. I knew that I had to do something. I had to be the one to lead the charge on her healing since it seemed that no one else could.

By the grace of God, I came across information regarding the Specific Carbohydrate Diet on the TACA (Talk About Curing Autism) website. It made total sense on every level to me. When I read Elaine Gotschall's book, "Breaking the Vicious Cycle," I was sold. We knew that she was ridden with yeast and bacteria and the idea behind this intervention was to stop feeding the pathogens in the form of food. The work of it all seemed so daunting, but not as daunting as the idea of my daughter continuing to be in pain. We noticed a change right away. For starters, she stopped screaming. She was talking a little more and just more alert. Could it be that after almost four years of biomedical and dietary interventions, we had found a treatment that packed the most punch? Let me say this again. It took us almost four years to find the intervention that has helped our daughter the most. It makes me shudder to think what would have happened if we would have given up searching at year two or three.

Don't act like everything is okay to your family and friends for the sake of being strong. Post autism diagnosis, I spent so much time putting on a brave front, pretending that we were all good and didn't need anything from anyone. Yet I always wondered why family and friends weren't coming to our door with casseroles and offering childcare along with loving support and kind words of hope. They had no idea because I didn't let them in. I was so damn convincing in my "we've got this" mode. Sometimes loved ones want to help but they don't know how. This is the time when we need to be brave enough to ask for exactly what we need.

Do not spend too much time on the people that just don't get it. You know the ones I'm talking about. The people that continue to question the validity of what we know happened to our children. Even after you provide them with the studies and the resources, they aren't ever going to be receptive if they aren't ready to have their mind completely blown by the truth they will discover. If they aren't willing to listen to your story and learn from your experience, it is wasted time and energy that could be given to your child instead. If there is anything positive to come out of our daughter's diagnosis, it's that the right people have stayed or been brought into our lives and the wrong people are no longer there. End of story.

Finally, don't buy into the theory that there is a window for your child to improve and to even recover. It is never too late to start the healing process! Over the years, it has always been interesting to me that people look at our daughter and see the obvious improvements but never ask what we are doing to bring about these improvements. I guess they think that because she still has limited verbal capabilities, and she still has the autism diagnosis, they assume that she has just grown out of the screaming and the hair pulling?

We've had financial woes, a new baby and jobs to manage. Admittedly, we've sometimes lost our focus. She is 10 years old now and we are still learning the roots of her autism and the best course of treatment. She has made tremendous strides because of diet but we've also learned that she responds very well to homeopathy and we're extremely excited about what is to come. As a parent, I share our story and learn from others who do the same. We find doctors and practitioners that know what has happened to our kids and put themselves out there despite the efforts of a government and mainstream medical system that wants to continue to deny that we even exist. We are writing our own pages of healing and recovery for our children. I will never give up until Lily can look at me one day and say, "Mom, remember when I used to have autism?"

PHOENIX

"**Y**ou are doing everything you can." said our pediatrician when I told him of our autism diagnosis, and he confirmed that we were receiving Early Intervention services. Everything I can. Fifty to sixty hours of Early Intervention services a month for a not even two-year-old. It wasn't helping. He was getting worse. More autistic. Less the boy I knew. How could I resign myself to this, when just three months ago, he was perfect? I had spent those three months getting Early Intervention services in place. A terrible agency, then a great agency, then an autism specific agency. Months of paperwork, agonizing decision making, months of further regression. No progress.

Meanwhile, I was reading. I had gone to the library and taken out every single book about autism they had. I didn't know anything about autism. I didn't know a single person with this diagnosis. I had no clue at that point that Andrew had about a 1 in 30 chance of becoming autistic in 2012, just by being born a boy.

I wept as I realized what had happened to my son. What I had allowed to happen. I learned about vaccines, the neurotoxins they contain, the heavy metals. But most importantly, I learned that there were things that I could do, that autism was a medical condition, and that I could improve his symptoms. I learned about biomedical treatments and diets, and later about GMO's. I convinced my husband to let us try going gluten-free with Andrew. Just for a month, as it was expensive. I agreed that if nothing changed, I'd drop it. Just three days after eliminating gluten from Andrew's diet, we had eye contact from our sweet boy who hadn't looked at us in months, and we were hooked. There was no turning back.

Deeper and deeper I dug. As a stay-at-home Mom of three, (Ava was turning eight, and Andrew has a twin, Benjamin) I didn't have a lot of spare time, but I was literally frantic to help Andrew. With every free minute, I networked, I researched, and I found mothers of children with autism on the same path. I was waking up, and I was very, very sad. I learned that thousands and thousands of children are sick here in the U.S. You know the story now; you've read the first Thinking Moms' book. You know about vaccines, about neurotoxins, about giving Tylenol before and after shots. You know about how GMOs create holes in the stomachs of lab rats. You know about MTHFR mutations. I didn't even know about regressive autism!

You are supposed to be born with autism, and my son wasn't. He was born unbelievably beautiful, with a full head of dark hair and two strong cowlicks on his hairline. He was happy and healthy and hit every milestone either on time or early. He was the earliest crawler of my three children. Sure, he was pretty cranky as a newborn, but he always had eye contact and smiles. As soon as he was mobile, he turned into the happiest child you could hope to meet. The doctor said the bowel movements he'd have once a week that would rip him open and make him bleed were nothing to worry about! He had dozens of words, he took steps. Although he wouldn't officially walk until 17 months, he had been adeptly cruising full-time since nine months.

He was even developmentally ahead of his twin. Way ahead actually, all along. Andrew sat at six months, Ben sat at eight months. Andrew crawled at eight months, Ben crawled at 12 months. We were actually worried about Ben, not Andrew. There were little things I remember now that might have been clues. All three kids were eating one day, Ava and Benjamin were making so much noise, and my mother commented how Andrew never talks anymore. Or the time when we went to the park, Andrew would bee-line it down the hill to try to get to the stop sign across the street instead of playing on the slide. But overall, Andrew was totally under our parental worry radar.

Until he wasn't. Until we realized that he had never really fully come back to us from that 104 degree fever that lasted four days after his 15 month shots but "wasn't related because he didn't have seizures." And then he was slipping away, day by day. Then, all of a sudden, Ben, who had been globally delayed all along, was doing things Andrew wasn't. We kind of looked at each other and said "What the hell happened here?" What did we miss?

Early Intervention, on their first trip to the house said he was deaf or autistic. Deaf!!! That made sense. Yes! He was deaf. That would suck, he'd have to get hearing aids and we'd all have to learn sign language, but no big deal! People who are deaf are not doomed! He could have become deaf from the high fever! He failed the regular hearing test, so we set up the sedated BAER, and prepared ourselves.

But then we realized he could hear us. Even though he didn't flinch at the loudest of noises or respond when we called his name, anytime I sang, no matter how softly, he would look for me, look at me. Fuck. He wasn't deaf. The BAER confirmed it, two weeks before Christmas, but we'd wait another month for the official autism diagnosis. We still didn't know what autism was, but we knew it wasn't good, because all our family and friends had said for months was "Better something wrong with his ears than his brain!" And that sounded right to us. Ears you can fix, brains you can't. Right?

But it was autism. We continued with full-time specialized autism Early Intervention services that were ABA based. I was in love with the therapists, and even though life was very busy, it was helpful to have people coming into the house in the beginning who knew what to do about autism. I sure didn't. I felt inadequately equipped to deal with this diagnosis or with my sudden son-stranger who appeared to view me no differently than the furniture surrounding him. He had no interest in anything except his little wooden street signs, or his puzzles. Shapes. "Pre-math," the therapists called it. Great! He'll be an engineer, I thought. If he can ever talk again. Or, you know, look at people.

But I kept digging. We received a grant from Generation Rescue, and took part in a three month program — an "Intro to Biomed," if you will. A new supplement every week. Andrew's ATEC (Autism Treatment Evaluation Checklist) before we started the grant, was 106. Anything higher than 104 is considered "severe" autism. At the end of the program, his ATEC was 84. We were watching our little boy come back to us, inch by little bitty inch.

We fought our homeowner's association and fenced in our backyard, so our happy little wanderer could stay safe and play outside. That was our only big, major, monster autism grievance — the scary, scary elopement tendencies. We knew how many children with autism drown each year, as they wander and are drawn to water. We knew how many were "lost." We knew autism was deadly. We were so lucky that he's never been a screamer, never violent or angry. He was our happy little Buddha baby. But he was only two. We didn't know what our future would hold.

I dug deeper every day into the world of biomed and recovery. I was so angry. My little guy was improving, finally, but it didn't seem to have anything to do with Early Intervention. I was so angry, so angry, that I had to find out the truth myself. Angry that I had to find out that vaccines are dangerous, that our food is poisonous, that Tylenol is really, truly poison, and that there were things I could do to help my son, and the doctor didn't even know about them. I was so angry every single minute of every single day, it hurt to breathe. I was mad at everyone who had made the same choices I made, and whose children were perfectly fine (they only have ADHD, allergies and asthma…but they have a future). I was mad at our doctor. Pharmaceutical companies. Monsanto. I was mad at everyone. Of course, I was more angry at myself than at all of that put together for my blatant ignorance. I had unknowingly sacrificed my son on the altar of the fictitious greater good.

Our ABA therapy picked up intensity. Andrew was becoming extremely resistant. He was actually losing play skills. At the onset of therapy he could put together any puzzle, knew dozens of shapes, and had very strong pre-math skills. Now if we put a puzzle in front of him he wouldn't even lift a hand. The therapists would try to do it hand over hand and he would scream and cry real tears and yell "No!" over and over. He would meet my eyes across the room, with a look that said "How could you let them do this to me?" For hours each day my little Buddha baby, so happily encapsulated in his own world, was trying to tell me that he hated therapy. But what the hell was I supposed to do about it? All you hear about is how important ABA is for children with autism. The therapists were deeply conflicted. He was not responding, he was even losing skills, and his behaviors were getting worse with each week. We spent many hours problem solving, with no compromise.

It was then I read The Thinking Moms' Revolution's book, "Autism Beyond the Spectrum." I wept as I read pieces of my own story, over and over and over. And I read Princess's chapter, "SonRise." My heart knew this would be important. A good autism mom friend (you know her as ShamROCK) knew her personally. She asked Princess to call me. The rest, as they say, is history.

My husband and I watched the videos of the therapists working with the children. With SonRise therapy, love and respect are core. We quit ABA because though it has helped many children, it was not the right program for our son. Autism is a lot of things, and expensive is one of them. Doctor bills, supplements and diet costs run our budget really tight, especially as there is no possible way for me to work. But we fund-raised, and I packed my bag and headed to the Option Institute for the SonRise Start Up program, and my very own path to recovery.

Everything fell into place, from the funds to attend, to my Mom's willingness and availability to stay with my children for the week. I started to see, really see, the good in the community that surrounded us. The friends and family who want to see Andrew succeed, had faith in me and sacrificed their own time and money to help me pursue this road for him. Before I left for Option, I already had a number of committed, loving, wonderful volunteers, willing to give up their time to be a part of our family and this journey.

At Option, I learned everything I needed to do to set up a full-time volunteer based SonRise program for Andrew in our home. I learned that my son is doing the very best he can. He is a magnificent being who has learned to do what he needs to do to deal with the overload of sensory attacks and the unpredictable world around him. I learned that my son processing things differently means he is more acutely in tune with my feelings and the environment in our home. If I am around him and I feel perfect acceptance and love, he will know, and he will respond. If I am around him and feeling the deep, deep grief I had been living, what must that feel like to him? Did he take that on? Did he think or feel for a moment that it was disappointment or sadness about something he did?

I learned that I get to choose. He stims and I get to choose how that makes me feel. I can see it as socially unacceptable, and try to stop him. Or, I can accept who he is, knowing he is doing the best he can, and be at peace with what he's doing.

As an example, early on, Andrew was passionately in love with road signs. My father-in-law bought him these beautiful wooden road signs, and Andrew loved them. He carried them around with him and would sit and play with them for hours on end. It was a visual stim for him and as such, the therapeutic approach to dealing with this is to take away the stim item. So his beloved stop signs were packed away for six months. Then we learned that he used those stop signs to deal with the world around him, how secure and happy they made him feel, and we realized we'd made a terrible, disrespectful decision taking them away from him. When we unpacked those signs and gave them back to him, he laughed…belly laughed! He was totally delighted. He was so happy. And now that he's had a couple of months of unlimited access to them, he doesn't even use them anymore. That's the magic of SonRise.

As the week at Option passed and I learned more of these gems, my whole thought process changed, and so much healing took place in my angry little heart. What a gift to look at my son and not see a baby damaged by corporate greed who needs to be fixed. I just see my sweet boy, doing the best he can, and my intense love for him is no longer marred by the things that went wrong. I am thankful every minute of every single day. Now, I know, for sure, that things have to change. We cannot continue on this path, as a world, with this generation of sick children and the generations to come. And I am devoted to doing my part to bring awareness of regressive autism, of GMOs, of vaccines, of Tylenol. I am devoted to encouraging the people I encounter to THINK.

Thanks to the Option Institute, I can operate from a place of peace and thankfulness, and not one of self-consuming bitterness. I no longer spend nights pissed off after debating vaccine/autism connections in public forums. I can choose to participate, or not. I can choose to turn off my phone. I know I cannot carry the world on my shoulders. I know I am not the only warrior out there. I can remember that not long ago, I was fighting for the other team.

Andrew now sees a DAN! Doctor who is also a homeopath. She is treating his MTHFR mutations, and clearing the vaccinations he reacted to. We are literally seeing our son grow by leaps and bounds every day. His ATEC score is 35. Less than a year after diagnosis, his score fell from 106 to 35. And I know in my heart that that needle will keep moving, until there's no place left to move. I know it won't happen without a fight and a lot more blood, sweat, and tears, but I am prepared to move Heaven and Earth to help Andrew be his best self.

My other two children's lives are forever altered. Ava is a compassionate force, and she is Andrew's biggest cheerleader. He tells her how much he loves her with his eyes. She understands. Benjamin, in many senses, lost his twin to autism. They have not developed into playmates or best friends. In fact, Andrew spends a great deal of time avoiding Ben, because Ben is very loud and unpredictable. I spent a lot of time being very angry that their twinhood was stolen from us all. But Ben intuitively knew how to do SonRise therapy. He intuitively knew that his best chance for eye contact was to join Andrew in Andrew's activity. He sneaks into Andrew's crib in the early morning for cuddles. He is mostly gentle and kind, and thanks to biomed and diet, completely on track developmentally now. I know that Ben and Ava will both be forces of truth in their generation. They know what happened to their brother. They know intimately what autism is, and what it does.

Some people believe that our recoveries, mine and Andrew's, will be a mirror of each other. That may be true. We've come a long, long way.

We've got a lot of work to do, but we are so happy to be where we are, and determined to choose happiness for the remainder of our journey. That, I believe, is truly the road to recovery.

We are largely supported by the community around us. I am often told that I am admired and how people don't know how I do it. How proud I should be for working so hard to recover Andrew. How amazing it is, what we've done. And it is indeed hard work. There are days where I feel like I could scream if I have to syringe one more disgusting supplement into his mouth, or fix one more allergen-free meal. But I know the cost of giving up. I know the precious gems that reward me for my fight. The work I do now is the reason I was put on the planet. And I say, like the Kaufmans before me said, "It was all for me."

MUSCLE MAMA

"It shouldn't be this hard." This is what my husband said to me as he stood in our kitchen in our third home in Missouri, watching me as I wrestled our 16-month-old down to the ground, trying to put his shoes on just so we could go outside. Hard? This wasn't hard...training 36 hours a week as a national gymnast at age 16, while going to school full-time was hard...dieting for five years and competing nationally as a fitness competitor, while holding down two jobs was hard...moving to the United States as a Canadian, a newlywed, and having to leave my career, family and friends, and everything I knew to be familiar to me behind, was hard.... This was just my son being stubborn, as he always was, day in day out and it just meant I wasn't working hard enough with him.

"I raised my nephew and I know how a child this age should act. It shouldn't be this difficult," my husband continued to say, after I had finally succeeded in getting our son's shoes on, his little face wet with tears. "He's fine and it'll get easier" I told him. Surprise, surprise, it never did, and then one day my husband threw the word "autism" at me. My heart almost stopped beating. What? Autism? How could he have autism? If anyone would know if he did it would be me because I spent all day, every day with this kid. Nope, no way, I just needed to try harder. Talk about denial at its best.

My husband saw what I did not. A few weeks later he came home with some literature explaining what autism was along with some case studies to go with it. Apparently, he had been speaking to a co-worker who also had a son on the autism spectrum, and my husband was convinced that our precious little boy was headed down that same road. His co-worker had suggested we get an appointment with a neurologist as soon as possible just to make sure, so if he did have autism, then at least he would have a medical diagnosis which would allow him to receive services. At this point, I was angry. I took this very personally and recycled the information he brought home. My response to him was "I think you're wrong and I'm going to prove it." I was so convinced that I was right that I proceeded to call the local school district to set up an appointment for preschool screening, and then the neurologist to set up an appointment to confirm my beliefs. How dare he think our child had issues, when he was meeting all of his developmental milestones? He might be difficult, but sure as hell did not have autism.

A few weeks later, a nice woman from our local school district showed up at our door with toys in hand, and forms for me to fill out while she proceeded to test Kameron on our living room floor. By the time she was done, she had grown very quiet and then gently showed me the results. She said he had scored in the black, and I remember asking her what that meant. "It's usually an indicator that he needs further testing." Oh great, what does that mean? Suddenly, a sinking feeling came over me and I asked her flat out if she thought he had autism. She replied that she was not qualified enough to make that kind of decision, but highly recommended we get further testing.

It was early spring and one of our neighbors decided to host a "Social Tea" with some of the other gals in the neighborhood, giving me an opportunity to meet some new people. I became quick friends with a fellow mom who also had a son close to Kameron's age. As we discussed our boys, I of course told her about my recent event with the early childhood center and their findings. She quickly recommended her developmental pediatrician and suggested that I go see her right away. So I called her pediatrician and scheduled a meet and greet with her doctor whom I will refer to as "Dr. M."

She was very friendly and kind, and waited patiently as I went down my list of concerns, and disappointments about prior visits to other pediatricians I had seen regarding the same issues. Oddly enough, Kameron had remained calm throughout this visit. Any other time we stepped foot into a doctor's office, he would start to scream inconsolably until we left. So I looked over at him, and noticed he was using my velvet hair scrunchie, which was his comfort object that we never left the house without, and was rubbing it up and down his arms. I thought this was kind of strange, but was happy that he was actually being quiet enough so I could have my conversation with the doctor. When I was done, she looked at me and said "Has anyone ever mentioned the word autism to you?" I told her not yet, but my husband had had some suspicions and I asked her why she asked. She proceeded to tell me that from what I had explained to her, and what she was observing, pointed to autism and sensory integration issues.

She suggested we look into the First Steps program, which was a service provided by the state for kids with special needs, and that we needed to get him in right away. In that moment, my heart sank, the room got smaller and I started to cry. Dr. M. looked at me and felt horrible that this was this first time I was hearing this. She handed me a tissue and tried to console me, but our time was up because this had only been a meet and greet appointment. Had she known, she would have booked us more time. I told her it was ok, and that I would go. I thanked her for her advice, took my information, and left to go home. I fought so hard to hold back the tears as I left the building, and how I even drove home is still a blur to me.

So this was real...my son had not only something wrong with him, it had a name and it was what I feared most. Autism. I had no idea what it was or what it meant for him. My husband had been right and I had been wrong. As soon as we got home I broke the news to him, and it only verified his suspicions. "Let's wait and see what the neurologist says and then we'll know for sure." Our appointment was still three weeks away, so now what? Well, for the next three weeks I cried daily, wondering how this happened to us? To him? How did he get this? And it had a name. A horrible, ugly "A" name that I couldn't even bring my-self to say for the longest time because it made me so angry to say it. I even referred to it as the "A word" for the longest time and it was never spoken by me in our home.

So all the difficulty that I had with him, which started at around 13 months of age, had been one of the biggest signs of autism. Regression. We didn't have a clue that it was even happening, but knew something wasn't right because it manifested itself slowly enough that to the un-trained eye, you wouldn't have noticed right away. By 16 months, he had lost all his speech and pointing skills, and then the aggression started. When he didn't get what he wanted, he would resort to eye gouging, hair pulling, and even scratching and biting. I used to wonder how this little person could be so angry all the time? How naive had I been?

A good way to describe regression is to say it's like watching your child die right in front of you, but yet they are still there, walking around and breathing right in front of you. No matter how hard you try to reach them you can't. Nothing you do helps, so you stand back and watch helplessly, as your child becomes worse and starts to withdraw more into themselves every day. It is one of the worst feelings in the world not being able to help your child. You wonder if you will ever feel any different.

I think the toughest part as a Mother during this time was that I knew that my child needed me, relied on me, depended on me, but there was no connection or acknowledgment of any kind. This expressionless little round face would just stare blankly back, and it was never directly at me, just slightly somewhere past me. There were no sweet sounds, no smiles; no intimate snuggling that a mother and child share. Just a rigid child who screamed when he didn't get what he wanted because he had no words and screamed himself to sleep because self-soothing could not be learned. He woke up every night and stayed awake for three hours at a time because his sensory issues would completely override his nervous system. Every day he led me around the house by my finger hoping that I would be able to figure out what he wanted.

It was finally time for our neurologist appointment. We saw a doc-tor, whom I will refer to as "Dr. C." He was much younger than I had expected, and his short time in his profession was greatly reflected in his bedside manner, with horrible sympathy skills. He asked us a lot of questions, and was observing Kameron the whole time, who was well across the other side of the room, sitting comfortably in his stroller, and again, rubbing my velvet scrunchie all along his arms. Then we moved onto the physical part of the examination, and of course Kameron started to scream because we had removed him from his safe place in his stroller. Once the doctor had completed his exam, he sat back behind his desk, looked us straight in the eyes and said: "Your son has autism. You can call it Asperger's or whatever else you want, but it is autism." He then pulled out a handout with a case study about a boy with autism, and then the appointment was over.

No "Good Luck" or "I'm sorry, I know this is a lot to take in right now," just, "Here's an explanation of what your child has and we are done." I was speechless as we walked back to our car and that horrible sinking feeling started to consume me again. This time, my husband was the one to take the brunt of the devastation, the helplessness and then the despair, because his worst fear had just been confirmed. His world came crashing down around him. He spent the rest of the day at home with us instead of going back to work, with a bottle of whisky that he nursed in a glass all day. I remember looking out at him through the window, while he stood motionless outside, watching Kameron attempt to play in our backyard, and I could see all of his dreams for Kameron slowly fall from his heart, one by one, and crash to the ground. It's a moment I will never forget. All of the dreams that every father has for their first born son died for him.

We found solace in each other's arms later that night, holding onto each other tightly, wondering what was to come. We had so many questions with no answers. How were things going to be for us? For him? And for the new baby inside of me that was now 11 weeks gestation? How were we going to do this? How was I going to do this alone while my husband worked all day? Where was my support system going to come from when all of my family lived in Canada? Who was going to help me?

As the next few months unfolded, we were thrown into meetings, and testing, and pages of paper work to fill out, and then more testing, and therapists, and it seemed to go on and on. Because Kameron was two years, four months old at his diagnosis, we had a lot to get done before he turned three, otherwise he would be too old to qualify for the First Steps program. So we got to work. We tested him for placement at our local school for their early childhood program, we set up our in home ABA program, and then managed to qualify to get into the Judevine Center for Autism, for a three week boot camp that they had for families with kids on the spectrum. I was now very pregnant with our daughter trying to juggle all of this, and an emotional hot mess just trying to grasp all of the change going on around us, and extremely overwhelmed by the intensity and speed that things had to be done. We had a deadline and that was to get this all done before Kameron turned three.

Finally one of the therapists that was scheduled to work with us took pity on me and told me there was a mom that I just had to meet. She had a little boy Kameron's age, and was going through the same thing as we were, but were just a little further ahead in their journey. This is when I met "M," who I commonly referred to later as my angel. She became my saving grace, the support system I so desperately needed. She would become the one to help me navigate through a world that was so uncertain and turbulent, and find strength and courage in my most desperate times. She was the one I cried with, shared my anger with, as well as my triumphs, (they were small, and few and far between, but triumphs none-the-less).

We talked about IEP's and ABA therapists, biomedical doctors and the latest therapies that were slowly surfacing out in the autism world and sometimes even each other, when the rare opportunity presented itself. Our families became friends, and it was so nice to finally be able to spend time with someone that you didn't have to explain to why your child was doing what they were doing. It was just understood and we finally began to experience and embrace our "new family dynamic." It wasn't what all the other normal families of America were experiencing, but it was definitely a step up from where we had started and it was going to be ok.

I look back on those years, and they were some very dark times for me. I am amazed at how I got through them. I slipped into a deep depression, was extremely sleep deprived, and put on a lot of weight. Even though I had "M" to fall back on, I still became so immersed into my son's world that I sometimes forgot what it was like to function in a world without autism, and it had now become the basis for every decision that we made. Thank goodness we had our daughter because she would quickly snap me out of it, and remind me that there was another little person who needed my attention, love and compassion. She would, as the years would go by, become my ticket to a world I thought I would never be a part of again, and in earlier years had resented so much. The best part of it was that every smile, every hug and every giggle that came out of her was for me and me alone, and slowly our family dynamic began to change. Not only because she demanded it, but also because Kameron's journey was beginning to change direction. We were all in this together, as difficult as some of those times were, and she was determined to be a part of it all every step of the way.

The next few years revolved around having therapists in our home almost every day, sometimes twice a day for ABA (Applied Behavior Analysis), RDI, listening therapy and private speech sessions. We transformed our basement into an amazing sensory gym because Kameron's sensory needs demanded it, and it became the new home to our continuing ABA program. This basement was so awesome that we hosted our kid's birthday parties in it numerous times. We had everything from swings, to ball pits, to roller machines to a bouncy house. My daughter soon became the girl with the "cool basement" and slowly she started to realize some of the perks that came with having a sibling with autism.

Another move transpired, but this time it was back to Michigan, which is when I met TMR's "SNAP!" even before she had become "SNAP!." She introduced me to HBOT (hyperbaric oxygen therapy) and many other amazing interventions, and SNAP! would become my new angel. We bonded quickly and banded together to conquer the school system and autism as we knew it. We spent many afternoons discussing our anger and frustrations with a school system that seemed so broken, but were determined to fix no matter what. She kept me focused and kept me strong and in the process we became dear friends.

There were always many struggles in between the small victories, like not being successfully potty trained until six years of age, not wanting to venture into dark places ever, especially barns, making school trips to a farm very difficult. Hearing his sister cry was the biggest challenge, because he would physically go after her to shut her up, and if I didn't get there in time to intervene it never ended well. Having to police my children every hour was no easy task, but it was just one more thing that just needed to be done. Transitions were also very difficult for Kameron, and having a written schedule for almost every part of his day became a necessity.

Thank goodness he was diagnosed with Hyperlexia at a very young age, which is defined as a strong affinity for letters and numbers, by a speech therapist that was part of our initial testing in the early years. We learned then that he was able to sight read even though he wasn't speaking yet, which allowed us to label everything in our home. With a lot of tough love, we would have him read the labels when he needed something, and he wouldn't get what he wanted until he pointed to it and later, when he found his speech again, use his words. Words were soothing to him and meant a beginning to an end that he could finally understand. As he got older, he eventually learned to ask me to "write it down" for him, because sometimes he was so mad that he couldn't find the words to express how he was feeling, or wasn't able to handle the unpredictable events as they were unfolding. But once those words were on that page, and they were numbered in a sequential order, life was good and he was able to move on.

So where are we now? Well, we ended up moving one more time and now live in a small town in the state of Illinois. Kameron just turned 13 years old and this birthday came with a lot of emotions for me. First, I had a lot of disbelief that I now officially have a teenager. Second, I had a lot of sadness because I had made up my mind, many years ago on our journey, that I was determined to have him recovered by the time he turned thirteen. Unfortunately that day has not yet come for us and we are still fighting the big fight. Is he better? Yes. Has he made progress? Absolutely! This young man went from being a non-verbal, aggressive and severely autistic little boy, to a teenager who now looks me in the eyes and smiles. A boy who can deliver two to three exchanges in a conversation, will seek me out when he has a comment or a question, which does not come easy to him, and most importantly can tell me that he loves me. It took him nine years to do that independently but he did it, and with such tenderness that for me, was one of our biggest victories.

He will engage with his sister occasionally, but always shares a deep concern for her especially when it comes to her emotions and mood, as any older brother would. He loves to hear her sing, and has quite the singing voice himself. We discovered just recently by total coincidence, that he is extremely talented on the piano and he will now be participating in the next talent show at his middle school. He has recently joined the Special Olympics Track and Field team with his fellow classmates and has finally showed an interest in our family dog, whom he engages with daily and dabbles a little with training him with simple commands around our home. Puberty still evades us but I know it's coming. I am terrified as to what it will bring, but I am already mentally preparing myself for the storm and tapping into my resources.

If there is one piece of advice that I can pass on to you is to not lose yourself. Autism will consume you and not always in a good way either. It's all about finding balance and support in those tough early years and remembering that if you don't take care of yourself, you will never be well enough to take care of your family. I know this for sure because I experienced it first hand and my husband and I almost lost each other along the way. Take the time to connect with friends, use your family or sitters to watch the kids as you go away for that long overdue trip with your husband. Have a glass of wine now and again, and when it really gets tough, just breathe. This too shall pass and brighter days are to come, this I can promise you.

Most importantly, when your journey is over and you have accomplished the unthinkable, pay it forward. Your journey is not only about paving the way for your child, but also about paving the way for the other families that come in behind you. It's your duty to help those families not have to struggle like you did, to not waste endless hours online searching for the right protocol, or doctor or therapy that will help further along their child. It is in that moment that you pass the torch and inspire the warrior mom that is within all of us, to move forward, to press on, to fight until you win, and most of all to spread hope. A hope that only you can portray because you have lived it, believed in it, and can now see it and hold it in your arms as it smiles back at you. So eat, pray, and sleep hope, my friends, and one day you and I will cross that finish line.

MONARCH

"I never thought your life would turn out this way" my mom said to me in a whisper with a crack which exposed her pain and undermined her attempt to keep her composure. Her efforts were too late as I had noted her eyes rimming red. The words hit me like a truck. We were separate from the rest of the family and near the couch during Thanksgiving dinner at my house. Only a few people sat as the table was being attacked by little fingers belonging to my four-year-old twins, who reached from behind chairs grabbing at plates and scooped little fists full of food only to smell it and drop it to the floor, smear it on the wall or rub it into the carpet.

The twins kept the dinner lively with meltdowns, shrieks, wails, outburst of aggression and throwing of toys. As the topic of conversation was kept light to balance the tension and obvious abnormal circumstance of the meal, suddenly her words, meaningful, sorrowful, and heavy, felt like a gash, an old wound opened in my flesh. Her simple statement broke through my façade and I felt my life exposed. "This way" was all that was needed between the two of us for her meaning to be perfectly clear. The loss, the constant struggle, challenges, exhaustion, financial devastation, frequent medical appointments, and fight against multiple agencies and entities that had become my norm were all brought to the surface by her innocent admission. My mother never thought my life would turn out this way. She never thought I would have children with autism, two of them.

How could I be surprised by these words as we were surrounded by the noise, the wails, the children's refusal to sit and the throwing of toys swirling around us? Despite my days of cleaning, toys covered the floor in rooms with torn furniture, carpet ruined by urine, feces, vomit, spit up supplements, and numerous foods that were refused and hurled across the room. The old saying goes "if these walls could talk," my walls did talk and revealed my life inside them to all. My walls held back no secrets nor hid any events. They spoke volumes. The once pristine walls were covered in marker, pen, holes, cracks, chipped paint, large patches of drywall ripped away from toys being flung against them and hundreds of dents due to repeated hits with a toy. Not one wall was without a battle scar.

I was in one of my moments where I had to turn down the chaos, the crying, the screaming, and the throwing of objects past me and attempt to focus on what to do next. Should I calm four-year-old Nathan, who was wailing demands that none of his toys be moved from their obsessively positioned places, or pull Nathan's twin brother, William, off the coffee table screaming and shrieking while punching himself in the head? The chaos began to escalate as Willy ruined Nathan's carefully laid out pattern causing Nathan to disintegrate into shrieks of panic, obsessive word repetition, and intense biting of his forearm. Willy attempted to hit and shove anyone in his personal space to quiet the unwanted noise. He began his own screaming, slamming his head with his fists and claw at his neck with his fingernails. Nathan screeched again and again, "He broke it! He broke it! Bring it back!"

The words, while painful, loud and angry, were still pure music and joy to me. Thank God for his words. Although not conversational, he was able to express his frustration through his tears and screaming. He wanted control and the small order he had found in his spinning and unsteady world was now demolished. Willy was rendered with no way to express his anger, sadness, internal chaos, continual abdominal pain, and his feelings of being overwhelmed in his surroundings except to explode into aggression and screaming. He hung his head, sitting still but body shaking and heaving with silent sobs. No feeling is more complicated and painful than watching the people you love the most in the world be controlled by pain inflicted by the thing you hate the most in the world. Looking at my sons, I simultaneously see the most beautiful part of my life and the most painful.

My heart ached to look at them, and yet I felt a certain hope. Having a child with autism, one must always search for the hope and continue moving forward. You must be diligently treating the bodily injuries that are causing their behaviors and use even an emotionally charged moment like this to step back objectively to determine and monitor the effectiveness of the path you're on to heal them. Healing and improvements, although slow and wrought with setbacks, had occurred in my sons due to continued treatments and diet. Nathan was expressing his frustration and Willy was calming himself. We had come so far and yet had a long journey ahead of us.

I continued to watch Willy and refocused on my mother, right by my side attempting to calm the storm, one of many that day. Her comment had now fully taken possession of my thoughts. I analyzed her statement and questioned what response she was seeking. I had no answer. How had my life turned out? The statement was one of pity and empathy, almost an apology. She meant well. I inhaled now feeling my eyes begin to sting and remained silent as to not reveal my own cracked voice. The words were ambiguous to a degree. "This way." My mother never thought my life would turn out "this way." What was the "way" in her comment? The diagnosis of autism in my twin boys, one profound and severe and the other moderate was the obvious answer, but the autism diagnosis was just a label.

In what "way" had autism stolen my family's normalcy, its sense of safety and protection, its place in society, its ability to engage in the average events of day to day living? Was it having four year olds in diapers? My sons' bodies, internal systems and organs injured and overloaded with toxins? Willy's non-verbal state except for the almost constant screaming? Nathan on the verge of an uncontrollable meltdown at the most innocuous events?

The financial ruin of my family? The loss of friends and family as the twins grew and the autism became more obvious, more undeniable? The necessity for me to become a 24-hour caregiver? The way we stood out in public like the neon lights of Vegas as the boys got older and their lack of language and infantile behavior became more pronounced? No words or narratives are sufficient to accurately and completely describe the life of caring for a child with autism. Life with autism is a personal experience and challenge for every family which is constantly changing and evolving.

I was being naïve and thoughtless. Her statement was sincere and her disbelief understandable. In fact, if she had not been shocked that I became a mother of twins with autism, it would be unusual. Of course my mother was stunned by the events that unfolded in my life. None of this was supposed to happen. When she raised me, autism was not part of the national vocabulary, not even a blip on the radar. Autism was not discussed, not feared, regarded, and not part of the American conscience. Our family's journey and familiarity with autism began before I was even born and not yet revealed itself for its true nature.

Autism entered her sphere of awareness at a time when autism was rare, 1 in 10,000. Long before autism became part of the national fabric and a medical and cultural phenomenon, it had already touched our lives and shaped my mother's thinking and perception of autism. She had understood autism as a mysterious psychiatric condition that surely would never touch her life, let alone have two grandsons struggle with the condition. However, even then, as I was a child of the '70's and becoming a teenager of the '80's, the stage was being set and the pieces put into place for the most wide sweeping epidemic of our modern age.

We entered an age of tremendously increasing toxicity in our environment, and those toxins were directly entering our bodies. The pharmaceutical companies were competing in a vaccine race to create the first vaccine for any given disease in order for it to be added to the childhood vaccine schedule. The FDA and CDC, with its links to Congressional politicians, whose campaigns are largely financed by pharmaceutical companies, were poised and ready to support these national advancements in healthcare. Toxins from new products to make our lives easier and more efficient were introduced into our environment at an alarming rate and advancements in agriculture and food production were being widely studied and utilized such as increased pesticides, additives and preservatives. We were so woefully unaware, so painfully ignorant to the storm coming to crush our world along with hundreds of thousands of other families. My mom had come miles from her 1970's perception of autism. She was the first to meet our enemy.

The 1960's and 1970's were a time of experimentation, civil unrest, and the idea that the individual could change the world. During this turbulent but exciting climate, Vivienne, a young graduate student studying Child Psychology and Development at the University of Illinois, and also my future mother, stood with her fellow classmates outside the Adler Zone, the university's psychiatric unit. The professor, having talked up this outing in the prior class, had left the students with hopes of something rare and exotic behind the door. The year was 1969 and it seemed at the time that the study of psychiatry had already firmly defined most deviations of the brain, behavior and thought. What could be so new, rare, and unexplored that these students, lacking in experience and having not yet earned their advanced degree, would be permitted to examine and observe. Prior to opening the door, the professor said something that haunts me, the daughter of the young and eager graduate student, even now in moments of exhaustion and frustration. He spoke with intent and the rambunctious group became quiet at his words, "You are extremely lucky to observe this subject. I promise you, no matter how far you go and despite how long you pursue your careers in psychology, you will never witness this again. Never." The excitement quieted to a hush. The door opened to reveal a 14-year-old boy. His diagnosis: autism.

My mother's assignment was to use basic ABA (Applied Behavior Analysis) to modify his behaviors. His mother was always present during the sessions. My mother recalls often thinking how his mother must feel being so isolated, having no answers, knowing no others with a child suffering with the same condition. Little did she know how intimate she would become with the thoughts, fears and hopes of another mother with a child with autism.

Since my mother's first introduction to autism decades ago, autism has become a national epidemic and crisis. The year my sons were diagnosed in 2009, the US autism rates were released by the CDC on my birthday, an astonishing one in 250. I was devastated and angry. All these injured children could have been prevented. As I write this, the latest number released by the CDC is one in 50 school aged children. These numbers will continue to rise as our children are assaulted with ever increasing toxins while a majority of society remains complacent. However, there is a whisper, a ripple, even a current, of change in the climate. Mothers and fathers are learning the truth and sharing their stories. More doctors and specialists are questioning how and why our children are becoming sicker with each generation.

Forty years after my mother provided ABA to the boy with the extremely rare condition known as autism, I frantically called my mom on a Wednesday night in July of 2009 to hysterically proclaim that my 17-month-old twin sons, William and Nathan, had autism. She laughed. Trying to calm me she reminded me of my exhaustion, lack of sleep, tendency to worry excessively about the twins and told me to simply relax. Everything would be fine. After all, she had just been there only 10 days earlier during the weekend prior. Their behavior was typical, playful, curious and affectionate. She would know, having a Masters in Child Development and Psychology. She could not understand that the unfolding of the events in a mere 10 days changed my life, my sons' lives and my family's lives forever.

Five days before my desperate call, my typical twin boys had received their MMR shots and three other vaccinations. The nurses reminded us to administer Tylenol before they went to bed to reduce soreness. By that evening, the Tylenol seemed like a good idea as both were hot and sweaty with fever. They were listless and barely resisted the Tylenol syringe as they typically did. The next day, the boys were agitated with fever and unable to sit still or rest as if their skin or bodies were being irritated. They were not interested in their favorite toys and activities. That evening as I sang to Willy and I held him in my arms, he stared, almost without blinking at his nightlight turtle. As I blocked his line of vision with my face, he would simply move his head and continue his glued gaze at the light. He persisted to fixate on the turtle as I headed for the door and for first time ever did not cry when I left the room. He did not even notice. Nathan, slick with sweat and pink from fever, was already asleep when I entered his room. His face was not the relaxed and slacken face of a slumbering toddler but tight and crunched. He tossed and kicked all through the night. He woke often and rambled gibberish to the walls as he ignored me and my gentle kisses. He got out of bed in the morning glassy eyed, dazed and his usually bright eyes were distant and bland.

As their fever and "sickness" passed, something greater and more profound had taken hold. They seemed changed, different, distant, even younger and more infantile. They lost interest in toys, began flapping their arms, toe walking, licking and mouthing every surface including the floor and walls. Their personalities, so bright, big and luminous, became flat, lifeless, expressionless and irritable. Their language was gone, their sense of wonder at new things transformed from exploration to staring at fans and any repetitive motion or sound in an object. I knew instantly and completely that something immense, affecting their whole body and biology had changed. They had not simply developed unusual tendencies or lost a few new behaviors, they were different children. I stayed up night after night with my computer and every search returned the same results: autism. We immediately set up for a team diagnostic testing of our sons to determine a diagnosis. Six months was the average wait time for the appointment.

I found myself falling down a dark black hole where no air, no life, no light could penetrate the deep darkness that had swallowed me. I did not know it then, but the person I had been, the foundation upon which I based my life was about to disintegrate and I would now move forward with no ground beneath my feet, but proceeded with eyes wide open where once they had been unknowingly closed. Ignorance is bliss and my own Eden had just been set on fire. The institutions I trusted, the moral code I believed we as a community of humanity upheld, the safety measures and protections created and enforced by my government, the belief that modern medicine and the healthcare system which existed to ensure my well-being, and the food that nourished me, the very basis of my intricate understanding of the world all no longer existed, never had, and my prior life, my prior self were dead.

I felt lost, alone, and in a deep despair that left me deflated and disoriented. The world seemed colorless. I felt my family played no part in this world, had no role in society. Everything was a reminder of our differences. Every child on the playground, every picture on Facebook of a child proudly holding their honor roll certificate, every television show and commercial with precocious and clever kids outwitting their parents and neatly navigating their way through the world were all reminders of what my sons could not be, a reminder of all their potential that was lost.

In the very early stages, despite my despair, I could not wait to begin treatment, any treatment. I needed movement, regardless of direction. My sons were different, faded, and seemed ill. I was losing myself, yet I continued to fight for my sons. However, because I neglected to take care of myself and manage my devastation, my decisions for my sons' treatment and care were affected. I was moving too fast with no direction or path. I wanted to try everything and try it now. If I read something worked for someone on Facebook or a support group, I chased it without reason. Any new treatment or latest supplement became my next pursuit in healing them without actually understanding their underlying medical conditions. I was utterly destroyed and incapable of seeing the bigger picture in terms of their treatment. I wanted relief from a particular behavior, really a symptom, right away. The overall treatment of the complex integration and synthesis of the body's processes and systems were not part of my rationale. I wanted to run the sprint, not the marathon. I was lost and so was the path to their healing.

I started using biomedical treatments and ABA therapy in the home at 18 months, but I knew recovery was not promised. Despite my moving forward with treatments, I was still blind and weighted down with grief and the need for immediate and immense progress. Without that clad tight promise of defeating autism, I felt as though I had no ground beneath my feet. I wanted a guarantee. I was chasing random treatments without proper research or guidance in my decisions. I found myself and my sons spinning in circles and progress was slow. I couldn't sit on my hands and do nothing and wait six months for these appointments to tell me what I already knew. I took to the internet for answers.

From day one, I accepted the challenge to take on autism rather than simply accept it as an untreatable condition. I researched and read every free moment. I absorbed as much information as I could. I joined support groups. Initially, my research was random and rushed, leading to treatments based on popularity rather than my sons' unique medical injuries. Seeing no progress, I quickly began to approach my research in a more methodical way and used the data and labs from my MAPS doctor to decide our path. The amount of books, studies, research and treatment options were overwhelming. In my mind, I began to divide the treatments into two approaches.

The first theory was that autism was a set of behaviors that could be shaped and controlled with therapies and reinforces. I ordered book after book about engaging autism, games to play, and behaviorism to name a few. Every word was a painful swallow of a drink I did not want to imbibe. All the "answers" were how to manage autism, to contain it and control it. I wanted it gone. I wanted to cure it. I wanted my babies back and nothing less. They were ill. In my mind, shaping their behavior alone did not resolve how one day a bright eyed curious child became a sick sullen isolated shrieking ball of pain, bumps, rashes, diarrhea, constipation, inability to sleep and refusal to eat all but three foods. I did not know the extent or nature of their injuries, but I knew they needed more than stacking blocks and matching pictures.

As I rapidly began to refine my research and understand my sons' injuries and interpret their labs, I found myself drawn to the second school of thought which argued that autism was a medical condition often brought on by injury or trauma to the infant or child through toxins, vaccines often being the biggest culprit, entering their bodies and wreaking havoc on the delicate balance of their various organs, biological systems and even cells. We are bombarded with toxins every day, in our foods through GMO and pesticides, in our home cleansers, pesticides, fertilizers, and unnecessary medications. I would not accept living this way. I had chosen our path. I was going to treat my sons' injuries, heal their guts and inflamed immune system, take control of their diets and supplement their nutrient deficient bodies.

As we waited for the months to pass to be given an "official" diagnosis from a team of experts who would examine the boys' behaviors to determine their condition, I had already taken them to see a MAPS doctor, ran a panel of tests, completed a stool testing, began a GFCFSF diet, become an involved member of a biomedical information and support group, had met other mothers on this path. I had listened to their stories of treatments and healing such as HBOT, chelation, various diets for healing the gut, viral treatments, homeopathic treatments, herbal remedies, and countless other treatments. The initial tests revealed how sick my babies were. Their guts were full of yeast, their count literally surpassed the top of the chart. They were deficient in multiple nutrients, their metals were past normal limits, particularly aluminum and mercury. Their viral counts were out of control. Nathan's measles and rubella titers were so high that he tested positive for both diseases and we were actually contacted by our state's Department of Health and had to get a note from the pediatrician in order for him to return to school. As we advanced into testing we determined both of them suffered from Mitochondrial Dysfunction and Willy had lactic acidosis. I will not catalog all of their ailments and disturbing test results, but the tests were clear and absolute; my children were sick. Test after test revealed disturbing results and two children with countless injuries and traumas.

I learned of how my taking a strong antibiotic a month prior to labor had disturbed my son's delicate gut flora. The gut, being the center of the immune system, once compromised, creates infants and children with weak immune systems and inflammation. My sons' guts had formed holes allowing toxins to easily pass through to their bloodstream and through the blood brain barrier causing neurological injury. After delivery, I remained in the hospital for five days for a severe infection with three IV's pumping me full of what the nurses assured me were the three strongest antibiotics they had. I was breastfeeding. I was destroying their guts, I was causing inflammation, and their immune systems were being challenged and taxed.

They had their first pediatric gastroenterologist appointment at four weeks. Over the next year, they would see three more GI specialists with no results. They screamed and cried as they ate due to reflux. They were endlessly restless, irritable and inconsolable. They had already experienced their first injury prior to birth and their bodies were weak, inflamed, and immune compromised when they received their 15 month vaccines. Once the vaccines entered their weakened bodies, the real damage began, the injury and trauma to their bodies began to take hold of my sons and they began to fade from me.

The more I learned about autism as a medical condition, the more hope swelled up inside me. Medical conditions can and are treated. I sensed that though the undertaking was enormous in scope and extremely complicated, with the information and support of the autism community, and the various treatments from the handful of doctors that recognized autism for its medical nature, that autism was not in control of my life. Autism could be managed and treated. We began treating our sons with guarded enthusiasm and I had to learn to follow my sons' lead by their behavior and reaction to treatment but understand that I was the one in control, not autism. I saw gains, stagnation and glimpses of hope. I realized that a promise of recovery was not what I needed to create a new identity to navigate this world. As I began to see my sons peek through their shells, I began to withdraw from mine.

Autism was no longer a monster that had a hold of my sons. Autism was a complex medical condition caused by vaccines and environmental toxins and I controlled the treatment, the protocols and the path of recovery. I was in charge of my sons' recovery and thereby I was in charge of the "autism." We have used multiple biomedical approaches. Some have yielded great advancement, and some have had little effect. For me, to climb out of the darkness and into the light and become a real fighter now was not always about winning, but the awareness that I controlled the path. I did not have to be at the mercy of endless diarrhea and bowel issues, viruses, inflammation, immune compromise, and Mitochondrial Dysfunction. I realized that I had endless resources of books, studies, research, other caregiver's stories and MAPS doctors to guide my decisions. I. Could. Think. I am a Thinker.

Thinking is empowering. Thinking puts you in charge of your child's recovery, of their treatments and path. Thinking shrinks autism down from a stomping and uncontrollable monster consuming your life and dominating your fears, your pain, and your dread of the future. You can slay the monster and reduce it to a medical problem which can be revealed through labs, stool cultures, and other testing. Thinking means you understand that autism is avoidable, treatable and recovery is possible. Thinking does not guarantee recovery but guides you and your next step to fight autism. Even when autism seems to deeply have its claws in your child, never forget you are in charge, even when your child is banging their head against the wall, or smearing feces on the carpet, or is melting down right in front of you, you are in charge. You have the power to examine and determine the underlying reasons and attack them with might, determination and science based treatments. This revelation saved me, pulling myself out of isolation, despair, and my beliefs that our future was set and bleak.

I grew from a caterpillar crawling on the ground with one perspective seeing only what was right in front of me, never seeing the path ahead, the view around me, or the possibilities. I could no longer stand living with such limited vision, not able to see the big picture. I went through a transformation, a rebirth, a chrysalis period where I learned the causes of autism, that autism is an injury, not a set of behaviors, and that autism is treatable. I carved the path using my children's behaviors and medical tests. I researched endlessly, devoured books about various treatments to heal the body and grew wings to fly. Now, like a butterfly soaring high in the air, I could look down and see it all: the path, the paradise in the distance, and the hope of a better future. I recognized that I didn't need the ground beneath my feet and the stability that I had believed a guarantee of recovery would provide me. Letting go of your loss and need for a promise that every treatment is the right one and that recovery is around the corner frees you of your grief and your need to hold onto what should have been. It allows you to focus on treatment and finding the right path. You will make mistakes. You will spend time, money and energy on treatments that don't work for your child, but these are not failures. These are just road blocks turning you to take another direction. Keep moving forward.

Knowledge is Power. Ignorance is Bliss. One may choose to live in blind happiness, or one may choose to live an informed and purposeful life, but at a cost. Along with knowledge, one must face and internalize harsh truths about our society, corruption in our government, our corporations and our medical community that keep our children sick. I hate autism. I hate what it has done to my sons, my daughter, and my family. If autism would not have entered my life, I would probably be living my typical American life with my three kids, a career, two cars in the garage and a nice modest home. However, I would also be drinking diet sodas, eating pesticide laden foods and processed "foods" with no real food in them but toxic GMOs instead of nutrition. I would be vaccinating and getting flu shots and filling my body with neurotoxins and poisons that attack the immune system, the gut, the brain and causing havoc in my body so deep and profound that it has the power to injure and change the function and health of my cells. I would also be doing this to my family.

Autism gave me the power of sight. Autism first broke me, and then sent me on a journey for answers which changed me and my entire perspective and understanding of society, government, medicine, corporations and science. The more I learned, the stronger I became. I gave up crawling on the ground and eating the crumbs dropped down to me from the powers above. I grew wings and soared above the lies and corruption to a state of truth and empowerment. Ignorance may allow you blind happiness and a simpler life and allow you to enjoy the fast food, cleaning supplies, and processed food. But if that is bliss, I chose knowledge and power. We, the mothers and fathers and caregivers of injured children carrying the "autism" label are the holders of the truth, which gives us tremendous power. We have an enormous responsibility to spread this truth, to never allow it to be buried or covered and to continue to fight for our children.

Our mission is to spread this truth to every community, every parent, and every individual. Change begins by sweeping away old dogmas and lies told by corporations, agencies and the government. Our biggest weapon against their forced propaganda and cover-up attempts: our stories. We begin to spread the truth by telling our stories of what happened to our children, how they became sick, and how we are healing them. Our stories will shed light in the darkness and pull others out of the darkness of ignorance, even at the cost of their false bliss. Our stories will enlighten the world and change society's perspective, shake them out of complacency, allow them to begin to ask questions and initiate their own research. The truth will set you free, and our stories are our truth. We will change the world perspective if we are not afraid to use our voices and share. Hundreds of thousands of us have a story to tell. This one is mine.

LONESTAR

I've heard it said that parenting your first child is kind of like the first pancake in the batch — your attempts are throwaways because you haven't adjusted the temperature of the pan or you flipped it too early or too late. When I got pregnant with my second daughter, I definitely felt that way based on all the things I'd learned (some that needed to be unlearned) along the way during my first go at motherhood. My oldest had only breastfed for seven months, and I was determined to make it to at least a year with my second. Payton (my oldest) used disposable diapers, ate jarred purees, forward-faced in a car seat at a year and was fully vaccinated. I decided that Reese would be in cloth diapers (or none at all since I was researching elimination communication), she would benefit from baby-led weaning and extended rear-facing in her car seat, and she would be on a delayed and selective vaccination schedule.

Let me be clear — none of the parenting changes were influenced by autism. Autism wasn't on my radar any more than Pendred syndrome, encephalopathy, chronic diarrhea, seizures, or mitochondrial dysfunction. My decisions were only based on some sort of ideal I had at the time, the pursuit of crunchiness I suppose. Autism didn't creep onto my screen until Reese was a toddler.

Put simply, I was going to do better for Reese (and Payton) by being healthier and more "natural." But I now know that there is a huge divide between better and best. Being better, doing better, feeding better, treating better are all just statements of comparison with actions that are worse. I could say I'm eating healthier if I choose Chick-Fil-A over McDonald's and, technically, I might be correct, but I'm certainly not eating the healthiest diet I can. I learned these lessons the hard way when Reese turned one.

Disclaimer: I recount these incidents as though I was fully cognizant of them at the time; I wasn't. My hindsight is 20/20, so I've had to piece together events through photos, emails, and rough recollection. Until autism walked into our home uninvited, I wasn't a note-taker. I have no baby books for any of my kids. Now I have medical record binders and day planners full of notes about what's been eaten, what supplements were taken, what the mood of the day was.

On Friday, January 26, 2012, the day before Reese's first birthday, she had her one year well child check-up. Her doctor, who I adored, and I had agreed upon a staggered and selective immunization scheduled. On that date, she was in need of her Hib shot. I dutifully complied with the imposed rules. Two days later, as friends and family members gathered to celebrate her birthday, she seemed out-of-sorts. She sat quietly on her grandfather's lap, spending a majority of the party hugging a balloon. We don't have a single photo of her smiling that day.

From that date forward, it was one mysterious medical event after another. Unexplained fevers and rhinitis occurred in February. March started with her no longer responding to her name, followed by odd marks presenting on the front of her feet. Her doctor was perplexed by them because the marks didn't match any kind of common rash or dermatological reaction to chemicals, nor were they the result of trauma or intense heat. He mentioned the possibility of an autoimmune connection, but the marks eventually faded and disappeared completely after a month, so we didn't discuss a potential systemic cause any further.

Soon after, she experienced what appeared to be a gnarly diaper rash. Being the healthier, crunchier, better mama, I immediately busted out the coconut oil and slathered it on along with cow's milk yogurt applied directly to the area. Plus, she enjoyed frequent diaper-free time while we tried to start potty training. But it worsened tenfold and spread. She began bleeding and crying out in pain. Her doctor diagnosed it as yeast and then a couple of weeks later, he surmised that it had become staph. But, prescription ointments didn't touch it, nor did a broad spectrum antibiotic. And, just like the marks before it, the rash went away.

By May, I had decided to do a hearing test as it was becoming obvious that she wasn't attending to peripheral noise. In fact, one morning her sister came bounding down the stairs shouting "Good morning Reese!" Reese didn't notice Payton until she was directly in her line of sight. The ENT discovered fluid so thick that her ear drums couldn't move, yet she had never had an ear infection. Even though she had just finished a course of strong antibiotics, and he had determined that the fluid was uninfected, he wanted her to take more antibiotics along with steroids. I reluctantly agreed to the steroids, but refused the antibiotics. After three days on her meds, I found her to be aggressive and violent, plus she had vomited at least once, so we ceased that course of treatment.

I did some research and decided to have her seen twice a week by a chiropractor and administer mullein garlic oil drops at home. When we went to the follow-up at the ENT's office and I proudly told him how we chose to treat her ears, he quipped "I'm sure we will have to put in some tubes." Then he peeked in her ears and found they were clear and her hearing had been restored. He backpedaled a bit, but insisted that while the chiropractor didn't do any harm, it probably wasn't what worked.

That summer, her diaper rash returned, looking somewhat different than before. A dermatologist diagnosed her with Jacquet's dermatitis, a rare skin disorder brought on by prolonged exposure to moisture. She recommended using disposable diapers and declined to do any further testing, though Reese's PCP had referred us for that purpose. I complied with the recommendation and boxed up all the cloth diapers.

Not long after, Reese had her highest fever to date — over 104 degrees. She seemed perfectly fine otherwise, just a little tired. She drifted into a quiet sleep on my chest (I enjoyed her snuggles), and I assumed she would sleep it off and wake up cooler and happier. About twenty minutes into her nap, however, her body jerked suddenly. Though I noticed it, I wrote it off as just dreamy movements. Then another jerk, and another. I rushed her to urgent care and was told to give her Tylenol for the fever. Confused, I asked the doctor if that would just prolong it and even increase the risk of the fever spiking back up and causing another seizure. He stated, rather frankly, "Yes, but if she's hot, she's uncomfortable and you want to make her FEEL better."

Throughout all this time, Reese was a totally different girl than she had been as an infant. Her funny personality was gone. The words she had started using around eleven months were lost and she expressed little interest in learning new words. She tantrummed frequently, seemingly without provocation. And she stopped accepting affection; hugs and kisses had to be on her terms when she prompted them. All of these doctors, but no answers. I was happily given prescriptions, but no solutions. The light bulb went off as I left urgent care. What am I doing to myself and what am I doing to her? Why?

From then on, I was noting behaviors and symptoms — the staring spells, the hand-flapping, the toe-walking, the sensory-seeking, the lack of awareness of danger or her surroundings in general, poop play, spinning, humming, fingers in the eyes, aggressive outbursts, violence, parallel play at preschool, red spots around her mouth, dark circles under her eyes, uncontrollable bowels. To this day, I come across misplaced pieces of paper with my scribbled notes and find lists I wrote on my phone.

The mountain of evidence was growing taller and taller each day, yet her early intervention therapists who had started coming to the home seemed unconcerned. Twice a week they came and paid no mind to the fact that Reese regarded them as strangers every time. I had to push for an MCHAT, which I was told she "failed."

So began another long series of specialist visits, a series that has yet to conclude. Neurologist, ENT, audiologist, allergist, gastroenterologist, geneticist, endocrinologist, DAN! doctor, MAPS doctor, naturopath, speech and occupational therapists. By now, though, I had learned my lessons: Do not take "no" or "I don't know" for an answer. Do not accept defeat. Do not fill prescriptions unless there is imminent danger from not doing so. Do not do anything but the best for her. Do not ignore my gut. Do not ignore my child.

As I look back and add up all the pieces in this awful equation, I see dominoes toppling over. The immediate brain fog — encephalopathy. The odd marks — immune system overload. The diaper rashes — goat milk intolerance and gluten sensitivity causing dermatitis herpetiformis. The glue ear, red spots, dark circles — more immune system overload. The staring spells — more seizures. The explosive poops —leaky gut, inflammation, mitochondrial dysfunction. The odd behaviors — manifestations and symptoms of larger systemic problems which all add up to an autism diagnosis.

Autism is now my life. It is my job. I'm like a clean-up crew after a natural disaster, or better yet, a crime scene investigator. All of the pieces need to be meticulously and patiently scrutinized and researched if I am to find a solution and recover my daughter.

Through tireless work I am doing just that — recovering Reese. I still see all of those mainstream specialists; if you're on a tight budget with bad insurance, it's the only way to get tests done without breaking the bank. But I take their advice with a huge boulder of salt, then have her MAPS doc (Dr. Dan Rossignol), her GI specialist (Dr. Arthur Krigsman), and her local ND review it all. And although I trust them more than other practitioners, I still make decisions based on my gut and my child. If it weren't for those standards I have set for myself and her treatment, I would not have discovered her genetic hearing loss, or her fecal impactions, or her night seizures. I push, I fight, and for good reason.

She has started coming back to us. Her eye contact is strong, her empathy improving. She finally recognizes herself in photos, and loves to be imaginative in her play. She drew a stick figure the other day and has started calling her sister "bubba" again! Reese is an amazing, brave and strong little girl. She has endured so much in such a short amount of time and we aren't even a quarter of the way there. Because of her, I am now the best mom I can be, and I'm no longer willing to settle for just "better."

GURU GIRL

As I sit on the bleachers next to the BMX track I watch my son ride his bike, and see him listening to his coach. I am in awe. He's *only* six years old.

I sit and reflect on the past six years of his life, and it all feels like a much longer period of time. How did my son that was born premature at 26 weeks, and diagnosed with autism spectrum disorder at the age of three, become this strong, determined, six-year-old boy that I see before my very eyes? My answer? Biomedical intervention healed him!

Anthony's birth was not what you would call a glorious affair. During my pregnancy at 20 weeks gestation, Anthony's twin sister Hailey passed away. My OB-GYN and other medical staff tried to keep me from going into preterm labor. But at 26 weeks gestation, my daughter was still-born. Anthony however, characteristic to his personality today, decided to do things his own way, and stayed inside me for four additional days. Yes, my twins have different birthdays. Anthony was born via emergency C-section, weighing 2lbs 3oz and 14 inches long.

His NICU experience lasted for 91 days. He had a grade 1 brain bleed, PDA ligation surgery at one month old (surgery by your heart), he had seizures, and his heart stopped beating a few times. He ended up coming home on oxygen and an apnea monitor for his first eight months of life because 80% of his lungs were scarred. But that being said, we were forever hopeful about the future Anthony would have.

The first year of Anthony's life was consumed with doctor's appointments and therapy sessions. Because he was born three months early, he was already considered a high risk for developmental delays and long term health problems. The first week he was home with us, we started physical and occupational therapy. It was at that point that I figured out that I was not only going to be my son's mother, but his medical advocate/in-home nurse as well. I learned how to change out an oxygen cannula and apnea bands, how to feed a child that had a very poor suck/swallow reflex, and how to do physical therapy exercises with a child who was incredibly floppy from low muscle tone. But even with the extra stress, I always looked into my son's eyes and thought, "You are my hero! You are strong, determined, and amazing! I know there is nothing out there that you won't overcome."

It was at the age of two that I started to become concerned about autism. Anthony had caught up with all of his physical milestones at the time, but he was very behind in speech. At 15 months old, Anthony had started to babble and had a few words. But as time went on, his words disappeared and his babble turned to humming and grunting noises. I would describe the sounds as if you had duct tape over your mouth and were trying to speak.

Anthony began speech therapy along with occupational therapy. He was diagnosed with speech apraxia and sensory processing disorder. Along with not being able to speak, Anthony started drooling. Whenever he would get excited, over stimulated, or touched a texture that was new to him, the drool would start flowing. He started rubbing his head on the carpet, and pushing his body into people. He also started hoarding food in his mouth, and while eating a meal, he packed his mouth full of food until he looked like a chipmunk.

As months went on, the issues started stacking up. There was talk of ADHD, OCD, and of course the conditions he was already labeled with, apraxia and sensory processing disorder. Each evaluation Anthony had was worse than the one before. There was no progress being made. On Anthony's exit evaluation from the Regional Center, he was a year behind in speech, gross motor, and fine motor skills. I vividly remember sitting in my car reading his evaluation report and the tears flowing down my cheeks. The therapy that all the doctors had pushed for was not helping Anthony. Not one bit. Something had to change! Therapy was not enough! There had to be something else going on inside my little boy. Something his current doctors were not aware of.

It was soon after this that I spoke with an online friend. She told me about biomedical intervention, DAN! Doctors, and probiotics. She told me all about Autism Spectrum Disorder. The more she spoke, the more this sounded like what Anthony was dealing with. The very next morning I found a DAN! Doctor, and made an appointment.

While we were waiting for Anthony's appointment date, I started him on probiotics. The first week he was on them, he spoke ten words! And for the first time in his life, he kept them! As the weeks went by, my formerly non-verbal son started gaining new words every day. I was shocked and in disbelief! Why? Because after two years of intensive speech therapy, my son had not gained one word. But after a week on a simple probiotic, he gained ten words! It was during this time that I started to feel hope, and knew that biomedical intervention was exactly the treatment that would heal Anthony.

That first year of biomedical intervention was intense. I could never downplay that. Anthony was diagnosed with Autism Spectrum Disorder, many food allergies, high yeast levels, mitochondrial dysfunction, methylation issues, oxidative stress…the list just went on and on. While I was overwhelmed with the news, I had hope! We could fix these issues. We had reasons behind the diagnosis!

Life changed for my whole family that first year. We had to adapt to Anthony's new dietary needs. Not only did we have to go gluten/casein free with him, but we had to avoid thirty other food ingredients as well, based on his Alletess IgG and IgE test results. After we received Anthony's Genova Diagnostic NutrEval test results, we started Anthony on many supplements, including a stronger probiotic with S. Boulardii, Omegas, Vitamin D, methyl B-12 injections, and TMG, just to name a few.

Anthony's recovery started right away. It was obvious that biomedical intervention was helping. His speech was growing by leaps and bounds.

Even his speech therapist was amazed! She even mentioned that whatever we were doing, to keep doing it! After a few months of biomedical intervention Anthony's sensory issues improved. He stopped drooling. He stopped rubbing his head on the carpet and pushing into objects. He even started feeling temperature for the first time in his life. I remember him running to the refrigerator and saying "It's cold mommy!" Anthony's gross motor skills improved too. At three-and-a-half-years-old, he jumped for the first time. He learned how to do somersaults, kick a ball, and ride a balance bike. His fine motor skills improved so much that a month into biomedical intervention he no longer qualified for occupational therapy.

It was at this time that his speech therapist advised putting Anthony into a typical developmental preschool to see how he would do. So at the age of four, I enrolled him in school. I was nervous and apprehensive. But I found a preschool that had warm and loving teachers. The students were very friendly to Anthony. And while his speech continued to improve with the help of TMG supplements, his confidence soared. For the first time in his life, he knew that people (besides his mom and dad) understood what he had to say. He made his first real friend and had his first real play date that year.

At four-and-a-half-years-old, Anthony no longer qualified for speech therapy. I vividly remember that IEP meeting. I remember walking out of there with an IEP with no recommendations or goals written on it. I remember crying happy tears as I walked to the car. It was a little over a year since we had started biomedical intervention. And I knew that I had biomed to thank for that moment. The moment that my son became therapy free!

The past two years have all been about maintenance and refining Anthony's biomedical plan. As his body has healed, we have changed supplements. We have re-tested allergies and seen them vastly improve. He now only has one true allergy, which is gluten. And just a few food sensitivities. He use to have 30.

We have fine-tuned Anthony's methylation protocol by running the 23andMe test. We found out that Anthony had two BHMT homozygous gene mutations, and one heterozygous. This is the reason TMG helped him so much. We also found out that Anthony is heterozygous for the ACAT gene mutation, which is the reason for his mitochondrial dysfunction. We treat this with Cytotine and Co-QH. And because of that, for the first time in his life he is able to put some fat/muscle on his body and have more stamina.

Anthony is now six years old, and in first grade. He is in a typical, mainstream classroom with no aid. He is age appropriate. He is reading, loving math, spelling words (even though he says it's not his favorite), and playing with kids at recess. He likes to swing on the monkey bars and go high on the swing set.

Anthony likes to play video games on his Wii U. He likes playing with Hotwheels cars, and Thomas the Train sets. He likes cooking, eating all types of food, especially Mexican food. He likes to visit his dad at work and "help out." He also likes to go to the mall. But Anthony's favorite thing in the world is to ride his bike.

So that's where I am today. Sitting next to the BMX track, watching my recovered son ride his bike, listening to him talk to his coach, watching him speed around that track just like his peers. We still may not be a "typical" family. The four of us avoid gluten like the plague. I carry enzymes in my purse. I can talk for hours to a complete stranger about organic foods, GMO's, supplements, vaccines, DAN! Doctors, and methylation issues. And if we go to a birthday party, I'm bringing my own home-made gluten free cake; and no, my kids won't be drinking coke.

Being recovered and on a maintenance protocol doesn't mean there are no little blips or setbacks. They happen. Usually due to illness or diet infringements done by a third party, but the difference is, biomedical intervention has taught me how to handle it all. It has taught me not to fear the "blips." I know that Anthony will never go back where we started out before biomedical intervention. Having that knowledge, and the tools in your belt gives you comfort, confidence, and most importantly… HOPE! Hope that life will only continue to get easier and better for your child. Healing your child does not happen in a day, a week, or even a month. Biomed is a marathon! But is it worth it? With a lump in my throat, and tears welled up in my eyes I say, "Yes…my son is worth it!"

GUARDIAN

When I was a little girl, I loved roller coasters. We were fortunate because we lived approximately one hour away from a gigantic theme park. My childhood best friend, Angela, and I spent many summers going to this theme park and riding the largest roller coasters at the park. Little did I know, my love for roller coasters would be a representation of my adult life.

Mikey and I met in November of 2000. We were engaged six months later. We were married 13 months after that and became pregnant with twin boys three months after that. Roller coaster accurately depicts the start of our life as a family of four. Jaden and Kale were born at 38 weeks gestation via vaginal delivery after a Pitocin induced labor. They were healthy and large for twins, weighing more than 12 pounds between the two of them. Our roller coaster was moving faster than ever but we were holding on tight and enjoying the ride until it came to a screeching halt on January 10th, 2006.

Kale was diagnosed with Autism Spectrum Disorder and Sensory Processing Disorder. Six months later, he was also diagnosed with Apraxia. I knew it was all coming. My husband worked the midnight shift at the time and I had twin babies…sleep was overrated. I spent my nights on Google. I googled autism signs over and over again and I completed the checklists. I asked people in my family, friends that came over, therapists in Early Intervention…do you think Kale has autism? It was not a surprise the day he was diagnosed. I already knew. That was the day our rollercoaster jumped off the track and descended into the world of autism.

For four overlapping years of biomedical protocols, six years of dietary restrictions, two years of homeopathy and six years of traditional therapies our rollercoaster stayed derailed. Jaden and Kale were now 10 years old. How did that happen? They can't be 10 years old! Kale is too old to recover from autism at 10 years old! We missed the "window!" Now what would we do?

My hope of him recovering from autism waivered as I thought about the years and years we spent working towards recovery without making it to the other side. I fought with myself daily, and focused on hope because I refused to let despair take over. I refused to give up on my son just because we had not found the right protocol or the right therapy before his 10th birthday. I knew it was out there. I just needed to research more. So, I did. I spent hours upon hours on Google again. Social media did not exist back when Kale was diagnosed. That's right people, there was no Facebook! We had Yahoo groups and I joined many of them. To this day, I still get email updates from the Yahoo groups that are still active, but I rarely participate anymore due to my obsession with Facebook.

One night just after my boys had turned 10, I was lying in bed reading through my emails. For some reason, I clicked on one of them and that is the night our roller coaster got back on track. I read a feed in that email about Homotoxicology. I was immediately intrigued and I went to Google. I learned that Homotoxicology was developed by Dr. Hans Heinrick Reckewig. I also learned that Homotoxicology utilized homeopathic remedies that worked at both the intracellular and extracellular levels. It would get the inflammation down, address the overburden/toxicity of the organs and detox him. Homotoxicology worked to open up the detox pathways in the body, pushing the toxins out. There were different phases of Homotoxicology, and I remember wondering which phase Kale was in. Homotoxicology gave me that feeling almost immediately. You know the feeling I am describing — the one when you are reading and researching a protocol and that mommy instinct kicks in and next thing you know you are talking to your computer screaming, "Yes, that's totally my son!"

I called that next week and made an appointment. Homotoxicology would be our focus for the next 12 months. We started the protocol in late August of 2012. From the start, I knew it was going to be life changing for all of us. Regardless of Kale's age, my hope, strength and focus were renewed and onward we went. After two months of Homotoxicology, I noticed increased eye contact, moments of pure clarity where he would look at us with those gigantic brown eyes as if he were seeing us in a different way, more compliant and he was laughing appropriately. Kale also had some huge emotional ups and downs during those first two months on the Homotoxicology protocol. We even had a short return of some old behaviors, but they quickly faded again. According to our Homeopath…Kale was a great responder.

The first holiday during our Homotox journey was Thanksgiving. I wasn't sure what to expect because everything was still so new. We were still learning about the remedies and the way that the body detoxes. I have had anxiety around every single holiday since Kale was diagnosed with autism. There are just so many people around during the holidays, people that are not used to your everyday routine with a child with autism. There are also the dreaded food tables within reach of my son, who could never eat any of it because of his dietary restrictions. What kind of meltdown was that going to cause that holiday? Would he play with the other kids or stay in his own world while we were supposed to be "visiting" with friends and family? Would he break something at my aunt's house? These are all questions that build the anxiety within parents of children with autism around the holidays.

This particular Thanksgiving was at my brother and sister-in-law's new house. I had anxiety because it was not at my parent's house, where we know Kale is comfortable. I went with the flow of the plans and I was blown away. That Thanksgiving, Kale sat at the dinner table, surrounded by Mikey and I, Jaden and my parents. He sat at the dinner table and ate Thanksgiving dinner with us. That was a first in our history of holidays.

He had never sat at the table and enjoyed a holiday meal with us. I took pictures. I cried. My husband cried and my parents joined in. We were in complete amazement and we enjoyed every single second of it. My sister-in-law walked over to the table and I said, "Look at him." We smiled and enjoyed the moment. My anxiety dissipated and that was a Thanksgiving to remember. We had conquered that ride and it was amazing!

Next ride...Christmas. It's my most favorite time of the year. Many Christmas celebrations have been ruined due to my anxiety and the failure of the day living up to the picture perfect vision I had created in my head of what these holidays should be with my children. We have had a number of good or mediocre Christmases but we were yet to have a Christmas where my anxiety didn't get the best of me. I usually ended up crying for one reason or the other. For example, during Christmas of 2011, Kale didn't even want to open his presents. I cried the entire morning.

Our holiday typically begins on Christmas Eve with my in-laws coming over, having dinner and opening gifts with the boys. This year, Kale was in a perky mood all day. My anxiety, although present, was at an all-time low. I think this was in part because Kale was in a good place all day, smiling and laughing with Jaden. My in-laws arrived, we ate dinner and it was time for presents. Kale was all about opening presents that night. He wanted more, more, more. He was interested in what the gifts were, he verbally said "thank you" and he smiled a lot. It was breathtaking, literally. Mikey and I had tears in our eyes as we watched it all unfold. We tucked him into bed that night, with his brand new weighted sleeping bag, and we were blessed. We were thankful for those moments spent together, witnessed by others, that our son was truly excited for Christmas to be here.

Christmas morning arrived and Jaden came running into our room at the crack of dawn. Kale was also awake. They both looked over the railing and smiled. They saw their piles of presents and couldn't wait to get down the stairs. Kale and Jaden descended the stairs together and ran into the family room. Side by side, they sat on the couch while I grabbed for my morning caffeine and gathered my camera to get ready to capture every single second of this most special morning. The whole time I was wondering, is this gonna be it? Is this finally going to be my picture perfect holiday…my favorite ride in the park?

I watched in amazement that morning, as my twin babies sat together, opening their Christmas gifts from Santa. It was a ride that I hope every single one of my autism mama friends gets to experience with their children. It was that perfect. Once again, Mikey and I cried tears of joy. We had waited a long time to experience this type of typical holiday together. We were elated. The day continued with an annual get together at my aunt and uncle's house for Christmas brunch. Kale continued to have a great day. Jaden confided in me that he had noticed how well his brother was doing and that it made him happy too. When it was time for opening gifts, Kale sat in the middle of the large, over-crowded family room and he waited for his gifts to be passed to him. He looked at me for approval to open them and he tore into them. He smiled, he giggled and he opened. When he was done, he went around with my prompts and thanked his family members for their gifts.

The day concluded at my parent's house where we celebrate with my brothers and their beautiful families. It had already been a long day and Kale had already given us such happiness throughout the earlier hours of the day, that I really didn't have high expectations for him to be so engaged for the remainder of our time at the autism theme park that day. I stopped and caught my breath for a moment and realized I had no anxiety in that second. The anxiety that had been my partner during all holiday functions for so many years had left me solo to truly experience the moments of this holiday. Gladly, I was on my own for this one.

Kale surprised us once again and sat on the floor, amongst his brother and his cousins, and he opened his gifts. I glanced over at my mom and she was beaming. She was staring at him intently, with tears in her eyes. She looked over at me and we knew in that moment, he was coming back to us. Mikey and I packed up the kids haul from the day and we headed home. We got in the house and couldn't believe we had just experienced this day. We had just experienced the most picture perfect holiday I could have ever dreamt up for our family. I would forever cherish every moment of the last 24 hours in my heart. I was grateful and I was appreciative but most of all, I was excited for what the year of Homotoxicology had in store for us.

Next ride, Easter bunny. We had now been doing Homotoxicology for approximately seven months. I was learning so much every day. I was introduced to so many different brands of remedies. Additionally, I had a tight lock on understanding how Kale's body responded to most of the remedies, most of the brands, and how to support him during detox. Things were moving along and going well. We were having more good days than bad, although anytime a child is going through detox like this, you are going to have some hard days. This is why it is essential to know your child's body and how to support them during the process.

Coloring eggs is a tradition that Jaden LOVES and usually ended up doing with me because Kale wasn't really interested. This year, Kale sat and colored Easter eggs with his brother, independently. He didn't need me to help him dunk the eggs, he had it. All by himself, he had it under control. He woke up on Easter morning, ran down the stairs with his brother once again and they dove into inspecting their baskets. Before us, he smiled and giggled as he explored the contents of his basket. Again, I grabbed the camera, documented the moments both on film and in my heart and we went about the day.

Homotoxicology was bringing him back to us. He was improving right before our eyes. His sensory aversions were dwindling and it was an amazing sight to see. He could now sit in a chair and get his hair cut. He didn't need Mikey and I to hold him down. Mikey didn't have scratches on his arms and I didn't have hair clippings all over me from holding him during the haircut. He sat in the chair like a 10-year-old does and got his haircut. I grabbed the camera again and I videotaped the monumental moments that just kept happening. Ten-year-old "window?" Kids cannot recover from autism once they reach a certain age? Nonsense. My son was fighting through right before my eyes and I was documenting his every moment. Our roller coaster was picking up speed and we were headed into the corkscrew turns.

Mother's Day, 2013 was a colossal moment for our family. For years, we didn't go out to dinner like typical families, for many reasons. Dietary restrictions, sensory overload, difficulties with waiting for long periods of time, to name a few. I often found that if a situation created more anxiety than was already apparent in our everyday lives, I respectfully declined offers and we stayed home. This Mother's Day was different. All I wanted was to go out to eat with Mikey and the boys. I felt like Kale's progress was at a point where he could handle going out to dinner if we let him have a dietary infraction. Mikey said ok, if you are ready, let's do it.

We headed out that day in the early afternoon. My plan was to arrive at the family friendly restaurant early enough so that there wasn't a long wait time for a table. We lucked out because there was no wait time at all. We were taken to a table immediately. Kale grabbed a menu and began to look it over. I am not going to lie…my anxiety came to the restaurant with us. I was nervous. What was I thinking? Was this a good idea? Finally, I had to get a grip and order our food. Kale pointed to what he wanted in the menu and then proceeded to try to push me out of the booth as if he were telling me, "Ok Mom, I told you what I wanted, now go get it." I looked at Mikey and said "Wow, we have to teach him that the server will bring him his food, not Mama."

We lucked out again and had an amazing server that day. Everything came out really fast and we had everything we needed. While we were at the restaurant, waiting for our food, Kale and Jaden colored on the kid's menus, played tic-tac-toe with us and all was perfect on this ride, for that moment. Our food came and Kale was so excited. He ate his dinner and I noticed that he was exceptionally quiet. He had not been verbal stimming since we had arrived at the restaurant. Except for the fact that Kale had very little expressive speech, I really don't think anyone in that restaurant would have realized that he was a child with autism.

My Mother's Day was perfect. Again, I had tears, I took pictures and I keep those memories in my heart. That was the best Mother's Day I had had since my beautiful twin boys were born, 10 years ago. It was every-thing I had envisioned it would be, going out to dinner as a family. We continue to take the boys out to eat, once a month. This does nothing for their healthy diets, but it does wonders for the memories we are making as a family and that trumps dietary restrictions one time a month. Kale continues to do well when we go out to eat. We have learned that he can control his verbal stimming when we are out which is something we had no idea he could do.

Summer parties with the neighbors were fun and exciting to watch Kale interact with peers his age. He jumped on the big trampoline with the other kids, he swam with the kids and he laughed and enjoyed being the center of attention. It was the best summer of his life. It was a summer filled with roller coaster rides, the fast ones. The ones that flip, turn and descend into the corkscrews that life throws us. It continued to be a summer of firsts for our boy. He rode his big wheel around the entire block, chasing his brother on his bike, for the first time ever. He played baseball with a bat and a tee in the backyard with his brother. He spent time at the beach with friends and he was showing us exactly how he wanted to spend his summer days.

Homotoxicology gave us our son back. With our Homotox protocol, he was more engaged, more connected overall. His receptive language skills were increasing. He would come downstairs to see what I wanted when I called his name from the staircase landing. He looked at us with meaning in his eyes. He no longer had to carry around a stack of animal or sight word flashcards that was 10 inches thick. He didn't need to be on the iPad every minute of the day, stimming on his movies. He wanted to play with Jaden. He sat and played simple board games with me. His need to regulate his sensory system was diminishing and he was controlling his own sensory regulation in more age appropriate manners. He was controlling his verbal stims in public. This was all so amazing and overwhelming at the same time. We were on the right roller coaster, finally. All those years, and we finally found our favorite ride at the theme park called autism. We were on that ride and we were screaming at the top of our lungs, hands in the air! It was the most fun we had experienced as a family to date.

During this time, we also did seven months of Sublingual Immunotherapy. This allowed us to test Kale and remove the foods from his diet that were causing inflammation in his body. This protocol, in conjunction with Homotoxicology, was miraculous as well. Sublingual Immunotherapy taught me even more about my son's body and it taught me about the foods that were safe for my son to eat. I was grocery shopping and cooking more than I ever had before. Admittedly, I am no Suzy Homemaker. However, I enjoyed it because my kids were eating exactly what their bodies needed to heal. The inflammation decreased and I am forever changed because of that protocol. It required hours and hours of cooking on Sundays and prepping food for the week, but I learned so much. I will always be conscious of the foods I am feeding my kids.

Our journey through autism continues. Although Kale has made remarkable progress over the last 12 months, we still have a lot of rides to conquer in our theme park. Apraxia is located in the Northern area of the autism theme park. It's the biggest ride in the park. It's the ride that you can see from a mile away. You know when you are driving on the highway and you are almost at the park, and that first roller coaster track appears through the trees in the skyline? Yeah, that ride! We have gotten close to riding it, but something always gets in our way and we just haven't been able to tackle that ride yet. Well, this year, it will happen. This ride has one of those really steep inclines that needs to be climbed…click, click, click. With the right harness and lap belt, it can be done. I know in my heart that we will defeat that incline and after that…we will sit back and enjoy the ride.

Apraxia is our biggest struggle for Kale. No protocol has touched it. Therapy has been rough. Apraxia tries to take over my hope and bring me down. My response? To hell with you Apraxia! I am sick to death of you controlling my son and keeping us from full recovery. No more! You may have a tight grip on my son for now, but I am coming after you this year. I can hear his amazing voice in my dreams. Soon, that will be a reality. Positive affirmation is a powerful being and it's in our house, everywhere. It will happen. Jaden asked me a few months ago, "Mom, why can Kale get his words out sometimes and then others he just can't?" I explained to Jaden, that was the Apraxia and that mama was fighting it hard this year. Lots of changes on the forefront for our family this year so that I can make sure we get in line for that ride in the Northern part of the theme park and that I find a way for us to successfully climb that incline on that ride. Hope remains a constant in our family. I won't let the negative in. We will get over every last hill on those roller coasters and we will do it together.

One of the most significant happenings within the last 12 months has been the relationships that I have formed with some of the most remarkable autism mama warriors. I am blessed to have the support of many who are fighting the same fight, who are stuck on the same roller coaster, who have conquered every ride in the theme park. I am supported, I am loved and I am honored by these women who I can call my autism family. The relationships that are built upon this journey are life changing. Without the support of these warrior mamas in my life, I would not have the knowledge, the strength and the determination to wait in line and conquer every single ride in that theme park.

My fellow Homotox moms know who they are. They saved me at a time when I needed saving. I am a strong autism mom. I support, love and guide many families on this journey. Sometimes, I am the one who needs the most guidance and I was so very fortunate to find it in these amazing women. Homotoxicology also brought me to The Thinking Moms' Revolution, where I was able to get to know a number of these amazing moms and dads. Additionally, I have a support system of warrior moms right here in my home town. They too, give me the unconditional love and support that is needed for this journey. My family, my very large family, Mikey's family, my friends and my best friend Katherine, continue to be there for us every day and are our biggest supporters.

My childhood best friend, Angela and I are still riding those coasters together in this autism theme park because she is Kale's Godmother. Little did we know how our love of roller coasters would be so significant in our adult lives. All those nights spent walking and talking the paved paths of the theme park are now spent in my kitchen, discussing our kids and their healing. Daily, we are able to share with everyone our stories of triumph from the autism theme park. My parents, there are no words for how much they love and support us throughout this journey. I love you deeply mama and daddy. To my Mikey…. I can never say in words how grateful I am that you chose me. I can only hope that you are proud of me and the work that I do and how hard I fight for our sons. I could not do any of this without you by my side. You are a true example of a warrior dad. You are among the best of them.

My hope, for all of you reading this, is that you find the support system needed to get through all of the lines in your theme park, on your roller coasters and on your journey through that "window." Conquer every ride in that autism theme park. If you haven't yet…you will, just like we will. Until then, hope will keep you going.

GREEN BEAN GIRL

"What I was really hoping to hear about was your experiences after HBOT and the chiropractor." My dear friend was trying to be as kind as possible. We met when our boys were in Kindergarten together. Two little boys with autism. We didn't have a clue what the future would hold. It seemed like a lifetime ago.

"And all the money you've spent on treatments with little to no help from insurance...I would write about that. Remember when they covered his probiotic, and then just quit?" I remembered.

A million thoughts raced in my head...things I try to keep quiet about and not think of often, like our mountain of credit card debt. I felt ashamed of it, even though I knew why it was there, relentlessly haunting me every month. I was grateful to hear an honest critique of my writing.

"I remember when Tristen first started getting adjusted at the chiropractor, and you were like, 'You have to hear his speech!' After talking to him on the phone, I literally cried! I know, I'm a big baby," she laughed. The thing is, she wasn't. She was one of the strongest people I knew, with the kindest heart. She loved Tristen from the first time she met him. I felt the same way about Caleb. "I'm not saying your rough draft isn't good." She paused. At that point, I knew our previous discussions about grammar and punctuation had been a stalling tactic. "But, I mean, your blog...is *really* good." Aw, crap. I need to re-do it.

She laughed uncomfortably. I really trusted her opinion. I *needed* her to be honest. "Thank you… I really needed to hear that! I am so nervous about writing this chapter! When I blog, I just write from my heart…I write what I'm feeling at that moment…and I don't really care who likes it and who doesn't. It's more of a therapeutic thing. But this…this…is going to be right smack in the middle of amazing stories about autism written by brilliant, educated, mother warriors…I don't know how I will measure up!" I went back to the computer to start from scratch.

I scanned the list of names. These ladies give their all, everyday, to their family, and to their community. What have I gotten myself into? How do I fit in here? I started to think about all the activism…the Facebook posts…the arguments…going toe to toe with the nay-sayers…the sheer *knowledge* of these women. Needless to say, I was overwhelmed.

I was drawn to the Thinking Moms' Revolution because I started to read about other moms who were living my life. Not just because they were parents of a children with autism, but because they were "thinkers" and "doers." It seemed they knew all my inner thoughts and worst fears. And they were healing their kids…just like me! They had read the same books and were determined like me to get their kids healthy, despite the effort and cost. That was something I had never seen in any other autism parent in my community. People couldn't believe the lengths I would go to get treatment for my children…they thought I was crazy. TMR showed me I wasn't.

So, what makes me so special? Why would anyone want to hear my story, if it's just like the others? I am not the only one with more than one affected child, health issues of my own or a limited income. I'm not even the only one with a husband with PTSD. What I CAN tell you, is what has worked for my child. I can join the ranks in proclaiming that autism is treatable! I can share what has helped him to make gains no one thought possible. I can prove that anyone provided with the correct information can make a difference in the life of their child.

I'm just a girl from a small farming community in the Midwest. People trust their doctors, and if something is not covered by insurance, they don't do it. For me, I felt like I was screaming in the middle of a crowded room of doctors and barely anyone noticed. How could I help my child when no one would listen to me? Why was I always brushed off? Why didn't anyone care? Why didn't anyone see my child as a human being needing help instead of an "autistic?"

My son was injured at two days old by the Hepatitis B vaccine. His perfect newborn cry turned into a jarring high-pitched scream. He couldn't latch on and threw up most of what he ate. He would gulp down his food for a few short minutes, fall asleep, and wake up wailing. He would only sleep for short cat naps and screeched every time he yawned. At his two week checkup, he had a fever, so he was immediately admitted to the hospital and given strong antibiotics through an IV in his forehead. After three days of treatment and all test results negative, they sent us home without any answers or explanations.

Just after the birth of my second child, I had the confirmation from the neurologist that my older son was on the autism spectrum. He did not have any language, make eye contact or play with toys. He liked to line things up in a long row, kneel beside them, and put his head to the floor to look at them with one eye. At that time, I didn't even have a computer, let alone the internet. There was no mention of support groups in 2000…not even book recommendations. A single piece of paper with a printed-out paragraph from the speech pathologist, who was working with my nonverbal son from the state's early intervention program, was the sole information I had on autism. So, I set out to really study my son to see how I could help him to learn and grow.

I had spent every minute with my child since birth. Much to the irritation of the maternity ward nurses, I wouldn't even let them take him from me for a bath or feeding. He was nursing so well (before the shot), and I didn't want to mess that up by having him bottle fed. I wanted to do it. They kept telling me I needed my rest, but I couldn't bear to be away from my newborn. My husband worked nights and slept days. I did it all. And I loved every minute of our time together. I wouldn't trade it for anything, but that doesn't mean it wasn't difficult to have a sick child. I believe that our time together helped me to better understand him. I knew every little detail about my son, what he wanted and when. I joked that he didn't need to talk, because I knew what he wanted before he did. He never went to daycare and was very rarely watched by anyone else, and if so, it was only for about an hour. When he started early intervention, I soaked in everything they taught me and worked every day with him at every opportunity. I took The Hannen Program (More Than Words) when it was offered to me.

I didn't have the internet in my home until he was about three and even then I didn't "google" autism. I knew what it was. If I had, I'm sure I would have found some of these types of connections back then. But what I didn't know, was why my child was constantly sick. Ear infections, sore throats, rashes, and fevers, fevers…fevers! That poor boy missed so much school from vomiting and fevers that I was frequently threatened with truancy. I trusted the army docs for way too long. Tylenol, Motrin and Zyrtec were handed out like Halloween candy.

My life was hectic with daily interventions for my son, done as if I were a single parent as my husband was deployed more often than home. Finally, I had had enough of doctors with no answers for why my boy was having cyclical fevers, and in 2007 I started to research illnesses. Not illnesses in correlation with autism, but what his symptoms fit regardless of that diagnosis. He had to have an underlying illness keeping him sick that no one was testing for. I thought that if I found it, then I would know what to tell the doctors to test for. They would see that I was not a crazy, overprotective mother with nothing else to do but bother them.

Hours and hours of research. Then, I read about encephalopathy. It fit too perfectly. Before I was able to get back to the doctor to share my findings, something changed our lives forever. In October of 2008, my mother-in-law sent me a gift for my birthday, a book called "Changing the Course of Autism: A Scientific Approach for Parents and Physicians" by Bryan Jepson. This book was about my son! This was exactly what I had been looking for! It had the answers to all my questions. The fevers, the vomiting, the constipation, the speech delays…I knew in that moment we HAD to find a Defeat Autism Now! Doctor to treat Tristen for his chronic illness.

The nearest doctor was in Milwaukee…a good three hour drive. It was do-able. I called to find out the cost. Now it was time to make this happen! The pitch: It went something like this: "Josh, the book your mom sent me? Well, it has all the answers to why Tristen is sick all the time… his fevers, his rashes…it even says the autistic symptoms get better as you treat the underlying conditions! I found a doctor who will do this stuff in Milwaukee. I was thinking, since we took away gluten and casein from Tristen's diet, he's been doing so much better. I said "good-bye" to him the other day when he left for the bus…like I've done every day since he was three, and for the first time, he turned back to look at me and said, 'Bye, mom.' I mean, I barely have to be at the school anymore, hardly ever get a phone call, and get all good notes from his teachers." I waited for a reaction. He was a little interested. I kept going.

"I saw in the paper I could be a substitute aide…they just call you when they need you. I think it would be perfect because if Tristen's sick or has a doctor appointment, I just wouldn't have to take a job that day. I think I could make about $80 a day because they don't prorate for the summer when you are a substitute. I should be able to save up enough money in no time to get him to see the doctor, and then it wouldn't add to our monthly bills. That way, we could afford it." Clenching my jaw, I held my breath. "If you can save up the money to go, I don't see why not." YES!

Money had always been tight. He tried to get work here and there for the first year of our marriage and soon realized he needed something more stable for our family. The army had never been his ideal job, but he signed up and left for basic training on Tristen's first birthday. I was thrilled that he would be getting a steady paycheck, even if it was only $800 per month. He was only in the army about four years before he was injured in Iraq. He came back with a crushed foot and was altered mentally and emotionally. PTSD and TBI is similar to autism in the sense that it also seems to be a spectrum kind of disorder. It can be worse for some than others.

Being honorably discharged because of a medical issue took away our family insurance and post privileges like the commissary. He struggled just living in the world and being around people. Work would go well for a while and then he would fall apart. He had mood swings and went into deep depressions. And that was before all the "help" from the VA, who had him on close to a dozen pharmaceuticals that caused him extreme illness and stress to our family due to side effects and the addictive nature of the drugs. The following years would prove very challenging, as we fought to stay out of poverty.

During the years we spent struggling just to put food on the table, we were very blessed with some generous grants that helped us with biomedical interventions. Every little bit helped, and I will be forever grateful. That being said, the money goes quickly. We were able to start IV chelation, which pulled out large amounts of heavy metals. At the time, Tristen had stayed at a first grade reading level for four years. After his treatment, he tested at a fourth grade level without any other interventions in place. We wanted to continue, but the cost of his supplements were $600 per month (and $300 more for his brother Tanner's supplements) and the grant money ran out just paying for their monthly regimen when we could not.

We were also blessed to be part of a grant program for HBOT (Hyperbaric Oxygen Therapy) in Madison. It was summer, and my husband was still out of work. We put the remaining expense on a Care Credit Card, used by only a few select number of doctors/clinics. We stayed at a friend's nearby home to make the cost for the treatments minimal as possible. HBOT was bringing old memories out of Tristen. It was as if you could watch his face and see how he was thinking and figuring things out that had never occurred to him before. He was talking so thoughtfully about things that happened when he was more severely affected by the autism and could not speak. With tears brimming his eyes, and a soft crack in his voice, he told me that his kindergarten teacher had spanked him. "I was just a little boy. I just wanted to go home." It broke my heart. He had kept that inside for nine years, and although his communication skills had drastically improved, he had never shared that before. This made me even more determined to share his progress with the community. How many other children like my son who could not speak for themselves were being abused?

I also learned about a new program in our area called The Autism Whisperers Program. I was intrigued to learn more and our insurance was approved for the boys to see a chiropractor. The program was exactly like the biomed protocol we were used to…the adjustments to the neck and spine were the missing piece to the puzzle. Even though the insurance later denied the coverage they had at first approved, we were able to pay monthly.

After only a few adjustments, we noticed Tristen didn't "look" the same. He had always held his head back in a posturing sort of way so he was looking down his nose. Soon, he seemed more relaxed, his head resting comfortably on his neck and he looked directly at us. After a week or so, someone commented that his head was finally looking in proportion to his body (He had always had a large head since he was a baby). His language and comprehension were becoming clear. He looked forward to his adjustments, and more than once he seemed to be getting sick before an appointment, but afterwards it never amounted to anything.

Moving to Texas in the summer of 2013 was a big change. Dad was working again, giving me the opportunity to teach the boys at home instead of sending them to public school. This meant less family income, but after so many years of fighting to get an education based on his learning level, and seeing the inside of the special education program first hand as an employee, it was well worth the sacrifice. The budget and staff cuts to public schools are real. An adult couldn't live on the aide salary alone, so very few even apply for those positions. Substitute aides can be literally anyone and more often than not, do not have a clue and basically are just in the way. One time, a substitute aide told me she took the job of caring for a particularly violent child for the chance to call the cops on him.

The kids who can sit in a desk and be (mostly) quiet and cooperative are put in classrooms. The teachers make it sound like it is because of the child's great progress and ability to learn at grade level, when the truth is, the staff is needed elsewhere for more severe children. Heaven forbid you bring up adapting the curriculum to a level they can understand if thrust into mainstream classes. Many do not want to do the extra work of adapting material. It gets worse as the child gets older. They learn less and less as the gap between them and their peers widens. Some teachers also feel very strongly they know better than the parent. I was surprised at how often my requests or hesitations were thought of as frivolous and unnecessary. With teacher and aide abuse running rampant in the news across the country, I needed to protect my kids. I knew I could easily teach them at home. The money would have to wait.

I will continue to fight. It's not over for us. As my kids reach 14 and 16 years old, I am still working for them to achieve their full potential. When I have money, I go after every option that makes sense, and when I don't, I focus on good, clean, healthy food, necessary supplements, and teaching them what they need to know to succeed in life. That doesn't mean it's over. I will do whatever it takes. If it means I learn how to cut my own hair by watching YouTube tutorials, if it means my clothes come from the clearance rack at Wal-Mart, if it means I never get a manicure or pedicure, if I have to go to the food pantry, if it means I drive a tiny Kia Rio because it's paid off, and even if I have to work nights and teach during the day…I will do it all without complaint for my children. I never want to look back and regret what I didn't sacrifice for them. My time, my money, my sleep, my effort…my everything. They deserve it. Everything else is just "stuff."

FRANKIE

"Is the game on yet, Dad?" my son, Josh, yells from the top of the stairs. "Almost, you've got ten minutes until it starts." "OK. I'll get my Seahawks shirt on."

This has been a regular exchange at my house during football Sundays this year. It's not that my ten-year-old son loves football, or any sport for that matter really (except for swimming, he would definitely choose to live in the water if we let him.) But he knows how important the game is to his Dad, and he's been putting forth an effort to connect with him on what he's interested in.

Football Sunday used to be my errand running day, but now I prefer to stay at home and watch the game. Well, not *really* the game. I mean, I enjoy the game, but I'm not a die-hard fan like my husband is. The best part for me is watching my son engage his dad over football. It's a common theme across America, fathers and sons bonding over their mutual passion for a sports team. Most people don't even think about it, it's just a given. But when you have a child affected by autism, one thing you know with all your heart is that there are no givens. Everything is painstakingly worked for.

Josh has come so far since he was diagnosed at age three with PDD-NOS (Pervasive Developmental Disorder — Not Otherwise Specified). At the time, he was stuck in his own world of spinning, tantrumming, dragging his head on the floor, and lining up his toys. He didn't communicate verbally, unless you count the screaming, and was constantly plagued with diarrhea. The specialists we looked to for answers told us he would only progress minimally with traditional therapies (i.e., Speech and Behavioral). They stressed that the best thing we could do for him, for us, was to accept this fact and begin planning his future. These "experts" recommended looking into group homes, state run facilities or other living arrangements for him when he reached adulthood. They told us not to waste our money or place hope on the promises of alternative medicine doctors — they were snake oil salesmen preying on desperate parents. The gluten and casein free (GF/CF) diet? Dangerous. Supplements? Not effective. Postpone vaccinations? Deadly.

Well, the experts were right about one thing, Josh was only progressing minimally with traditional therapies. Not because they are ineffective, but because Josh would only participate for a half second during his therapy sessions. The rest of the time was spent corralling him as he ran around the room like a madman. I knew there had to be more — more for my son's life on this Earth. It's a very scary place to be, when your child is suffering and the people that should help, don't, won't, or can't.

After spending nine months after Josh's diagnosis seeking help from doctors to no avail, we accepted the fact that our son's health and future was completely in our hands and it was time to get to work. I got my Google on, searching for alternative treatments for autism. My search led me to the Generation Rescue website, only weeks after it had gone online. That's where I read the words that would change the course of my son's life: **AUTISM IS REVERSIBLE**.

I had opened the information floodgates and spent every hour I could keep my eyes open taking it all in. The Autism Research Institute's website was also a valuable guide. I only wish TMR and TACA had been around at that time, as I think they are amazing resources for knowledge, hope and support. Dr. Kenneth Bock's book "Healing the New Childhood Epidemics" helped me a lot as well. Being a military family and living in a small town did not leave us many options for alternative care. The closest doctor that practiced what used to be called the DAN!

(Defeat Autism Now) protocol was five hours away and had a year-long waitlist. Not wanting to waste any more time, I developed a plan of what I could do on my own to reverse Josh's autism, and with my husband on board, we started implementing it.

We started the GF/CF diet and saw our son's behavior transform. We also saw his very first solid bowel movement. When you have a child who has only had diarrhea their entire four years of life, this is a very big deal. I was tempted to dip that log in gold and mount it on the wall! His tantrums were noticeably decreasing. He was looking into our eyes and connecting with us more. His therapists noticed a big change in how he was participating in his sessions. All of these accomplishments in just two weeks of changing his diet! Yep, the very diet we were told was "dangerous" was bringing our son out of the pain he had been in since birth. His severe colic early in life was always chalked up to being "one of those things some babies have." Now I understood that his body had been under severe distress. He was hurting, and the only way to communicate that was by screaming.

Motivated by the changes the diet had brought about in Josh, we started implementing the rest of the plan I had drawn out. We used magnesium salt baths to detox his body, and we removed all toxic cleaners and other products from the house. We started giving him SuperNuThera vitamin supplement, MB12 nasal spray, and probiotics. All of these things were making improvements in Josh's behavior, his ability to focus, and his language development.

We decided to put his vaccines on hold, as other parents were connecting the MMR with their child's regression into autism. Although Josh had received every shot on time, he never had a regression, so I didn't believe that vaccines were a factor for him. Yes, I would love to go back and smack myself in the face. Even though we didn't see another surge in progress like we had when we implemented the diet, he was slowly and steadily making progress.

Life was moving forward. After spending six years in the military, my husband decided it was time to move on and create a more stable home environment for Josh. We relocated to California where there were more resources for children with autism. We were beginning to let ourselves feel hopeful and optimistic about the future that was unfolding for us.

But, as with every underdog story, there comes that twist where doubt creeps in and the chance of overcoming adversity is put at risk. This moment happened in our new pediatrician's office as Josh was getting his physical to enroll in school. The doctor took one look at his vaccination records, and went into attack mode: "Do you know you are putting your son at risk of death?!" "This is the most irresponsible thing you could do as a parent!" "If you walk out of here without getting some of these vaccines, and he contracts an illness and dies, how are you going to live with that the rest of your life?" Cue the inner doubt dialogue: *What if I am putting him at serious risk? Maybe just one, as long as it's not the MMR. That's the only one being questioned as a link to autism anyways. Josh never had a sudden regression after his shots in the past. Just one. Then I'll know I'm not putting his life in danger.*

It only takes a few seconds to make an irrational decision based on fear. This was one of those moments, and is now one of the biggest regrets of my life. I left the office in tears, knowing I had made a serious mistake allowing Josh to receive the DTaP vaccine. Within forty-eight hours, Josh started losing the gains he had made over the last year and a half. Words disappeared and were replaced with crying, his eye contact decreased, he started withdrawing into his own little world again. It's hard to write about this because of the emotions it triggers within me. I don't know if I will ever be able to forgive myself. I try not to think about it too often because when I do, it takes me to a dark place and when you are trying to save your child, you don't have time for dark places.

I immediately went back to the Generation Rescue website and contacted one of their Rescue Angels looking for a referral to a DAN! Doctor. My intervention plan had been child's play and I needed the big guns to undo the damage of the DTaP vaccine. I was referred to Dr. Karima Hirani near Santa Monica and I loved her from the get go. It was such a relief to finally find a medical professional who could, would, and did help us. We started the Valtrex/Nystatin protocol, IgG and IgE tests for food allergies, vitamins, minerals, amino acids, MB12 injections and within a few months, we were able to bring Josh back to baseline (where he was developmentally before the DTaP shot). Dr. Hirani had suggested chelation after getting labs back because Josh's aluminum and arsenic levels were high, but I wasn't comfortable with it. From the little information I had looked at about chelation, I thought it was too aggressive and too hard on the body.

Over the next six months, Josh continued to slowly progress from baseline, but he seemed to be hitting a plateau. After revisiting the research on chelation, I decided it was the right time to try it. Josh's vitamin and mineral levels were looking good. Chelation can be hard on the liver, so it's very important that liver function be monitored throughout the process. Dr. Hirani reassured me that his liver was healthy and able to handle it and that she would closely monitor the situation. My motivation for trying interventions for Josh has always been the fact that I don't want to look back ten years from now and say I wish we would've tried it. That's not to say I am willing to try everything, but if I feel there is little risk and the effectiveness has been shown, and I feel it is a good fit for Josh, then I climb onboard.

We decided to go with the suppository chelation as I felt it was less demanding on the body than the intravenous version. Two weeks after starting the treatment, I got a call from Josh's teacher asking me what we were doing with Josh. As with any treatment we've done, I refrain from informing his teachers/therapists of what we are doing so we can have an unbiased opinion. I told her I didn't want to say anything yet. "Well, whatever you're doing is working. Josh has a surprise to show you when he gets home. I am so excited for you to see what he's doing!"

Josh got home from school, walked through the door and said, "I want paper and pencil." He had never used the phrase "I want" before. This was huge! I happily obliged and figured he was going to scribble as usual. What I didn't expect was to look down and see him writing the entire alphabet! This is the same child who fought me so hard on tracing over the letters of his name, who made me write the alphabet on the chalkboard in his room ten times every night, but would scream if I even tried to put the chalk close to his hand. I remember starting to shake as he showed me his finished work, and with a huge grin said, "Alphabet letters."

Then Josh asked for more paper, at which time I handed him the entire stack of printer paper. He wrote the letters out again and this time added his name and the numbers one through fifteen. I called my husband at work and asked him to come home. I was scared it was just temporary, and I wanted to make sure my husband got to experience it. Well, he did, and we were both puddles on the floor.

The next morning, our oldest daughter came running into our room. "Mom! Dad! Did you guys write words on Josh's chalkboard?" Still half asleep, my husband and I opened the door to Josh's room to see him standing in front of his chalkboard, chalk in hand, and the words BOX and FOX written on the board. I barely squeaked out, "Josh? Did you write those words?" "Yes — box, fox," he said, with the largest grin I think I've ever seen. My tears were starting, "Josh, can you write more words?" He turned to the chalkboard and wrote "MOM" and "DAD." I looked at my husband with my mouth hanging open, and with tears rolling down our faces, he said, "We are going to Disneyland today." We did, and it was one of the best days of my life.

Josh continued to make progress in leaps and bounds. We tried a couple more rounds of chelation, once intravenously, but never saw the huge spike in improvement like we had the first time. He was mainstreamed part-time in kindergarten and also in first grade. He was always ahead academically, but socially, emotionally and behaviorally, he lagged behind his peers.

In second grade, Josh was mainstreamed full time. There were a few bumps (mostly behaviorally), but he was able to maintain a B+ average. Third grade proved to be more difficult, because he was no longer ahead of his peers academically. I had always thought that if Josh could get to the point where he was fully mainstreamed, autism would be behind us for good. I've since learned that recovery is an evolving journey for us that never really ends. Some people are lucky and cross that recovery finish line and never look back. For now, I feel that we've crossed many recovery finish lines, but the race ain't over yet.

I had heard of a fairly new treatment for autism called rTMS (repetitive Transcranial Magnetic Stimulation) being done by The Brain Treatment Center in Irvine, CA. We decided to have Josh partake in the trial to see if he was a viable candidate for treatment. It was a weeklong process, and on the first day, Josh's EEG indicated his brainwaves were not in sync, garnering him a go ahead on the treatment. Dr. Jin and his team were caring, insightful and a goldmine of information. That alone made this treatment worth it for us. We ended the week with a second EEG to see if the rTMS was working well enough to justify continuing treatment. We, as well as the team, were surprised by the results. Josh's brain had responded so well to just four sessions that he was no longer a candidate for treatment! This did two very important things for us. It took his brain's functioning ability out of the equation as a hindrance for him. It also allowed me and my husband to let go of some of the worry we carried about his future. We've shifted our focus on doing what we can in the here and now to provide him with the tools he needs to flourish.

Looking back at our journey of recovery with Josh, there have been so many moments that at one time I thought would never happen because I was told they wouldn't. Hearing him say "I love you," going to a friend's house to play for an afternoon, competing on the school's swim team, and now, sitting with his dad, enthusiastically cheering on his team — these moments are never taken for granted, as each and every one of them has been worked so hard for.

Looking forward, we know this journey is far from over. It is constant. Ebbing and flowing. We are still faced with challenges and setbacks, but we know that we have the ability to change the course and affect the outcome.

CREOLE QUEEN

"**S**ince the Lord is directing our steps, don't try to figure out everything that happens along the way." "Trust in Him" Proverbs 20:24. My faith is everything to me and when things happen, no matter what happens, I choose to be happy. My advice is to have patience with everything unresolved in your life. We women have to be strong. There is really no other choice.

My story is no different from any parent when their child is diagnosed with autism. Your heart drops, you're confused, you are going through your whole pregnancy before delivery. "What happened? How? Why?" You're asking the doctor but he cannot tell you how it happened, or why. Okay, breathe. Let's go. Our goal is recovery.

What is recovery? According to the dictionary it's an act or process of becoming healthy after an illness or injury. The act or process of returning to a normal state after a period of difficulty. Your recovery may be different from another's recovery. Through trial and error and research, you can eliminate the things that didn't work for your child and put your time and energy into what does work for your child. On the path to autism recovery, remember you're the expert. You know your child better than anyone else. Follow that gut feeling, ask questions until you understand. Research, research, research; and with patience, prayer, and repetition — recovery can happen.

At the age of 27, my doctor broke the news that it would be impossible to have babies. Can you imagine that? Near thirty, wanting to have kids, being told it couldn't happen. We talked about IVF and adoption. I couldn't believe I was having this conversation. A couple of years later at the age of twenty-nine, I discovered I was pregnant. I couldn't believe it! I guess the doctor was wrong. I can remember that day like it was yesterday.

My adorable baby boy was born in February 2008. Full term. Healthy. I remember holding him in my arms for the first time. Oh, my goodness! He was beautiful! Gorgeous blue eyes, nice round head, just handsome. I stayed in the hospital for three days. He cried. But that's what babies do, they cry. I was a first time mom, so that's what I expected. I didn't see anything wrong. No sleep, who cares? He didn't want me to leave him. He wanted to be near me at all times. I didn't focus on that. I was just enjoying my beautiful baby boy.

I didn't start to ask questions until he was a month old. I noticed he would cry and he wouldn't allow me to cuddle him to comfort him. I had to figure out what position he wanted me to hold him in by going through multiple holding positions. I would go through the steps of making my baby happy. I checked his diaper to make sure it was clean, I patted him on the back to burp him, I timed his feeding to make sure he was fed and full. Oh, I was doing all of it. I didn't care what I had to do. I enjoyed being a mother, but it really made me sad that he would cry and that it took a lot to comfort him.

I took him to the doctor. I was told it was colic and bad gas. I was given a colic medicine to soothe his stomach. Oh, it would make him fart, but my poor baby would still cry. As time went by, I noticed he would not allow anyone to hold him but me. He would not sleep in his bassinet or crib. He slept by me every night. If I had to take a bath, he had to be near me and see me. Later, I noticed he did not want to be in a crowd of people. I always had get-togethers in my home. That completely stopped, because he would cry the whole time others were there. I did not know what was going on.

We purchased so many baby things: a bassinet, a crib, a play set, and so many toys. He didn't want to sleep in his bassinet or the crib. He didn't want to play with almost any of his toys. Momma was his enter-tainment. I would sing the ABC song, Twinkle Twinkle Little Star, and talk about anything that would keep his attention and make him happy.

As a first time mom, I got no sleep. I thought that was normal. I was still excited that God blessed me with a baby boy. Sleep will come later, I thought. He just cried a little bit more than other babies. I stayed positive. I memorized the things he did not like. I knew he didn't like a crowd of people, loud noises, certain textures, certain sounds, and riding in the car.

I went through this journey with his pediatrician. A concern came up when I noticed he wasn't talking a lot. He was one and a half at the time. We went through questions and an evaluation and she said some kids take a little bit more time. At two, she put in a referral to Early Steps. I remember the first visit, it was the first time I heard the word autism.

The Service Coordinator noticed that my son was playing with his ABC toy by himself. He never looked up to say hello. He never ac-knowledged that she was in the room. He continued to play with this toy. She called his name, "Brian." He didn't respond. She called again. No response. Now, Brian did respond to his name at this time, but only if mom or dad was calling him. So, she kneeled down to be on the same eye level as him. She asked if could she see his toy, he said "No." He started to talk to her without looking in her eyes.

During that visit, she said "Mrs. Hertzock, I'm concerned your child is showing signs of autism." I asked her "What is autism?" She responded, "Difficulty with verbal communication, using and understanding language, difficulty with social interaction, difficulty changing routines, repetitive body language, doesn't make eye contact, doesn't smile when smiled at, doesn't respond to his or her name, doesn't wave goodbye or point, doesn't initiate or respond to cuddling, does not like to play with other people, cannot make basic requests." The list went on and on.

As she was talking, I checked my list of the things he didn't like. "Oh, my baby," was all I could say. I couldn't believe it. She advised me to see a neurologist and a psychologist. I have to add that during this visit I had my one-year-old there. Yes, I became pregnant again when Brian was six months old. I began to notice these same signs with my second child.

As a baby, my second-born didn't really cry. We had to check on him constantly because he was so quiet. My major concern was that he wouldn't eat. I tried to feed him baby food at six months, but he didn't want to eat it. I took him to the doctor. They didn't find anything unusual and suggested we give it some time. Months later, he was still not eating and not speaking. He only said "mama" and "dada."

I had no idea what to do. I was puzzled. I didn't picture my second child having autism, but what parent does? I knew this wasn't the time to stop and ask why, as my kids needed me. I needed to learn what to do for them. There was no time to sit back and think about what had happened. I had to move forward and we needed to make progress.

When you have a child or children with autism, you meet many different doctors. Some doctors will say or do things that make you not want to continue service with them. I was asked to sign a contract before one doctor would help my child, stating that I would not have any more kids, because I had two kids with autism and there was a chance that any subsequent children might have autism as well. I told him I would not do such a thing. All kids are beautiful and all kids deserve to live.

We then met a doctor, a neurologist, who was the most amazing woman. She explained everything to me. She was involved with their recovery. She was very informative and resourceful. She gave me hope. I stayed with her until she retired. My neurologist gave me a diagnosis, but once you get your answer, you cannot stop there. You have to come up with a plan. The kid's neurologist, pediatrician, and psychologist all had an input for creating their plan.

Remember to stop and take a deep breath. It will be ok, even if it isn't. Take it one step at a time. Prayer and patience is everything. It's awesome if you have family for support. If you do not have family, create your own supportive circle. I really didn't have my family for support. It's unfortunate, but what are you going to do? My support became my friends and other parents that also have kids with autism.

I found parents fighting the same fight as me, fighting for recovery. We understand each other and we do not judge each other. It hurts when the people you think will be there aren't. But let that go, and put that energy in what matters — and that's recovery.

Today, my kids have increased their abilities. Their behavior, speech, social skills, and communication have improved. Ryan, my second child, is still a quiet child. He will talk with his favorite cartoons, sing along with his favorite song, play pretend and talk with his favorite toys, and sign for his formula. He was born with a hiatal hernia and reflux. He is not eating solids yet, but he had surgery in December, 2013 (nissen fundoplication) to treat his reflux and hiatal hernia. I am hopeful he will eat solids soon. His sensory and social skills have improved. He hugs you; he loves to cuddle and sit in groups.

Brian, my first child, is amazing. He is very smart. He is talking and loves to talk, and is expanding his vocabulary every day. He loves to cook and always wants to learn how to make more foods. He does very well solving problems. His sensory and social skills are skyrocketing. He hugs me, kisses me and tells me he loves me. I remember the doctor saying I might not ever hear the words "I love you." He was so wrong.

My third child Zion is showing signs of ASD. He is two years old now. I will go through the same steps with him. He is currently in speech and occupational therapy. Every day he is making improvements. I am a parent that's winning with three handsome boys. All three of my boys are gifts from God. My instruction manual to raise my kids is somewhat different from other parents.

Parents that have kids with autism are judged so harshly sometimes, because people only see our kids on the surface, "Why is he acting like that?" "Does he cry like that all the time?" "You must not be doing something right." I've heard it all and I was ripped apart, because it mostly came from people that were close to me. The outsiders are quick to say we are bad parents and our children are not disciplined. I would like to say these people that do not understand, "Do your research. Get to know us. You really do not know the life we live and we need all the love that someone is willing to give to us."

My journey has taught me compassion, discipline, patience and the real meaning of love. We are still on the road to recovery, but we have come such a long way. It's a battle. Stick with it.

KARMA

I am considered a "stay-at-home" mom, which is ironic when you consider the fact that I drive my four children with different needs a minimum of 60 miles each day to two different schools, and we spend upwards of 3 – 4 hours per day on the road.

In February, our drive changed when, after one semester of first grade and 40 hours of IEP meetings, my twin boys' names came up on what seemed to be the permanent waiting list for multiple services at our local autism center. We had spent two years at this location already in feeding therapy, parent training for feeding and behavioral strategies, and behavior intervention training for all four kids and I as a group. Now we're going back for intensive ABA therapy five days per week, as the boys have continued to struggle at school and at home. I had to withdraw them from school after working so hard to determine the cause of their lack of progress. I have been the parent member of IEP teams for four children since 2009 when the twins entered the public school system in a self-contained classroom. Just the tip of the iceberg of all that entails: weeding through reports, data and evaluations all while integrating a speech-generating device to facilitate development of their communication skills.

Our commute begins at 7:00 am; stop number one is Hazel's school. Our middle child, a four-pound preemie born at 32 weeks, she miraculously only stayed in the hospital for a week under the bili lights for jaundice. She was a tiny red doll that needed little medical intervention, which was a relief. But Hazel ended up having her time in the hospital right before her third birthday. What started out as a stomach bug with diarrhea on the hottest day of the summer 2007, resulted in a two-week hospital stay for E. coli poisoning. I have never seen anyone so sick in my entire life as our little girl with the big brown eyes who said nothing the entire time as I stayed by her side. When her kidneys shut down, she was put on dialysis, then blood dialysis on a continuous veno-venous hemofiltration machine in the pediatric intensive care unit (PICU). The nurses brought her a birthday cake, presents and signed a card. Her older sister was admitted a few days later for the same infection, but luckily did not end up with hemolytic uremic syndrome, or hepatitis like Hazel. I do not have fond memories of the month after she was discharged, as I had to take stool samples on a weekly basis to the county health department to ensure that she no longer had the E.coli in her system, something the hospital had neglected to tell me.

Before Hazel's second birthday, we took her to be evaluated for speech delays by the state early intervention program therapists, but they declared her "within normal limits" and denied services. I dismissed her sensory-seeking tactile issues and odd walking as imitation of her younger brothers. She was kept on the vaccination schedule even after her illness, as she was about to enter a preschool program that required them. Red flags continued as she entered kindergarten. She was sent to the principal's office the first month of school, because her teacher thought Hazel's refusal to join the group in circle time, or to leave the sand box full of sensory input, was defiance.

I was so wrapped up in IEP meetings for her siblings that I was completely caught off-guard when the school contacted me. They had the district autism specialist observe both girls who then identified them as possibly having Asperger syndrome. Talk about being blindsided. Now in fourth grade, Hazel is struggling to find her place in the regular classroom. She loves cats, requires constant sensory input and will only talk about her favorite online game to the point of driving her sister to shout "THAT'S ENOUGH!!" at the top of her frustrated lungs. It gets very loud in our car, and between all the ruckus and the boys constantly unlatching their seat belts, it's a wonder we don't all have PTSD. On second thought, we probably do.

Our older daughter, Irene, is dropped off next at her charter school a few miles away. A fifth grader full of humor and artistic talent, she has struggled the most as the oldest sibling of two younger brothers and a sister on the spectrum. A few weeks after being discharged from the hospital for E. coli poisoning in 2007, she started a pre-K inclusion program at a local university autism center, where college students are trained to work with ASD kids in the classroom. Her brothers were diagnosed a few months later; somehow it must have been on my radar subconsciously that we would need their help. We kept her on the recommended vaccine schedule in order to attend school, despite the fact that she spent a week in the hospital after birth with a severe case of jaundice. Looking back years later, I believe the jaundice was a reaction to the hepatitis B vaccine. A full-term healthy baby, she was readmitted to the children's hospital PICU after her pediatrician proclaimed her "orange enough to be placed on top of the Christmas tree" with a dangerously high bilirubin level at three days old. No one connected it to the shot, and I had no idea.

At age five, not long after Irene's hospital stay I noticed she was blinking excessively and making small jerking movements and vocalizations. I brought her to the pediatric ophthalmologist I took her brothers to, thinking it was her eyesight. The doctor proclaimed her vision to be perfect, prescribed drops for allergies and, when I asked about vision therapy, told me it was useless. The vocal and motor tics remained, and at age six she was diagnosed by her pediatrician with Tourette's syndrome and ADHD. Having already experienced ASD with her younger brothers, the minute I saw she was unable to complete worksheets and exhibiting handwriting problems in kindergarten, I started the evaluation process with the school. After she was observed by the district autism specialist in first grade, I brought her and her sister to the center for evaluation.

I had no idea it was possible to have two more children with autism. It was something I had never heard of.

We were still trying to wrap our heads around all of the medical issues with the twins, who were diagnosed with autism in 2008. How can you have four children with developmental problems? Isn't it rare? Both girls went to evaluations at the same place, same time in 2010, but Irene came out with a confirmed ADHD diagnosis with the therapist stating that she had characteristics of autism, but was not on the spectrum. Her younger sister Hazel emerged with the Asperger label. You would think that we would be used to it by then, but truthfully it is always a shock to hear those words. With girls, it is supposedly unusual to identify it at such a young age.

Pulling away from Irene's school, we head to our third stop, the autism center. The 20-minute drive is bumper-to-bumper traffic of college students, hospital workers and CDC employees. Driving past the CDC, a gleaming fortress of solitude, while taking my twin sons to the autism center for behavior therapy is an irony that is not lost on me. My heart aches as I wonder why it has come to this. I am grateful for the opportunity for our boys to finally get ABA, but why is this the only way? Our insurance doesn't cover it, neither does Medicaid, nor does the school provide it.

Last year I went to the state capital with another mom in the boys' classroom to get the state representatives to hear a bill called Ava's Law, which provides insurance coverage for autism services in the state of Georgia, with ABA being the most important. After years of languishing in committees, with politicians blocking it for fear of raising insurance premiums for constituents, this year it was finally being heard. As we were starting this new treatment program, Ava's law finally made it through the state senate with a unanimous vote, but with an age cap of six and a behavior therapy cap of $35,000. Ultimately it was not passed by the House due to the objections of a few lawmakers, one of whom has a major insurance company headquartered in his district and has vowed to never vote for it. Turns out, it would raise insurance rates an average of 50 cents per month. While Ava's law would be a start, the boys are now eight and would be excluded if it were passed.

So much has happened in the past eight years. In March 2006, my water broke on a Monday morning when I was 25 weeks pregnant with identical twin boys. I entered the hospital expecting to remain for a few months. Instead, they were delivered at 26 weeks via emergency C-section due to a prolapsed cord. Sometimes I reach in to a junk drawer and pull out a plastic sandwich bag containing a tiny diaper that fits in the palm of my hand and remember the months we spent shuttling between hospitals, with their toddler sisters in tow, to visit our two-pound babies.

Before their birth, I was given antibiotics for strep, steroids to mature their lungs, and shots to stop premature labor. Examining my medical records years later, I found that a lung surfactant given at birth to prevent Respiratory Distress Syndrome has serious risks not revealed by the drug company, addressed by the FDA in a warning letter to the manufacturer in 2011. What was striking to me is that their drug trials on premature infants listed the many serious conditions associated with prematurity as side effects of the drug. Our sons, especially the most affected one, had almost every condition listed. As I read this, I wondered how we would know if they were "born this way," or if all of the complications were not caused by this drug.

To stop premature labor, I was given shots of Terbutaline, which has since (2011) received a black box warning from the FDA advising against its use for prevention of preterm labor because it "may cause harm to the mother and/or the fetus." Terbutaline is also implicated in lawsuits which link it to the development of autism in twins. It crosses the blood-brain barrier in fetuses and can predispose them to developing autism as well as increase vulnerability to environmental toxins. The more I read, the more studies I saw linking its use to neuro inflammation, microglial activation, behavioral issues and developmental delay.

There are many reports of antibiotics wiping out the good gut flora in newborns, especially those born via C-section, and I was on IV antibiotics for all three births, as well as lots of acetaminophen, which has also been implicated in autism and ADHD in recent studies.

The boys were at separate hospitals because one twin developed necrotizing enterocolitis requiring emergency surgery as he clung to life. Was the enterocolitis connected to the fact that he was tube fed milk-based formula as an underdeveloped newborn? The research I did after the fact revealed evidence that premature infants are not able to process milk protein, which causes the intestinal tissue to die and rupture. His brother got off lucky; he only had a chest tube and contracted a staph infection. I will never be able to comprehend why our sick newborn, discharged from a four-month hospital stay after multiple surgeries, and living on a diet of TPN and prescription hypoallergenic formula, was "caught up" on his immunizations before his release without our knowledge. Forty-eight hours after he came home, he was back in the emergency room projectile vomiting and very jaundiced, something that was attributed to his medical and birth history. We weren't even told that we had to order special hypoallergenic formula from a pharmacy and mistakenly picked some up at the grocery store.

We care for our children in the aftermath of all of the chemicals, medications, vaccinations, genetically modified food and environmental insults. I feel like I should have been wearing a hazmat suit instead of maternity jeans when I think of how my pre-pregnancy body was a toxic waste dump. I did not know a mouth full of 20-year-old leaking amalgam fillings that needed to be removed could go bad and leak mercury into my body, exposing the babies in each successive pregnancy. In the end, there are so many environmental factors that contributed to their fragile premature state, creating a perfect toxic storm that a two-pound baby could not withstand.

Karma is the principle that "what goes around comes around." The energy you put out into the Universe is returned to you. The concept of Karma, in the most basic terms, is that every action has a result. One frequently hears "Karma is a bitch," meaning that all of the wrong things people do will come back to get them in the end, a form of cosmic justice delivered by the hand of destiny. Karma has reared its ugly head and bitch-slapped us all as a planet. Only recently has any mainstream organization acknowledged that yes, there are environmental factors influencing autism, not just genetics. Unfortunately, most people don't realize that genes can be altered by their environment, including all the chemical insults that have become pervasive in everything we are surrounded by.

I keep putting out positive energy into the world that comes back to me in the form of hope, which should never be taken from anyone, yet is done so on a daily basis at the doctor's office when they tell you there is nothing you can do for autism because, "We just don't know what causes it for sure." I call bullshit. I think my biggest regret in life is that I have never had confidence. I relied on others to tell me what I should do because they were "experts," and I was "just a mom." While others were critical of Jenny McCarthy for going on Oprah and speaking about her son's autism, I watched intently. Then I dismissed her truth. Not because, as many people love to exclaim, "She's a playboy bunny!" but because she was a mom like me, so what did she know?

I started looking at biomedical treatments a year after the boys' autism diagnosis in 2008. It was time to see what we could do, even when I knew we couldn't afford it, because it had to be better than doing nothing. At night, I scoured the web for ways to fund treatments but came up short. I had visited the Generation Rescue site a few times and realized that Jenny, a fellow mom, had helped her son by doing the very things I was doing — researching. And then I saw it — GR was accepting applications for the first round of their Rescue Family Grant program. HOLY SHIT!! There was no way we were not going to get in on that! I filled out all the paperwork and nervously waited for notifications. I will never forget the day I got that call. I started screaming out of sheer relief. FINALLY we were going to get to try biomed for real.

In 2014 we are six years down the road of our journey. I have been inspired by many in the autism community along the way; this is what has kept me going. Talk About Curing Autism, Generation Rescue, and the Thinking Moms' Revolution have been my anchors while I leave no stone unturned in getting to the bottom of my children's challenges. Sometimes I feel like these stones line the riverbed of our existence as the steady current of stress, illness, and isolation often rush over me and threaten to pull me downstream.

The other truth about Karma is this: it is not predestined. You have the power to alter your course and therefore influence the outcome. Nothing is written in stone. I strongly believe that, although the progress of my children has been slow and the fight has been exhausting, things will continue to improve. The more that individuals believe they have the power to enact real change, that change will come. Instant Karma is knowing that you, the parent, have the power to shape your family's destiny. It is up to you to enlighten yourself with the knowledge and confidence that you will make a difference. Remember, what goes around comes around.

CRUSH

I remember the day my daughter Cali received her diagnosis; it is burned into my soul. The words that were said to us that day will never be far from my thoughts. Seething words that shatter parents' dreams, just rolling off the neurologist's tongue as if this were just an everyday conversation about the weather. These phrases would be repeated over and over by medical professional after medical professional so many times in the first few years that they are never far from my thoughts, even today.

"Your daughter has autism. There is no known cure, no known cause, it will not get better, and it is likely to get worse. She will never speak. She will never have friends. She will never be able to function in a normal school setting. There really is nothing to do. She is a danger to herself and others. We can try medication, but there is no guarantee. I don't know how to explain to you that this is just something that goes along with autism. We can't help you. You need to consider putting her in an institution."

"YOU NEED TO CONSIDER PUTTING HER IN AN INSTITUTION!"

We were told by the age of four that we should just stop bothering. Cali was never going to be anything more than what she was, and it was time to walk away. But this made no sense to me. How do you tell someone that there is no hope, and in the same conversation admit that you don't even know what is wrong? How do you walk away from a child, just give up on her, when you haven't even tried to look for the answers? How do you say there is no possibility if you don't try? There are a number of things I took away from those conversations: disgust, anger, sadness, frustration. But never did I leave an appointment and think they were right. Never.

Looking back, we didn't start out here. We started out with a baby that by all evaluations was deemed a perfectly healthy child (although now it's clear that this was likely not the case). There were issues before pregnancy (environmental toxins, family health history, medications) that should have been considered. There were issues during pregnancy for myself (illness, health, adverse reaction to RH shot, strange rashes) that were dismissed by my team of providers. There were issues at birth (delayed birth, lack of oxygen, medication, poor medical care) that are inexcusable. And there were issues after birth (surgery and health issues for myself, and food intolerances, GI problems, reflux for my daughter) which were swept under the rug as normal.

And yet somehow with all of that being said; Cali was a beautiful happy baby who had normal scores at birth, normal well-baby visits, and everyone said she was doing great. By all appearances, she was our perfect amazing little angel. We followed every guideline, listened to every word of advice the doctors gave, read every baby book, and took her on time to every doctor's appointment. She smiled, rolled over, re-sponded to her name, walked, played, and started talking, all on time or early. Life was good. And we were proud parents who were completely unaware of the storm that was brewing, the pieces piling up and the life changes that were shortly to come.

March 1, 2004 was the day that changed everything and would rock life as we knew it. I brought Cali to our trusted pediatrician for her 12 month well visit. I remember hearing babies crying, and trying to keep my daughter distracted by reading books, playing with toys, and smothering her cute little face in kisses so she would giggle. We weighed, measured, talked about how adorable she was and I signed the papers for her shots. And then I held my child, and told her it was going to be okay while they injected her with the MMR and Varicella vaccinations. And within hours my beautiful smiling daughter was gone. "Encephalopathy" from vaccination. Those are the words that are listed on her records. The promise of it being okay forever stuck in my heart. It wouldn't be okay that day. Actually, it wouldn't be okay for many years. The storm had hit, the tipping point was toppled, and our world would never be the same.

I retreated to my bathroom floor, shut the door and tried to breathe. Sitting on the cold tile, tears running down my face, I prayed (often begged) for answers. I was not in a spot where I could even grasp looking ahead, or believe in hope, or what our life would ever be, I was stuck in survival mode. Cali was three and half, and the days of before were barely recognizable. Hurting so deeply, I looked into those same beautiful eyes for a glimmer that showed that Cali even knew who I was and searched for any signs of my child that used to be.

Our days were on repeat, hours of pacing the house picking up objects trying to find something that would satisfy the screams. I wrapped my arms around her so tightly and rocked her because letting go meant she would harm herself. The fourth copy of Aladdin we had purchased played in the background from her favorite spot because it was the only thing she seemed to hear. Alarms were installed on the windows and doors just in case she found a second that we were distracted and decided to elope. We couldn't leave the home or be around new faces because it produced an epic meltdown. The home had become both our safe place and our prison.

There were emergency room visits for hernias, ear infections, strep, GI problems, and injuries that she didn't feel. Tylenol and round after round of antibiotics had become the recommended staple from the physicians. I watched for any sign of the skills that had disappeared, and in fear as the ones she retained had become so structured that we couldn't sway from routine even an inch. Friends had disappeared, doctors were completely clueless, and our family was trying but unsure how to help. Our marriage was falling apart, we worried about the safety of the baby on the way, and the bills stacked up as autism was an insurance "exclusion" at the time. My world was crashing down around me. Sixteen hours a day of screaming and that little spot on the bathroom floor was all I knew to do when she finally rested. Alone, without hope and praying for miracles had become our life. Cali was in her own dire world and we had no clue how to get her out.

Miracles sometimes come in the most unusual ways. Cali was four and a half and little had changed. I had been working from home as a travel specialist, assisting groups in planning vacations. This memorable morning, I headed to the airport to see a group of high school students and their moms off on a trip. I arrived early, checked the departures, and gathered my paperwork for the group. Shortly the travelers began to arrive, the excitement filled the air. This was a group of fun young women, that I have enjoyed working with. The mom who organized the trip was a special education teacher and we have shared many conversations.

This morning was no different as I welcomed her, and immediately she asked about Cali. As we were chatting, one of the fathers who had brought his daughter to the airport, walked over, apologized and interrupted our conversation. My first thought was that his daughter had forgotten her ticket or he had a question about luggage. Little did I know that he was about to change my life. He explained that he overheard our conversation, and that he didn't mean to interrupt but had to say something. He went on to tell me that I had to speak with his wife, and that he couldn't give me all the details because it was his wife who had really done it all, but that his daughter too was once diagnosed with autism. He shared that his wife had done all these "alternative things" and then turned to point out his daughter.

She was in my departing group. I had no clue. Here before me stood this beautiful young lady, surrounded by friends giggling about the plans they had on their trip, who at one time was like my daughter? I knew this young lady from our planning meetings and was aware that she was graduating and headed off to college out of state on academic and athletic scholarships. She was popular, smart, had a boyfriend, and spent her free time like any other teenager. And she had a proud and very nervous father willing to walk up to me and share with me the first glimmer of hope I had in years. A random kind man, who would change everything in a matter of one small conversation. My miracle.

We didn't have time for but those few words as the group was due for their flight. I watched the girls and moms head to the gate, and the dad disappeared to his car. I gathered my stuff and headed to my car and sat there with the engine running and for the first time in four years I cried like a baby. Tears of pain, sadness, guilt, anger…all pouring down my face as I finally let it all go. Life was about to change again drastically. This time towards the promise I made to my daughter so many years ago. It would be okay.

Change doesn't happen overnight. Cali was now five. I was bringing in the groceries, arms overflowing as I had taken the opportunity to get out alone. I opened the door and Cali looked right at me and said, "Momma!" I dropped every bag I held and stood there for what seemed like hours crying tears of joy holding her in my arms. Never was a sweeter word said. It wasn't recovery or cure, but it sure as hell was one of the greatest joys of my life. Life had become easier. Once we changed her diet things began to shift, and the screams disappeared. The behaviors that once ruled our home were now gone. Cali looked at us again. She found language. She made a friend. She played t-ball. Life wasn't perfect and we knew we had a ways to go, but our path was paved by those before us, and we knew she was getting better. We became less concerned with what the world had decided for my daughter, and focused on what we decided for her. We began to see that we were not alone, and we had things to try and my daughter had a lifetime to prove them wrong.

First grade, six years old, and Cali was about to show the world that she is proof. I was sitting in a school meeting room, awaiting the arrival of those involved in the IEP process. The stress of these meetings was long gone, as I had become accustomed to this. They evaluate, and tell me how far behind my child still was, we set goals, I'd go home and try to find the strength to not focus on all the things she could not do, but instead focus on the things we have accomplished. But this meeting was different. As the binders opened and pens came out, I heard something about wanting to remove her IEP.

The shock rippled through me, as I realized that they were telling me that she was, by all evaluations, on the same level as her peers. I had no idea what to say or do, because I was prepared for the way these meetings went normally. One foot in front of the other, no looking backwards, celebrating every small accomplishment...that's how we roll. And yet, here I sat hearing that my once nonverbal child, whose evaluations showed her at a nine to twelve month old's skill levels after the regression, and according to the doctors would never make it in school, was being removed from services because she didn't need them. The pieces were coming together.

In 2010, I took my daughter back to her original diagnosing neurologist. I have to admit I may have just done it with an agenda. Cali was eight, and we were moving across the country to where my husband was being stationed for military duty. I probably needed to get all of our medical records in order, but mainly I just wanted to show him how totally fucking wrong he was.

It was clear from the moment he walked into the room that he didn't really remember my daughter. He asked why we were there and I explained that we wanted to have our last annual exam as we were moving. He asked my daughter to hop up on to the examination table and she walked over and bounced right up there smiling. As he examined her eyes and tracking, she casually told him how she was a straight-A student, that she loved sports and playing with her friends. I could see the confusion growing, but he said nothing and continued her exam, measured her head, checked her reflexes, and listened for signs of repetitive language. He asked about her emotions, her health, and life overall. After searching, he finally helped her down from the table and told her she could play with the toys he had in the room while we talked. I gave Cali a smile and walked over to his desk.

The dreaded desk that we had sat at so many times over the years. The desk where he had told me five years ago that Cali had autism. The same desk that he scratched out a list of things to "not" look into as things that might be causing autism. The same desk where he told me there was no known cause (yeah right) and no known cures (ha!). The same desk where he sat a year later when he told me she would never get better, and likely get worse. The same desk where he uttered the phrase, "You need to consider putting her in an institution." The same desk where he told me she would never speak, never have friends, never make it in a school setting. The same desk where he said none of those "alternative things" would help and we would just be wasting time that we could use to deal with reality. The desk from hell. But not that day, not ever again.

He opened her file and began scanning through the notes. He read them out loud, phrases and words like "danger to herself and others," "violent," "psychotic," "severe," "institution," and "medications." I wanted to laugh out loud at the things he wrote knowing he had to be wondering if he had the right records. I just smiled and listened. And then he closed the file and said, "Well she sure seems to be doing well on the medication." I said very nicely, "Oh she isn't on any medication." He opened the folder to look again and said, "I prescribed medication back in 2007 to address some of these issues." I explained to him that while he had suggested that, my husband and I opted to go a different route. Confused but still unwilling to admit that we had found answers that he didn't provide, he started to applaud the ABA therapy. Again, I explained that while he had suggested that, we opted to treat the medical issues instead. No ABA either. Frustrated with the conversation, he picked up his pen and asked what it was that we had done. And then he started writing.

I explained to him that we began looking into those so-called alternatives, such as considering diet and treating underlying issues. I added with a big fat smile, "You know all that stuff you advised us against; biomedical care." And I continued, "Within a matter of months we had eye contact, no more meltdowns, no behavior problems, and she was in school. Within a year, she was caught up to her peers, and within two she was testing in the top 1 % of the country. She has friends, plays sports, is not in pain and is happy."

He looked back into the folder, took a deep breathe, closed it again, and then leaned across the desk from hell and said, "I need to shake your hand." I didn't know whether to fall out of the chair, cry, or punch him in the face. He proceeded, "If I could bottle up what you have done, I would be rich." And because I came there determined to show him this child, whom he long ago dismissed, and the truth about hope.... I said, "You can. You can tell every parent who comes here from now on that there is hope, there are answers, and do not let them walk out of this office believing the things you told us over the past six years." And we left the office and headed home floating on the belief that maybe, just maybe this neurologist would be the start of other families seeking answers, believing in the possibilities, and knowing there was so much more.

Even looking back seven years later is very difficult. It seems like I am looking back on someone else's life. Today there are very few traces of autism. Cali still struggles occasionally with very chaotic or loud places, has some health issues and nutritional deficiencies that we manage, and she still can't grasp why people are mean or why doctors aren't helping all the kids who are like she once was. She is a straight-A student, plays sports, and loves theatre and film. She has best friends, sleepovers and covers her walls in the latest boy bands. She teaches her peers about what autism is like and loves to explain why nobody should move to Mississippi because of their limited vaccine rights. She has the biggest heart and shows more empathy and compassion than most adults. She writes stories, and loves helping other kids with special needs. She is her sister's best friend, and their giggles are priceless. She never misses a moment to say how amazing parents fighting for their kids are, or how thankful she is that we never gave up.

She will change this world, I have no doubt. She changes lives every day. She inspires people, and she brings hope. While I know every story won't look like ours, and recovery is a word that can mean much; I know that every little change, every step forward was so worth it. Hope is there, every single day. I struggled with that for some time, but it was there, it just needed a push. I needed someone or something to remind me that we were stronger than we knew, that we were filled with courage and fight and that nothing could stop us. I needed to be reminded that life was what we made of it. That it is okay to look forward, even if it's just a small little glance to remind us to keep going.

I have those before us to thank, those who were in the trenches, pushed the science, demanded the answers, fought for change, and inspired us. The strangers in the airport, the friends online, the doctors who get it, the parents going through the same struggle that many of us don't even know, and the loved ones who stand beside us. I could never have done this without all of you. You did this. You helped me keep that promise I made so many years ago on that awful day. It will be okay.

Not only does life look different today for our family and for my daughter, but my own personal journey is nothing I imagined. Today my focus is on others, on being someone else's stranger. It's come full circle for me. I fight now for those who are sitting on their cold bath-room floors trying to find a way to survive the day, who can't imagine their life ever being different, who haven't yet found the strength inside themselves, for those who can't bear to hear anymore comments about no answers or no hope. For those parents who today will be told it won't get better…I say to you IT WILL! We are friends, given to each other, determined to change this world, and we have each other's back. Nothing will stop us now. We are healing, and we are finding hope. We are changing the course of medicine and science.

We are in a revolution!

And we are going to CRUSH those who stand in the way of our children!

CHIEF

"Is suffering really necessary? Yes and no. If you had not suffered as you have, there would
be no depth to you as a human being, no humility, no compassion. You would not be reading this
now. Suffering cracks open the shell of ego, and then comes a point when it has served its
purpose. Suffering is necessary until you realize it is unnecessary."
Eckhart Tolle

(To Madison, my toughest, yet greatest teacher: You have taught me the most valuable things a person could know. Without you, I wouldn't be a fraction of the person I am. I am forever grateful for you.)

I n the fall of 2002, I left my job as a Registered Nurse at a local hospital to become a full-time stay-at-home mom to my daughter, Madison. My pregnancy seemed uneventful, aside from the vicious morning sickness (which was all day) that had forced me to take a leave of absence from my job and wish for death. After that first trimester of hell, all was going very well. I was enjoying my daily Diet Cokes and fast food. I developed a strong aversion to coffee and ground beef, but I could eat Taco Bell like it was nobody's business. My new BFFs were

Krispy Kreme doughnuts! Minus the horrible eating, I did everything just right. I went to all of my prenatal appointments, took my vitamins (synthetic, I'm sure), had an ultrasound or two, bought the top of the line baby bed and car seat, beautiful nursery, new and bigger car — the works!

I was completely submerged in mainstream everything. I had no idea there was another perspective. I had no idea I was actually setting my baby up for the catastrophe that would follow. Madison was born on a Monday night, three days before my due date. Of course, I had an epidural and Stadol and an antibiotic. Why would I not? These things are all perfectly safe. We wouldn't put them in pregnant women if they weren't, right? Oh, and Pitocin: a necessity to delivering a baby now days. My membranes had been ruptured for more than 24 hours, so immediately following her birth, she had a gastric lavage to check for meconium. She appeared healthy and her Apgar score was good.

She latched on like a pro when I put her to my breast (one of the only smart things I ever did). We stayed in the hospital for four days so she could be treated prophylactically with antibiotics. She also received a healthy dose of Thimerosal from her Hepatitis B vaccine. It was important to give her the Hep B at birth, so that when she got home and started shooting up with dirty needles and having unprotected sex with multiple partners, she would be protected. You just can't be too careful. All in all, a great start, wouldn't you say? Geez…

Madison was a colicky baby. She cried a lot. She had horrible gas and would wiggle and squirm and grunt, even in her sleep. She never slept soundly her first few weeks of life and this concerned me, knowing that infants require a lot of sleep due to a rapidly developing brain and body. Along with the lack of sleep and colic, she developed a rash, mostly on her face. It wasn't raised like baby acne, which is what her pediatrician said it was. This rash was macular and I felt certain that she was not tolerating the formula I had begun to supplement. So at six weeks, I switched her to a soy based formula (Do not roll your eyes at me if you are in the know!). Success! Her rash cleared, her gas resolved and she began sleeping through the night. Can I get a big amen on that! Everything rolled along fairly smoothly after that, for a while anyway.

She seemed to be developing normally in all areas. I was diligent about her well baby appointments. I never missed one, and she was fully vaccinated. Of course she was. What kind of fool doesn't vaccinate their baby? I didn't bother looking into it. It was never a thought. You vaccinate. Period. She was good on the growth chart, rolled over, sat up, babbled, smiled and made eye contact. Perfection! At her six month appointment, the pediatrician noticed that her head was a bit misshapen and we were sent to a pediatric neurosurgeon to make sure her cranial sutures were not closing prematurely. She also received five vaccines for seven different illnesses at her six month appointment. A week or so later, the flapping would begin. I had no clue the two were related. I didn't know why she did it. I just thought it was "her."

Cognitively, she remained intact. The appointment with the neurosurgeon went well and we were sent to a physiatrist to determine if she would need a helmet to reshape her skull. She was diagnosed with torticollis (a shortening or contraction of the sternocleidomastoid muscle in the neck, which can result from several causes, one being a toxic brain injury) at that appointment, and underwent stretching therapy to correct it. At a follow up appointment when she was 11 months old, I commented to the doctor that she was not yet crawling. X-rays revealed bilateral developmental dysplasia of the hip, and we were referred to a pediatric orthopedic surgeon who performed bilateral adductor tenotomy to release the ligaments and allow proper placement of her hip bones. She was placed in a body cast for 12 weeks following the surgery.

It was a few days before her surgery that she received her 12 month vaccines, which included five live viruses. At the time, I didn't connect the symptoms and regression with the vaccines because of the surgery and casting. Plus, I was a wreck due to everything that was going on with her. I was scared and worried and so very naive. Right around this time my perfect sleeper began waking in the night and screaming. I had never heard screaming like this. It sounded as if she was being tortured. Later, I would find out that was exactly what was happening. She also stopped making eye contact, her language stopped progressing and she became incredibly cranky.

Over the next two years, things progressively got worse. Of course we blamed everything on the cast. Her surgeon had informed us that being in the cast would cause a delay in her development until around age three, at which point she should be caught up with her peers. By three, she was not caught up. It was becoming more obvious that something wasn't right. I had no idea what it was, and anytime I expressed concern, I was always met with a reassurance that "She's only two" or "She's barely three, and she was in that cast." I hate to confess this, but I remember telling my husband she was retarded. I didn't mean it in an ugly or degrading way. It's just that some of her characteristics reminded me of someone who was mentally retarded, and I didn't know a better way to describe what I was seeing in her.

However, she did do things that were advanced for her age, too. For instance, she could count to 20 in three different languages when she was two but she didn't have a lot of original speech, just a handful of words. She screamed and threw fits constantly. It seemed that if I breathed wrong it would set her off and all hell would break loose. You really had to walk on eggshells around her. And that was really what led me to seek help, because it wasn't like I didn't try to discipline her. It was that no form of discipline worked. It never carried over. She never learned from it.

A few weeks after she turned three, I took her to the pediatrician and expressed my concerns about her behavior and development. My instructions from the pediatrician were to read a book about strong willed kids. So, like any good mother, I followed her advice and read the book within a few days. I didn't even get halfway through it before I knew I wasn't just dealing with a strong willed child. It just didn't fit. At this point, I felt completely lost. I had a child that was out of control behaviorally. She seemed so unhappy. Why should any three-year-old that is in a loving home with everything they could ever want and a family that dotes on them be unhappy?

I had just given birth to my son and had gone through a scare with a post-partum hemorrhage, I was raising my two stepsons, who at the time were 15 and 11, and I was very active in my community with volunteer work. My plate was full, and I was exhausted. When I think back to that time I really don't know how I kept it together.

I began praying for Madison every night. After she was asleep I would sneak in her room, lay my hands on her, and beg God to show me what was going on with her. Maybe that sounds ridiculous, but I didn't know what else to do, and no one else seemed to share my concern. If I could just figure out what I was facing, I could work on it and I could make it better for her. For all of us. I can only imagine what my other children must have been feeling. What it was like for them when she was so out of control? It seemed like forever, but without fail, I laid my hands on her and prayed for an answer every night.

It was also during this time that she received her Hepatitis A series, and "coincidentally" developed the most foul, horrid, green diarrhea that burned the skin off her backside. This happened about seven or eight times per day. Imagine trying to clean her up and having to rub those "burned" placed with wipes. Sometimes, they would be so bad, I would just try to rinse her a little with water to clean her. She absolutely could not stand for her bottom to be wiped, and with good reason. How would you feel if you had open sores and someone rubbed them several times a day? I can barely stand that memory. I was ignorant enough to assume it was just from her being in diapers, which is absurd, because wearing diapers does not cause diarrhea.

She had also started standing in weird positions (posturing) while flapping her hands (stimming). One night, I was in her room praying over her, and a thought popped into my mind. It was just one word, but it was so clear. That word was autism. I immediately got up and went to my computer to look it up. A lot of her behaviors matched. Now, most people would probably feel discouraged, angry, sad or scared, but what I felt was relief. I now had a name for what I was dealing with. Shortly after that, I made another appointment with the pediatrician, and discussed her behaviors and that I felt she had autism.

She agreed and sent us to a developmental pediatrician to confirm. It took several months to get in to see that doctor, which is a whole different story. Anyone who has gone through getting their child a diagnosis knows what I mean. By the time she was officially diagnosed, we had been through three doctors. I had reported the intestinal issues to each one and not one of them addressed it. Why? Because there was no standard of care for kids with autism and their physical symptoms are still to this day written off as part of their so-called psychiatric disorder. This is completely unacceptable. The medical community should be ashamed of themselves for allowing these children to suffer so horribly.

After she was formally diagnosed, I decided I was going to learn everything I could about autism so I could give her the very best support available. On one random day while she was at preschool, I went to a bookstore to see what they had that might help. That day my life would forever change. That day was the day that turned everything around. That day, the most important piece of information found its way to me and I have never looked back. As I was perusing the books, I had already found three or four and as I was finishing up, I picked up one last book and scanned the cover. At the bottom of the cover in small print it said, "A Mother's Story of Research and Recovery." Recovery? Wait. She recovered her child? Ohhhh, hell. If she can, I can. I immediately checked out and took my future home with me in a plastic bag! That book was "Unraveling the Mystery of Autism and Pervasive Developmental Disorder" by Karyn Seroussi.

As I read this book, I honestly couldn't believe what I was reading: the horrid GI problems, the vaccine connection, symptoms of yeast overgrowth and antifungals, special diets, urinary peptides, etc. There was a ton of science, but it seemed like science fiction. Except that my child had all of the same symptoms that this mom was talking about: the painful diarrhea, the rashes, the posturing, the flapping and stimming, the tantrums, the self-limiting diet. Most of what Madison ate contained gluten and dairy. In the book she talked about removing gluten and dairy from the diet as some children have an inability to digest these proteins. I knew I had to try it with Madison and see if it helped.

There was only one problem. I was married to a mainstream, western medical doctor with a double board certification and a healthy dose of skepticism. And I needed to tell him that it was plausible that for whatever reason Madison had reacted adversely to her vaccines, which had potentially injured her gut, and we were too ignorant to notice, and I needed to remove the two main sources of nutrition from her diet for at least a month to see if it helped. Oh boy.

On top of that, my youngest was eight months old, and I did not feel comfortable continuing his vaccinations until I could look into it further. I feared that this conversation was not going to go well. But, it ended up turning out much better than I anticipated. Not so much regarding the vaccines at first, but we did come to an agreement that we would give the diet a try. After all, it wasn't going to hurt her. She literally only ate about six foods anyway, it wasn't as if she was being properly nourished considering four of the six came from packages that listed ingredients on them that no human can pronounce, much less expect their body to assimilate into something useful. I was relieved that I had his support. Plus, with all the other things I was learning about, I was going to need his knowledge, training and expertise.

I have to say one of the biggest assets I've had is having an MD at my disposal. Being a nurse has definitely helped, but he just has that deeper knowledge and experience. Regarding vaccines, it would not take him long, after reviewing the literature and comparing it to Madison's clinical presentation, to see my point. After a short time of prep, I made the switch cold turkey. I was prepared for the withdrawal symptoms I had read about in other children when you remove their "drugs," but honestly, she adapted very well. I was worried that it meant it wasn't going to work, but I persisted. And then…a miracle!

It took about four weeks, and then one day it was as if she woke up. She became aware of the world around her. It's one of the most precious memories of my life. She was alert and made eye contact. Not a lot at first, but she would turn and look at you if you called her name. These diet changes had brought her back to Earth; back to me. After that, nothing was going to stop me. You cannot imagine the fire that grew within me that day. It's just those types of successes that motivate you, keep you searching, keep you digging, and keep you fighting. She was GF/CF for about two months before trying anything else.

In the meantime, I had gone to speak with a DAN! (Defeat Autism Now!) Doctor, and left feeling overwhelmed with everything he suggested. Some of what he suggested was cleaning up her environment and decreasing her exposures. Things like water filtration, converting our pool to salt water, changing to non-toxic everything (cleaning supplies, personal hygiene products), etc. It seemed crazy at the time because none of this had ever been on my radar. We also had a long discussion about vaccines and he provided scientific evidence of the damage that they do in fact cause, according to their own package inserts.

I had also been reading the Autism Research Institute website. I decided the next step was to start Madison on Super Nu-Thera, a high vitamin B6/magnesium supplement. Yeah, that didn't go so well. I tried three different times with different forms and each time she would become irritable and tantrum, and we couldn't have that! Let me just say that when you have a child who tantrums all day it really does a number on you, because your instinct as a parent when your child is crying is to fix it. Often times when the child is ill and in pain there is nothing you can do in that moment to comfort them. That is the most helpless feeling I have ever felt. So, when they begin to get better and then they get worse and start to tantrum multiple times again, it is distressing. You feel like you will lose your mind.

After she had evened out again, I introduced DMG. And…nothing. Crap. So I tried TMG instead. Two weeks later she began stringing together three and four word sentences. Yeah baby! And, that's how it's gone for the past seven years. Some things she does not tolerate and with some things there is no noticeable response. But, sometimes whatever it is helps, and you just keep building, keep working the puzzle. Eventually, we ran about every test known to man and were able to see exactly where her deficiencies were and supplement, and also see what was there that shouldn't be (e.g., heavy metals).

I could continue on here and explain to you in great detail everything we have tried. I know you want me to tell you how to recover your kid. If I just tell you, you will do it. I know, I wanted that too. I just wanted someone to tell me what I was not doing. There had to be a magic bullet.

But there's not. I can't do that for you. Believe me, if I could, I would spend the rest of my life passing out magic bullets. But, what I can offer you is hope. Please never give up on your child. They can and will get better. I cannot guarantee you that they will make a full recovery, but what does it hurt to believe they could? At the very least, their quality of life could be improved. You will have to go to war, but you can win.

I'm not the toughest or the smartest. Sometimes my willpower is pretty much at zero. But I get up every day with the intention to help my daughter. And that's where it starts. Your belief and persistence is where it starts. Some days I'm just maintaining. That's okay. It's a process. So, here is a list of mostly everything we've done. Diet has been the biggest component to healing, but not the only thing.

Diets: Gluten Free/Casein Free/Soy Free; removed IgG and IgE reactive foods; Specific Carbohydrate Diet (dairy free); organically grown foods when possible.

Supplements: Numerous vitamins and minerals, DMG & TMG, Enhansa, TruFiber, RepairVite, melatonin, probiotics, essential fatty acids, colostrum, biofilm protocol, digestive enzymes, Biocidin, acetyl l-carnitine, Coenzyme Q10, taurine, glutathione (oral, topical, nebulized, IV), N-acetyl cysteine, folinic acid, aloe vera juice, neurotransmitter support (niacinomide, GabaFlo, SerotaFlo, DopaFlo, Copper-Gold-Silver), Methyl B12.

Medications: Antifungals, Valtrex, Actos, chelation (oral, topical, rectal, IV), oxytocin (nasal), LDA (low dose allergen therapy).

Therapies: Speech therapy, occupational therapy, music therapy, Applied Behavioral Analysis, feeding therapy, social skills classes, cranial sacral therapy, Berard Auditory Training, Neurofeedback, Essential Oils, homeopathy, Epsom salt baths, Far-Infrared Sauna.

It has been over seven years now since I began to heal my daughter, and I couldn't be happier to tell you that Madison is recovered from autism! She has been discharged from all services and therapies, except for a social skills class. She still has some catching up to do in that regard. Her expressive language still needs tweaking, and she struggles with comprehension at times. She was at a six on the last ATEC I completed, and three of those six were for lingering health problems. Medically, she is not fully recovered. Her gut still does not function appropriately. She has great difficulty digesting carbohydrates and starchy foods. She still carries a toxic metal burden. But, I know with all my being that eventually I will find the last few pieces of the puzzle that will complete her recovery.

There is nothing more important to me than knowing that she is free. Free from a painful body, free from struggling because her brain is affected, free from every symptom of this iatrogenesis that is ridiculously labeled autism. Free to enjoy her life to the fullest, which is what she deserves. She did not choose this. I chose it for her in my ignorance. I have forgiven myself for that and I choose to move on. I hope that if you feel responsible for your child's injury, you will forgive yourself too for not knowing. It does not serve you or your child to carry that burden.

This is my truth. I wish it weren't, but it is. I wish I could spare my daughter the pain, suffering and struggle and I wish I could spare myself and those that love her the heartache. But, I can't. All I can do is tell her story and use it to help someone else. I want you to know that you can do this. Do not be afraid to do what you feel is right for your child. Never give in to that fear. No matter what anyone says, even if they are an expert. They are not an expert on your child. You are! Trust your instincts. Always. It's the one thing that will never fail you. It is your guidance system and it works beautifully when you stop and listen to it.

I have heard many times over the years from experts, doctors and scientists, that some of the things I have done to heal Madison should be considered child abuse and that these things are not scientifically based. That is not truth. It's a good thing that I no longer make decisions regarding the health of my child based on what someone else thinks, regardless of their qualifications. I did that before. Lesson learned.

Now, instead, I gather information from various experts, doctors or scientists and then I look it up myself, and learn what I can about whatever it is. So my decisions are never based on fear, but instead on knowledge. Also, I ask other moms. Yep. The women I have met on this journey are amazing! They have to be some of the most intelligent women in the world. I am constantly blown away by the amount of knowledge they have. Because, they too no longer have a choice. They have to do whatever it takes to heal their child. When you have to figure that out, you get smart real quick.

You see, we are not just moms, even though some folks out there contend that we are, and that we know nothing. We are doctors, lawyers, scientists of all kinds, nurses, social workers, teachers, pharmacists, activists, writers, and corporate executives. And when you put brains like that together along with the motivation we have in healing our kids, guess what? WE. GET. SHIT. DONE. We recover our kids. We fight for our kids. And we fight for your kids. Because the greatest reward, the greatest feeling aside from healing our own is helping others heal and preventing what happened to ours from happening to yours. Now, put on your war bonnet and get to work.

BEAKER

The gastroenterologist knelt down on the floor and looked my then one-year-old, non-verbal, failure-to-thrive daughter in the eye and said, "Sweetie, there is nothing wrong with you. You need to just tell your mommy to quit worrying about you so much, you are just fine." Then he turned to leave the room and looked back and said, "Get her off your breast milk, mom, and get her drinking cow's milk so she finally gains some weight." And the door shut behind him.

In that moment, I not only accepted that I was alone, but that I alone was going to have to get to the bottom of what was happening to my baby girl. My daughter had just turned a year old, and none of the five pediatric specialists (two gastrointestinal doctors, two allergists and a pediatrician) who we consulted with could find anything "wrong." However, they also offered NO explanation, and more importantly, NO relief for her pain, or other symptoms that worsened with each passing day.

For those first two glorious weeks of her life, my sweet baby girl nursed beautifully. She slept, she cuddled, she napped, she was the picture of health and perfection. I even recall my husband joking on the phone with his brother (who had two sons already), encouraging him to "Try for a third one," he said, "It is so worth it, dude, this girl thing is so peaceful!" Our first child, five at the time, was a boy full of noise, spunk, and energy.

By her third week of life, everything had changed. She began to scream. Not cry, not whimper, but scream. By her six week well-baby visit, the screaming had gotten worse and her periods of sleep had become shorter and shorter with each passing day. Her obvious discomfort required that we hold her upright for any of us to get any rest at all. She breast-fed non-stop and was voracious (almost like she could not get enough, ever). The pediatrician said it must be colic and sent us home saying it would soon pass. Before leaving, though, she had her nurse inject my daughter with four vaccines containing numerous antigens, and an oral live virus, for good measure.

;) WINK= <u>W</u>hat <u>I</u> <u>N</u>ow <u>K</u>now

;) *WINK #1 — There is no such thing as colic.*

Colic is a made up term left over from the 1950's that has little medical significance other than to describe a fussy baby. Sound familiar? Kind of like autism is a made up term to describe a child who doesn't look you in the eyes and has repetitive behaviors. Some of the causes of "colic" include: reflux, food intolerance (often the major culprit is milk), "rare" metabolic disorders, and weak muscles that control the LES (Lower Esophageal Sphincter). [Source book: *Colic Solved* (http://books.google.com/books?id=5kIEnXvfXXgC&printsec=frontcover&source=gbs_atb#v=onepage&q&f=false)]

The "colic" was unrelenting and we were soon back at the pediatrician, who began us on what I call reflux med roulette: Zantac, Prevacid, Bethanacol, back to Prevacid, add a little Carafate, put in some more Zantac. We would see a glimmer of relief with each new med change, and we would hold our breath only to see it evaporate a few days later. More shots at four months, right on schedule, and then six month shots, (all six of them). Then came the vinegar smelling poopy diapers. The blood curling screams continued, and no one in our house was sleeping, at all.

Our pediatrician finally agreed at seven months that we might need to see a GI doctor. So off we went to the first GI consult. Puzzled but intrigued, the doctor set out to help us figure things out. He changed some meds with no improvement, changed some foods we were feeding her with no improvements, and then started me on a breast-feeding elimination diet. First out went milk (which was not too bad since I despise the stuff, it was already mostly out of my diet). Then he pulled eggs from my diet, then soy, and then viola, for the first time in months our baby girl was calm and peaceful.

Being the engineer and scientist that my husband and I are, we launched into "experimental protocol mode." I grabbed a journal, which became my "lab notebook" and my husband eloquently pronounced, holding a peaceful baby girl for the first time since those first weeks when he bragged to his brother, "Beaker, whatever you did yesterday, whatever you ate, you have to repeat it for 14 days. If it is the food, then we will know for sure."

Easier said than done... So for 14 days I ate the same thing every day: Oatmeal, brown rice, ground turkey, mixed vegetables and a few fruits. I was distraught (not to mention sooo hungry). I went to a La Leche meeting in desperate need of validation and support from anyone who knew anything about breast feeding an allergic child. Instead, what I found was a leader who told me that it was impossible for a child to be allergic or even sensitive to a mother's milk and I just needed to eat anything I wanted and feed her whatever I was eating. These words crushed me. Once again, I was looking for support, but found quite the contrary. I was discouraged at that moment, but looking back, it led me to another WINK moment.

;) WINK #2: It is very possible for a baby to be "allergic" to breast milk if the baby's mother is eating foods that the baby cannot digest well or which they are intolerant to.

Later, I would find out a version of the breast feeding elimination diet we had created by trial and error is called a TED diet [Total Elimination Diet, discussed on the Dr. Sears website (http://www.askdrsears.com/topics/feeding-eating/feeding-infants-toddlers/food-allergies/elimination-diet)]. I also found a very supportive group of moms who knew the ins and outs of breast feeding an allergic/food sensitive child on a forum (http://community.kidswithfoodallergies.org/forum/breastfeeding_with_food_allergies) found at www.kidswithfoodallergies.org.

The 14-day experiment gave us our answer. What we didn't know then was that food was only part of the puzzle. By her first birthday, our daughter was falling off the growth charts (and her very hungry momma was not far behind her). We had a much more peaceful baby, but on the limited diet for both of us, we struggled to find enough "safe" foods to satisfy her body's demands. She also still seemed to have a constant round-the-clock need for food. We consulted a second GI, who sent us into panic mode with his urgent need to "scope her" immediately, declaring to us that we were witnessing a child with failure to thrive.

An endoscopy and colonoscopy followed. This included heavy sedation for the procedure and biopsy results that the GI doc pronounced normal. This lead to his pronouncement that all she needed was cow's milk and the condescending exchange that began this chapter. Then a couple more vaccines for good measure (including her MMR), and our little girl regressed before our eyes. Within two months after the last round of shots, and two weeks after following the GI doctor's orders to wean her to cow's milk, she began banging her head on anything hard she could find…including our tile floor. I watched in horror and held her in bear hugs, crying and pleading for her to stop and praying that I could keep her from hurting herself. We stopped the cow's milk immediately, although the doctor claimed there was no way that the milk could be related to the behavior. He stated that this could just be normal toddler behavior, yet if it continued, perhaps she should be evaluated for autism. By immersing myself in research into the late hours of the night, endless Google scholar, Pub-Med and scientific journal searches later led me to another WINK moment:

;) *WINK #3- Eosinophils in the gut, head banging, and failure to thrive are NOT normal, in fact they are quite abnormal and cause for great concern in ANY child.*

What the GI doc failed to acknowledge was that eosinophils [a type of white blood cell that can become active when you have certain allergic diseases, infections, and other medical conditions. Source: Medline Plus (http://www.nlm.nih.gov/medlineplus/ency/article/003649.htm)]

are not supposed to be found in anyone's gut and when they are in great numbers, it results an allergic, inflammatory condition called eosinophilic gastritis. The pathology report showed eosinophils in my daughter's GI tract but the doc claimed everything was normal... oh, and that I was worrying too much. But I wouldn't know just how big an issue this was for another eight months when a third GI, with whom we consulted, had the biopsy slides re-read and his pathologist found the same thing — eosinophils. The difference — this GI knew they were not supposed to be in a child's gut, or anywhere in their GI tract for that matter!!

Head banging is not normal and can be one sign of autism or other developmental disorders, in the form of self-injurious behavior. Possible causes include everything from seizures, neurotransmitter imbalance, food intolerance or genetic conditions. [Source: Autism Research Institute (http://www.autism.com/index.php/symptoms_self-injury)] And finally, failure to thrive: "Failure to thrive (FTT) is a term used to describe inadequate growth or the inability to maintain growth, usually in early childhood. It is a sign of under nutrition, and because many biologic, psychosocial, and environmental processes can lead to under nutrition, FTT should never be a diagnosis unto itself." [Source: AAFP (http://www.aafp.org/afp/2011/0401/p829.html)] Well that certainly does not sound normal or healthy for any kid. "A diagnosis unto itself," well, that is exactly what we got, until the next leg of the journey began.

At this point, we were close to giving up on the medical profession. None of what they were telling us seemed to make any sense and the advice we were given certainly wasn't improving the situation. In many incidences, the treatments they were recommending were actually making our daughter's condition worsen. So, we sought the advice of a naturopath who had experience with autistic children hoping to find some guidance on what we could feed our daughter since she was reacting to so many foods, both gastrointestinally, and neurologically.

This doctor ordered a stool test and gave us some dietary advice. He confirmed our suspicion and concerns about vaccination and got her started on a probiotic. The stool test came back positive for Clostridium difficile toxin A and B (Cdiff). How the heck did my 15-month-old get a bacterial GI infection that is common in hospitals, the elderly, or those who have been on frequent antibiotics when she had not had an antibiotic or hospitalization at this point in her not-so-elderly life? In trying to figure out what this meant for my daughter, I consulted with her pediatrician and GI doc for clarification, and this is the conflicting information I received.

Her pediatrician told me babies are carriers of Cdiff and never tested for it until after two years of age, so not to be worried about the result that the naturopath had told us was concerning and needed treatment. The following day, after seeing her pediatrician, we see the gastroenterologist and he walks in the room and declares, "She has Cdiff." "She does?" I question, explaining what the pediatrician had just told me. He proceeds to tell me the test was for the toxin, meaning that this was the active state of the Cdiff and since she was having chronic diarrhea, this could be the cause. We treated with an herbal treatment the naturopath had recommended, and the Cdiff re-test tests came back normal. I feel a WINK coming on…

;) **_WINK #4 Clostridium difficile (Cdiff) overgrowth and toxin is bad, very bad, and has been recently linked to use of reflux medications (Proton pump inhibitors such as the Prevacid our daughter had been taking) [Source: FDA Alert (http://www.fda.gov/drugs/drugsafety/ucm290510.htm)]._**

Remember that reflux roulette that the docs were playing? Ummm, yeah. Awesome. Oh, and in mouse models Clostridia bacterial strains can produce excess propionic acid which when injected directly into mice can cause them to look "autistic." [Source: Frye, et al. (http://www.nature.com/tp/journal/v3/n1/full/tp2012143a.html)] Coincidence? I think not.

I wish the story ended there, but the journey continued. Upon returning from a family vacation when my daughter was almost 18 months old, we reached what I recall as the bottom. As in rock bottom. Things got worse. Just as we felt we were solving the "mystery," we would find another clue. This particular "clue" came in this form: I was removing some of my nail polish using a non-acetone, alcohol-based remover. My daughter was playing in my closet quietly with my shoes. I had finished a few nails when I heard this blood-curling scream coming from the adjacent closet. My daughter was lying on her back in a back bend position, screaming. As I picked her up, she was as stiff as a board. I had no idea what had happened, she had no blood, no cuts and her brother was not in the room, so I could not figure out why she was so upset.

After nearly 20 minutes of trying to calm her down, and two frantic calls to the pediatrician and my husband, she took a sip of water. I had to go to the bathroom, so I took her back into my bathroom with me to keep an eye on her. The minute we stepped back into the doorway of the bathroom, she began to scream and stiffen again. I ran out of the room with her in my arms, out the front door of our house to fresh air. Within minutes she calmed down. It hit me...it was the nail polish remover chemicals, still lingering in the air of the bathroom. Over the next week, our observation and hypothesis would be tested. Similar "behaviors" and screaming ensued when her brother squirted hand sanitizer near her, when we sprayed our countertops with Windex and it evaporated near her, when we wiped her face with alcohol containing baby wipes and even when my breath (after an adult beverage) was near her face, she started slapping my mouth. The common ingredient was ethanol. My baby had a severe intolerance to inhaled Ethanol fumes. How did that happen?

;) WINK #5: The reflux medication Zantac (Ratinidine) in the syrup/ liquid form (for children and babies) contains ALCOHOL (ethanol).

"Zantac Syrup contains 7.5% w/v alcohol. Each spoonful (5 mL) of syrup therefore contains almost 400 mg of alcohol. This is equal to the amount of alcohol in one spoonful (5 mL) of wine or two spoonfuls (10 mL) of beer." [Source: Glaxo Consumer sheet (http://www.medsafe.govt. nz/consumers/cmi/z/zantacsyr.pdf)] So let me get this straight? The American Academy of Pediatrics encourages moms who are breastfeed-ing to limit alcohol consumption and delay nursing for two hours [source:

AAP position (http://pediatrics.aappublications.org/content/129/3/e827. full.pdf)] but the AAP's own member (our pediatrician) handed me a prescription for two spoonfuls of beer (plus some H2 blocker for good measure) a few times a day for my baby? I wish I had been a little less sleep deprived and a little more educated back then to question this, but sadly I was not. We were in survival mode.

The next morning after the reaction to the nail polish remover was my daughter's 18 month "well visit." I stayed up the entire night researching ethanol sensitivity and around 2am came to this conclusion that I wrote to my husband in an email: "We have to push for metabolic testing. Period. Love you…goodnight." The next day, I pleaded with our pediatrician to send us to a metabolic specialist. She told me the wait for a geneticist would be over a year, and sent us to a neurologist and offered my daughter another vaccination booster! No thanks, not until you tell me what the hell is happening to my little girl that she cannot tolerate the smell of the rubbing alcohol that you are going to wipe her skin with before you inject her!

The neurologist did the first tests for mitochondrial (mito) disease (blood testing for lactic acid and pyruvic acid) as well as many other conditions. The mito testing came back abnormal, so he repeated the tests two more times. All abnormal. The preliminary bio-markers were positive for mitochondrial disease. While we waited three months to see the mitochondrial specialist, our food discoveries continued.

Our daughter's diet at this point was dairy, casein, gluten, and soy free. In place of wheat flour, we were baking a ton with almond flour and letting her drink almond milk. On that family vacation I mentioned, we could not find almond milk, so we switched to rice milk for the trip. Upon returning, we went back to almond. She had few, if any, episodes while on vacation. So at some point after we returned home, it dawned on me that maybe there was another connection with all the foods she was not tolerating (the list was mostly made up of highly colored red, orange, purple fruits and veggies).

Being the geeky chemist that I am, I hypothesized that the food itself might not be the issue but perhaps the chemical that they all contained which made them highly colored, was the issue!! After many a google search, I found it…. They were all high in salicylates or salicylic acid… also known as asprin. I know what you are saying — "Aspirin in my strawberries, no way??" But it is true. Salicylic Acid is God's pesticide that the plant naturally produces and some foods have higher concentrations of this chemical than other plants. Not so coincidentally, ALL the foods she was reacting too were at the HIGH end of the Salicylate list. And guess what else was on there…almonds…they are very high in salicylates. So began experimental protocol # 3,486 — salicylate removal. Amazing result #3,487: Increased speech and lots of it. She had been acquiring speech all along, but the increased salicylate load seemed to somehow be blocking her from expressing it. Bye-Bye almond milk and almond flour, and hello speech!

;) WINK #6: Salicylate intolerance and toxicity is very real and causes severe health issues (both physically and mentally) for many children, as well as adults.

"Research shows that about 20% of adults with asthma, 60% of people with food-induced itchy rashes, headaches or migraines, 70% of people with irritable bowel symptoms and 75% of children with behavior problems may be sensitive to salicylates." [Source: Food Intolerance Network. (http://fedup.com.au/factsheets/additive-and-natural-chemical-factsheets/salicylates)]

Do you remember a condition called Reye's syndrome in the 1980's? This may be one of the most severe examples of salicylate sensitivity/toxicity. Children were becoming very ill, some dying, after taking aspirin with viral illness (like chicken pox and flu) leading to the warning on aspirin labels that it was not recommended for children under 19 years old. Epidemiological research has shown an association between the development of Reye's Syndrome and the use of aspirin (a salicylate compound). [Source: National Reyes Syndrome Foundation (http://www.reyessyndrome.org/aspirin.html)]

We found 30 healthy, low salicylate foods for our daughter (largely by trial and error and by consulting salicylate lists we found from researchers in Australia). We started feeding her these, rotating them, and trying to make them look and taste different so that she wouldn't lose interest in the diet that seemed to bring so much relief to so many of her other symptoms. We have stuck to this diet, the "cave-baby" diet, as my husband refers to it, for the last three years, slowly trying to introduce new foods when she is stable and holding our breath that she does not react.

From our perspective, the diet and environmental changes, as well as the avoidance of chemicals she is sensitive to, have taken significant burdens off her system. This has allowed her body to have peace and less pain. It has also allowed her brain to develop, and for her to grow physically, emotionally and developmentally. We have now seen well over 20 specialists on our medical journey. This prestigious list, includes four metabolic/mitochondrial specialists, who still can't agree on whether this is or is not primary mitochondrial disease, despite the fact that hundreds of thousands of dollars of testing have been ordered, reported, and analyzed. She has remained in the "suspected mitochondrial disease" diagnostic category for the last 3.5 years. As time has worn on, we have become much less concerned about the "formal diagnosis" and the "label." We are now much more focused on continuing to keep our daughter pain free, growing, developing, healthy, and smiling more now than she ever did her first three years of life. Recently we consulted with a developmental pediatrician. He spent nearly two hours going through her medical history with a fine tooth comb. At the end of the appointment he said, "You did it mom." Confused, I said, "Did what?" He replied, "You saved her brain." "I didn't do this, God did." I said. "Ok fair enough, but you listened," he concluded.

I trusted my gut, I researched, I made changes, I observed, I recorded my observations, I listened to that inner voice (which I truly believe was God's guidance). Our family witnessed my little girl retreat deep within herself, and we pulled with all our might to bring her back to our world. I have been blessed with a husband and family that support me, believe in my intuition and who help me do everything in our power to keep her here, each and every day. By making changes to her diet, environment and removing toxic insults to her system, we continue to see improvements, true improvements, and healing. After much searching we have found practitioners who truly "get it" and have helped us continue to help her. We still have rough days, but they are greatly outnumbered by the good ones. She is ready to enter kindergarten in the fall in a mainstream classroom. She is ice-skating, swimming, riding a bike, and having play dates with friends. She is prescription medication free (no more reflux roulette), and for us, these are all amazing accomplishments.

;) *__WINK #7: Mitochondrial disease can cause regressive autism and may be caused by a genetic defect, or triggered by environmental toxins, including (but not limited to): medications, anesthesia, vaccines, and environmental exposures including pesticides.__* [Source: Kennedy Krieger Paper: Mito/ASD (http://www.epidemicanswers.org/wp-content/uploads/2010/05/Dr.-Richard-Kelly-Autism_Mitochondrial_Disease.pdf), Mitoaction Drug Toxicity Webinar #1 (http://www.mitoaction.org/blog/medication-exposures-mitochondrial-toxicity) and Webinar #2 (http://www.mitoaction.org/blog/may-mito-meeting-drug-toxicity-mitochondria), Kennedy Krieger Paper Anesthesia (http://www.epidemicanswers.org/wp-content/uploads/2010/05/Dr-Richard-Kellys-Mito-Anesthesia-document.pdf), Poling Case Study (http://www.ncbi.nlm.nih.gov/pmc/articles/PMC2536523/), Mito Conundrum: Unraveling Environmental Effects on Mitochondria (http://www.epidemicanswers.org/wp-content/uploads/2010/05/Environment-Affects-Mitochondria.pdf)]

God really gets the last ;) WINK on our journey, without His eternal wisdom and guidance, the outcome would have been very different for our entire family.

John 8:32: *"And you will know the truth, and the truth will set you free."*

ZORRO

There was no starting gun to mark my son Connor's descent into autism. No abrupt loss of skills or speech, no seizures or fevers, just an imperceptible braking, until his forward momentum in life just rolled to a stop somewhere between 16 and 22 months.

I don't know if it was my own health — undiagnosed chronic Epstein-Barr and mycoplasma pneumonia that set him up; or my mouthful of leaky amalgams and 15 years of mercury-filled flu shots; or even the case of salmonella food poisoning that put me in the hospital for four days halfway through my pregnancy and stripped my GI tract. Could it have been the three ultrasounds or the 18 hours of Pitocin? Was it the Hep B shot at birth? My son turned blue less than 24 hours later, but the doctor assured us that was a normal stress response. The MMR? Total vaccine load? After every well child appointment I always had to clear my calendar for a week, because I knew I'd have an extremely fussy and feverish baby who would nurse constantly. Whatever it was, whatever lowered my boy's resistance and increased his risk, I'll never know with complete certainty.

By the time he was 22 months old, my beautiful boy was speaking less and less, having peaked at 16 months with the phrase "Too hot to eat the pizza!" His anxiety increased daily. We couldn't leave the house without several pacifiers — one in his mouth and one in each hand

— and his blanket, which he wrapped around his head. Three pediatricians in three states assured me that he was fine.

He wasn't fine. I wasn't fine. I assumed the full load of guilt — the guilt I produced myself in abundance, and the guilt lobbed at me by other people. There was something off about my kid, so as the mom, it was clearly my fault. I was reminded of this failing daily, from evil stares when I tried to contain monumental meltdowns while shopping or at the library, to helpful strangers suggesting my son would be fine if I just took a strap to him now and then, to flat out assessments that I was clearly a terrible mother and this was *all my fault*.

The summer of 2001 leading up to our son's diagnosis was particularly hard. He wouldn't let me get a toothbrush in his mouth to brush his teeth, so he needed to have two stainless steel caps and four amalgam fillings put in while he was under sedation. When he came out of it he howled for a solid hour. Howled like a wounded wolf. It was hideous. A few weeks later he fell and banged up his knees so badly he refused to walk for nine weeks. The pediatric orthopedic specialist thought he must have bruised the *inside* of the patella. No one could figure out why he wasn't walking and we didn't know if he'd ever try again.

We were drowning. Every day was a struggle and we didn't know why. Our pediatrician waited until my son was three to agree that it might be time for a speech evaluation. I didn't know that I could search that out on my own. It took six months to get an appointment. By then, I had to wheel him in the stroller to the desk because he couldn't or wouldn't walk. The speech therapist said that, in addition to pronounced echolalia and expressive speech in the 2nd percentile, our son had cognitive delays and we should get an evaluation. Looking back, she knew what was going on immediately, but couldn't say because she wasn't qualified by the state to diagnose. We found a special preschool class for kids with speech delays and got a referral for a neuropsych evaluation. Then September 11, 2001 happened and everything shut down, including our scheduled intake appointment.

One night in the midst of the multi-day assessment, I broke down crying after I'd put Connor to bed. My thoughts were reduced to a sobbing prayer of "Help us, please, help us." A very calm and clear message interrupted my sobs, almost like someone was speaking to me, and said: "Jill, everything's going to be alright." I stopped cold. There have been two occasions in my life when I've heard this tiny, powerful voice. This was the first. I think that raised my spirits enough that the rest of the process didn't overwhelm me as much as it could have, but it rendered me defenseless for the actual diagnosis.

Honestly, an autism mom could have taken one look at Connor, gripping a Thomas train in one hand and lining up rocks with the other at the playground at age two and a half and given me the same answer, but due diligence must be done, the piper paid, etc. And so, autism. A full 299.0 diagnosis, for what it's worth. Connor had some speech, but it was almost exclusively echolalia. He ran in circles, he jumped up and down for hours, he flapped his hands, he toe walked, he lined things up, he tantrummed, he'd flip out if I took an alternate route while driving, and he had no friends.

Dr. B., the psychologist who did the assessment, stopped after she made the pronouncement. "Mrs. R, are you breathing?" Not so much. I only remember snippets from that appointment, the highlights being: 1) my son would probably never make friends on his own; 2) we could take comfort in the fact that he wasn't technically mentally retarded because his IQ was above 70; and 3) he was too inflexible and anxious for ABA.

We were gob smacked. Autism was something at the periphery of my awareness, something that happened to other people, but only rarely. They couldn't mean my boy — he was so affectionate. What was autism? What was going to happen to my son? What could we do? I knew my mother-in-law would ask about dietary changes, so we asked Dr. B. about it. She kind of brushed that aside, mumbling something about no double-blind placebo controlled studies, and directed us to the Family Resource room at the clinic. We dutifully listened then headed home in a daze. I think I was able to talk about it for about 12 hours before the shock and adrenaline wore off and the sadness that comes in the wake of a diagnosis took over, but it was long enough to make a couple of phone calls to our families and a couple of friends.

I'm a die-hard bookworm from a long line of readers. My first step in the direction of *doing something* was to head to the bookstore. I cleaned them out of books on autism. In 2001, that meant five books. My mom, 2,500 miles away, found one book: *Unraveling the Mystery of Autism and Pervasive Developmental Disorder* by Karyn Seroussi. That was the only book on the shelf at Books-A-Million in Goodlettsville, Tennessee, so that was the one my mom bought. I had the same book in my stack, but it was at the bottom.

Two days later my mom called me, likely in tears because we were all a sobbing mess, and told me to put down whatever I was doing and read that book. Now! So, I did. That changed everything. That book saved my son.

My husband wasn't keen to change our son's diet. Connor was living on bagels and chocolate milk. I could see his point, but I had grabbed onto a shred of hope and I wasn't going to let go. I didn't care if it was hard. I was willing to crawl through glass for a 1% improvement. That book gave me hope, but more importantly, it gave me something to *do*. I took milk out of my son's diet the next day. I'd been on elimination diets myself for allergies, so I had a vague idea of what to do. My niece Chloe had a milk allergy, so I already had some organic soy milk in the house. Gluten presented a thornier challenge.

Taking the approach that it was easier to ask forgiveness than permission, I changed Connor's diet when my husband was on a weeklong trip out of town. I started by taking out milk. Within two days he'd stopped running in circles. Within two weeks, he had adopted his cousin's stuffed bunny, renamed him Carrots, started singing lullabies and pretending to put him to bed. There was no way I was giving that bunny back. Sorry, Chloe. My husband read *Unraveling* on his next plane trip and came home ready to dive into a 100% GFCF diet. Good thing I'd already started. And we were off.

I found a small group of parents who had started a local biomed support group. Those parents became a lifeline. They connected me to doctors and therapists, pointed me to online support and resources, and became my friends. A few months in we found a Defeat Autism Now doctor out-of-state who was a Godsend, Dr. John Green, in Oregon City, Oregon. He was our team leader and a true thought partner. It was such an enormous relief to find such a fabulous doctor. He helped us save our son, he's a wonderful human being who has compassion, who listens and who thinks outside the box. (We love you Dr. Green!)

Our first order of business was to safely replace the amalgams in Connor's mouth with composite fillings, ramp up his mineral intake, and get chelation going. I'm not sure if it was the action of removing mercury, the powerful antioxidant properties of the DMPS, or the giant bolus of sulphur it delivers, but Connor did beautifully with the first round of oral chelation.

The school week following our first chelating weekend was interesting. Two of the most skeptical therapists we had — top-notch speech therapists that had zero faith in biomed and special diets — both came to me to tell me Connor had turned a corner and they had seen significant improvement just that week. I mentioned to the first I suspected the new treatment we started was helping. She just rolled her eyes. When the second mentioned the slew of emerging skills, I just smiled.

We became early adopters of biomedical interventions. We tried chelation, IVs, targeted nutrition, antifungals, antibiotics, methyl B12, and supplements. I attended conferences. I read books, medical papers, and spent hours online. I took classes and even got through half of a degree in naturopathy before the school closed down. I was obsessed with helping my son improve. He had eczema, a million food allergies, sky high viral titres — especially for measles, intractable yeast and clostridia overgrowth, heavy metals, oxidative stress, nutritional deficiencies, low-level mitochondrial dysfunction, chronic diarrhea, bowel impactions, reflux, leaky gut, plus weak nails and brittle hair. For a year or two he didn't gain any weight and his sleep — which had always been good — went to hell when he was five. We tested everything: hair, pee, poop, blood.

Recovery wasn't even a concept I entertained. I couldn't think more than three months ahead until our next doctor's appointment. It was an immediate and narrowly focused life, but it paid off. My son began to emerge from the fog of pain and disconnection. He gained three years of expressive speech in 12 months. He stopped tantrumming. Life got easier for everyone and I had a fire in my belly.

By the time Connor was six, we were able to start thinking about that second baby we'd always planned on. We chose to pursue adoption and we brought our son Kyle home just before Connor turned seven. (The second time I heard that tiny powerful voice was when I took Kyle's birthmom to the doctor just before Kyle was born and heard his heartbeat on the Doppler. I had an overwhelming jolt of recognition "That's my boy!") By then, I was starting to consider the possibility of recovery. When Connor was in second grade, we had him re-evaluated. The psychologist didn't remove the diagnosis, but downgraded him to "very mild PDD." He also registered a nearly 50-point improvement in his IQ scores.

It was interesting to me that none of the psychologists or educational therapists involved in that re-evaluation asked us what we did, like that kind of overall improvement and a 45 – 50 point increase in IQ scores happens every day. Connor's recovery wasn't fast, cheap, or easy. He had several plateaus and at least two significant and scary regressions.

He made another huge leap in improvement after age nine when we added an extensive regimen of combination homeopathy under the direction of our holistic pediatrician. (We love you Dr. Elisa Song!) Every morning and evening I would mix his prescribed dose of up to 10 different remedies — 5 drops of one, 10 of another, 30 of a third — feeling like a mad scientist, but seeing definite improvement across the board. We prepped him for another round of prescription antifungals and the combination of the two approaches cinched it. We've never had to look at that kind of treatment since.

Today Connor is 16 and he has recovered from autism. He had a few bumpy years with depression and anxiety when he hit puberty (DO NOT underestimate puberty), but has come out the other side with the help of excellent medical and therapeutic care. A few months ago we ran a series of tests like we used to do when we first started. Everything looked great: the number and severity of food allergies (real IgE, histamine moderated allergies) has decreased dramatically and all the metabolic markers were normal. The tests for organic acids, dysbiosis and gut function were all pretty much perfect. I got teary looking at them and I swear I'd frame them if it wouldn't mortify him with embarrassment.

He's a lovely young man: kind, good-natured, and good-humored. He loves movies, heavy metal, and theater. He takes a stand on the side of social justice in all things and thinks about life and the people he encounters. I couldn't be happier or prouder. He's happy that he can have the occasional pizza out with friends with no ill effect. (Yes, the whole pizza. Teen boys and their appetites.)

So what did we do to get here? A fairly complete list includes: GFCF diet, with removal of all allergens, antioxidants, high dose Vitamin A, herbs, homeopathy, both classical and combination, antibiotics, antifungals, enzymes, probiotics, methyl B12, TMG, and folinic acid, DMPS chelation, both oral and transdermal, N-acetyl cysteine transdermal lotion, TTFD, glutathione (both IV and transdermal), cranial sacral therapy, BodyTalk, and lots and lots of prayer from every corner.

Keep in mind that this was in addition to occupational therapy with sensory integration two to four times per week, Special Ed preschool, full-inclusion through second grade, speech therapy, social skills groups, Floortime, RDI, special needs soccer, and karate.

There were things we tried that didn't work or caused a negative reaction. I had a very sensitive kid and had to go very slowly. For example I tried eight different enzymes before I hit on one that worked. I begged samples from my support group and went through them one at a time. One gave Connor stomachaches, another gave him an eczema flare, and a third triggered odd behavior. Vitamin B6 was pretty much a disaster. I never completely understood why, but it took six years of healing before we were able to introduce it in a very small dose in the P5P form.

Food allergies and his extreme pickiness limited his diet. A trial of the Specific Carbohydrate Diet exacerbated his eczema and food allergies, so we went back to what had worked before. Please note: I recovered my kid during a six-year period where he never ate more than eight different foods.

Yes, we were lucky. My son responded early and consistently enough to show me that there was a definite biological basis to his autism. But it wasn't just luck; we didn't give up when we got overwhelmed. I was devoted to his recovery to the exclusion of just about everything else. If something didn't work or he hit a plateau, I just maintained until I had enough energy or found a new approach to the issue and pushed forward. There was always something new on the horizon and always, *always* there was hope. In the end, that still, powerful voice was right: everything was all right. It just took a lot more time and effort than I ever could have imagined.

I was also lucky — and I'm still lucky — that my husband stood shoulder-to-shoulder with me on this. We never stopped moving forward. No matter how dark my own world was (at one point I couldn't drive my son to therapy without having a panic attack myself) or how expensive the treatments were, we didn't stop. It was worth it. Hope is always worth it.

EPILOGUE

W hen the original members of The Thinking Moms' Revolution
wrote "Autism Beyond the Spectrum," our goal was to share our
stories and inspire others to do the same, with the hope of reaching every
parent of a child with a developmental disability to give them the message
that they were not alone, and that there was hope for their situation.

At the time, a not-for-profit organization to help families financially
was an idea, the way the book, now realized, had been an idea the year
prior. I am happy that Team TMR came to fruition and that we can pay
it forward in the form of granted funds for treatments for families that
need help.

ShamROCK approached me about a year ago after reading *Autism
Beyond the Spectrum* with an idea that gave birth to *Evolution of a
Revolution: From Hope to Healing*. She was inspired after reading our
book and wrote her own chapter. She added her chapter to the back of
our book, and read it at her book club meeting. We blogged about it and
encouraged others to do the same.

After the formation of Team TMR, we reached out to Thinkers and
asked them to donate their stories of recovery to a special text, where
the proceeds would be used to fund our treatment grant program. The
response was overwhelming, and to keep the book manageable, we had
to take the request down after just one day.

What that tells me is that our stories are a powerful tool to spread hope to other families who do not yet know that biomedical and alternative interventions can really work wonders on a child with autism. The recovery stories in this book happened. And recovery from autism continues to happen every single day.

My hope is that you, our reader, will be inspired to write your own story. Share it with your family and friends, your book club, your bible study group, and your bunko pals. Together we are changing course. Autism is not a jail sentence that ends in institutional living as we are so often told by our neurologists. It is a toxicity problem that once addressed can reverse course. What are you waiting for? Get out there and change the world with us! To become involved with our mission, visit us at www.teamtmr.org

Helen Conroy

Executive Director, Team TMR

May 2014

ACKNOWLEDGEMENTS

We, the members of Team TMR who have contributed to this book, would like to thank all of the thinking moms and dads that write blogs and web pages on social media sites, the brave doctors who have put their careers on the line for the sake of our children and their health, the politicians who are trying to change the ways of the Government, the advocates who tirelessly work to pave the way for our children and the educators, paraprofessionals and therapists who took the time to care about and help our children.

There are certain organizations and individuals that have helped us on a profound level. They are: Generation Rescue, TACA, Jenny McCarthy, Stan Kurtz, Autism Research Institute, David Kirby, Autism One, Age of Autism, The Canary Party, Safeminds, Ginger Taylor, National Autism Association, Dr. Wakefield, Rob Schneider, and Aidan Quinn.

Whether we were introduced to the original members of TMR via their blog or their chapter in their book, we all agree that we felt an immediate connection to one or many of them as we read their words, their stories, their inspirational messages. As we read the blog each and every day, we all knew that we were no longer alone on this journey to ultimate health for our children.

Through their written words, we were made to feel as though we were all connected, united on this journey of healing and hope. TMR was and is a breath of fresh air in this community. We are so very proud, humbled and grateful to work alongside these extreme warriors and we are elated to be a part of Team TMR. Thank you to all of you, for guiding us, for sharing your stories with us and for taking us under your wings. Thank you for befriending us and showing us that hard work and determination can and will make a difference in our community.

<u>Team TMR Contributors to Evolution of a Revolution: From Hope to Healing</u>

Barracuda (Julie Clymer Pletner) — Mom to an amazing seven-year-old girl who has taught me the true meaning of love through the journey of recovery. Wife to a hands-on husband that shares my passion for recovering our daughter. I'm a stay-at-home mom that loves cooking, fundraising, and Will Farrell. Laughter truly is the best medicine.

Beaker — Started her professional career in the lab as a bewildered chemist who often felt she was a round peg in a square hole. After her daughter's multitude of medical issues, she found out the exact reason she had that graduate chemistry degree and put it to good use as she set out to restore her child's health. Along the way she found her true calling: sharing her family's experience with other parents (especially mothers) and helping them improve the quality of life for their children by staying true to their guiding light . . . their God-given mother's instinct.

Bling (Heidi Scheer) — I am a true girlie-girl that was raised in a house of boys. I am the mother of three incredible children and wife of the most amazing man on Earth. My middle son is recovered from autism and is, by far, my family's greatest example of perseverance, courage, and faith. As they say, it takes a village…and I am here to join yours!

Chief (Jennifer Young) — Southern born-and-bred, Registered Nurse, mom to Madison, who is recovered from autism. I have settled nicely into my crunchy-mom role, after years of working to heal my daughter. If you need me, check the grocery store or my kitchen, where I whip up gourmet SCD cuisine. Just kidding, it's chicken and carrots.

Co-Pilot (Heather Jung) — I'm a military spouse and mom to two beautiful children. My daughter, five years old, had autism and bowel disease. My two-year-old son is neuro-typical. My husband is a pilot in the Air Force. He serves our country and I serve our family. Though he travels a lot, he is very involved in our daughter's recovery and we make all decisions together. As the military life goes, we find ourselves on the move a lot and our lives can feel pretty hectic sometimes. But we always try to make time for the things we enjoy doing together as a family.

Cougar (Ginger Lee) — I'm mom to four children, two boys and two girls, the oldest of which is recovered from autism. A loyal friend, a loving mom and wife, and a lot of fun, I'm also fierce in my pursuit to right the injustice that's occurred to a generation of our precious children. I will not stand idly by while our kids are being poisoned. This will end. I am the Revolution! You are the Revolution!

Creole Queen (Keisha Hertzock) — RAWR! I'M A TIGER! I'm a southern woman from Louisiana. God, family, good music, good food, big dreams, and red lipstick are everything to me. My six-year-old son has autism. My four-year-old son has autism and digestive disorder. My two-year-old son is experiencing delays in his development. Through it all, my faith remains strong. My six and four-year-olds have made awesome progress and continue to shine, and my sleeves are rolled up, working with my two-year-old. Prayer is my steering wheel! REMAIN STRONG AND KEEP HOPE!!

CRUSH (Shannon Strayhorn) — I am a mom to two amazing little girls. Cali is my recovered eleven-year-old daughter who is going to change this world, and Melia is my eight-year-old daughter who is her sister's best friend and strongest advocate. In my home life I am a silly, laid back mom who has the good fortune of being married to my best friend. I celebrate life, and love nothing more than family, laughter, and time at the beach. In my "autism" life, I am a feisty, sarcastic, common sense thinker who is on a mission to CRUSH the limitations placed on our children, CRUSH the lies of these epidemics and CRUSH the people standing in the way of truth, hope and healing.

Frankie (Andrea Frank Giboney) — I'm mom to three amazing children who, along with my husband, are my heart and sou!. At the age of three, my son was diagnosed with PDD-NOS, and we were told his future would consist of group homes or state run facilities. With biomedical treatment (and a lot of sweat, tears, humor and love) he's now recovered. I tossed the rose-colored glasses, rolled up my sleeves and made his recovery my mission. I hope his story can inspire others to do the same.

Green Bean Girl (Meadow Davidson) — I am a Midwestern mom trying to adapt once again to Southern-living. My oldest son is 16 and has been on the autism spectrum since age two. My 14-year-old was diagnosed with Sensory Processing Disorder, Anxiety, and Aspergers two years ago. I worked as a special education assistant, but decided to teach my boys at home this year and we are loving every minute of it! We have a beagle, Maddy, and two cats named Aqua and Patches.

Guardian (Sadie West) — I am a wife and a mom to ten-year-old twin boys. I have lived in the suburbs of Chicago all my life. I am a Developmental Therapist and autism education advocate. My mission is to teach others about the strategies that work best in our educational settings so our kids can be successful learners. I love spending time with my family and friends and need more time to do it!!

Guru Girl (Kim Ruckman) — A SoCal mom to two wonderful kiddos. Wife to a very sexy Software Engineer husband. I'm a graphic designer-turned-biomed advocate, Grant Mentor to Generation Rescue's Grant program and Creator of Biomed Heals (http://www.biomedheals.com/), a website that chronicles my son's complete recovery from autism. I'm a problem solver at heart, and will never back down if I think something can be fixed. On my downtime I like to watch 80's and 90's tv sitcoms. Roseanne and Seinfeld are my favs! I'm a tee shirt and jeans kinda girl. When I'm not at home, you can usually find me out shopping at Target, at my son's BMX race track, or at my daughter's dance studio.

Hoppy — I'm a mom of two handsome little boys who light up my life (almost) every day! Proud owners of a brewery and farm-to-table restaurant, we believe that nature knows best when it comes to our bodies and our foods. I focus on having fun with my boys and my work and everything else falls into place!

Juicy Fruit — I am the mom to a beautiful nine-year-old boy who regressed into autism at age three. We have spent the last six years getting him back and he's very close to recovered now. I work in Corporate America by day and fight as a Mother Warrior by night. We have a punk poodle named Shanti who is our unofficial service dog and we live in Colorado Springs.

Karma — Is "just a mom" to four kids that spend way too much time navigating their dirty mini-van through the urban sprawl that is metro Atlanta. She proudly supports Generation Rescue in the role of parent mentor for their Family Grant program. When asked, "How do you do it?" the answer is simple: Coffee, Belgian ale, and an odd sense of humor.

Lioness — I am a forty-something mom to two girls: a nine-year-old with Down syndrome and autism and a fun-loving and spunky typical five year old. Before having children, I dabbled in bellydance, Native beadwork, and Tsalagi (Cherokee) language lessons. I even considered going back to school to become a zookeeper. After the autism diagnosis, I became a Lioness, protecting and providing every resource I could to ensure recovery for my daughter. I also spent a lot of time wanting to "attack" the predators of Big Ag, Pharma and Government for damaging our kids. But this last year brought some physical and mental changes that brought me 'round to myself and a lot of introspection. I renewed my love of Jesus and am providing for my own wants and needs. As a result, it has been slowly transforming my whole family for the better.

Lone Star (Michelle Taff Schneider) — I'm a proud Texan and a married mother of three. My middle child, now three-years-old, was diagnosed with autism at twenty-seven months, more than a year after her initial regression. I have no shame in admitting that her recovery, in one way or another, has consumed my life. I have discovered a level of strength and determination I never knew existed within me, and this journey has taught me so many things about her as well. Through this journey, I've met so many committed parents who also believe that autism is preventable and treatable, and I've made it my personal mission to support families and educate as many people as I can about the facts.

Monarch (Jennifer Swanson Collins) — I majored in philosophy in college and still believe in questioning and examining all issues, arguments and dogma. At heart, I am a humanitarian, a little quirky and a dreamer. I am soft spoken with a permanent smile, but I am a fighter and fearless when it comes to caring for and healing my children. I am the mother to a set of beautiful and sensitive twin boys diagnosed with autism. The twins have a toddler age sister who demonstrates symptoms of toxic injuries. She has been treated with natural supplements and diet since birth and is showing incredible healing. I feel my true purpose in life is to unite with other Thinkers and spread the TRUTH and a message of hope. I believe our children's stories have the power to change the world!

Muscle Mama (Mary McKnight) — Mother of two beautiful children, the oldest is diagnosed with Autism and Hyperlexia. I love working-out to stay focused and to never forget who I really am, and I love to educate people about autism and help families whenever I can. Favorite thing: Hugs from my kids because they are growing up so fast! Best trait: I don't give up…EVER. No matter how long it takes or how hard it gets, autism is going down and I have the muscles to prove it.

Oracle (Laura Hirsch) — has a B.A. in Speech Communications and is the author of three books. Her first book was an autobiography about her experience of being a young widow, which led to her investigation of mediumship as a therapeutic avenue for grief. She remarried and had two sons, the older one diagnosed at age three with regressive autism. Her love and devotion to her son led her back to mediumship for answers from her loved ones in spirit and others on how to heal her son. Working with a psychic medium and his wife, a spirit artist, they extended an open invitation to the spirit world to help solve the autism puzzle. Her third book, *The Other Side of Autism: Famous Spirits Unveil Regressive Autism's Causes and Remedies* is the culmination of their sessions. She is also a Non-GMO advocate and is featured in the documentary "Genetic Roulette" in the autism segment. Her website is http://www.theothersideofautism.com.

Phoenix (Lindsey Articolo) — Born again from the ashes of my life before Autism. Mom to Ava who is nine and twins, Andrew and Ben, who are three. Andrew was diagnosed with ASD at 21 months. The best part of this journey has been learning to enjoy it. At the same time, it is hard for me to pretend much else matters besides our Canaries.

Queen B (Christina Johnson) — I am a tried-and-true Midwestern girl and the mother of three beautiful and precocious children who are my everything. My ten-year-old daughter is diagnosed with autism but we now know the many underlying issues she has that make up that diagnosis. I am constantly researching to find the best interventions and figure out a way to afford them all. Our daughter didn't make significant progress until she was seven years old, so I know there is hope! I try to make it all work while juggling a full time job, being a mommy, and a wife. I have an amazing husband that supports my obsessive search for answers and an amazing support group of close friends (my Warrior Mom Tribe) that are there for me no matter what. Oh, and I like my occasional cocktail and ice cold beer to take the edge off once in a while too.

Rebel (Mary Pulles Cavanaugh) — Is a mom of three girls. She became an avid researcher in 2008 by necessity when she began the autism journey that led her to awareness of the sick-care system that is so prevalent today. What keeps her focused is the knowledge that we are fearfully and wonderfully made. She is most proud of her success using her compiled research to win her second appeal with her insurance provider proving what really happened to her youngest daughter. Rebel looks forward to a future with natural healers of the mind and body, and many future travels discovering new places with her husband of 27 years. Her current struggles include dressing for success, a clean house, and finding time to cook.

Rocky (Nikki Di Bari Roxby) — I grew up in large Italian family and still enjoy homemade gnocchis (organic & gluten free), wine and good conversation. Today, my passion is healing my four-year-old son. I believe anything is possible and I am known to jump in the ring and when the cause is important to me. It should be no surprise that my favorite Rocky quote is "Going in one more round when you don't think you can — that's what makes all the difference in your life." Whether you are newly diagnosed or have been at it awhile, always hope for more. Don't let anyone make you think otherwise. I have presented at Autism One with leading physicians and parents and my family will be featured in the upcoming trailer for the Canary Kids Film Project.

Rogue Zebra — Virtually lives in her own little world, far from the African savannah. Stroke, seizures, Asperger's and the decision to go GFCF "cold turkey" started our rogue adventure eight years ago. Next came virtual school, real learning from the comfort and warmth of home, with the flexibility of homeschooling and structure of brick and mortar. When not explaining the difference of momentum and inertia, RZ interacts in undiagnosed, mitochondrial and occasionally ASD communities. "When you hear hoofbeats, think horses, not zebras." is an outdated paradigm that needs to change. RZ is partial to "When you hear hoofbeats, THINK."

ShamROCK — I am a mother to three beautiful children, one of whom is recovering from ASD. I am a Thinker who won't stop until my son and family are healed, who won't stop until all our 'canaries in the coal mine' have returned to health. Our kids need help in their recovery. We can't do it alone. Peace, xoxo.

Shawty (Terri Burges Hirning) — I am a proud mother of three children: Two born to me and one I was lucky enough to get as a bonus gift through marriage. My son is recovered from autism thanks to some serious team work and the tireless help and support of my husband. As a result of my journey, I also work full time in the autism world helping others in a way I never dreamed possible. I also mentor and blog in my "spare" time. I am obsessed with allergen-friendly cooking, meditation, natural healing methods, crafting, gardening, sustainability, growing as much food as we can and just trying to keep up with our children, goats, chickens, cats, and dog. I'm Wonder Woman with a generous helping of attitude and a dash of ghetto-fabulous!

Spark (Jaima Gadeaun) — Mama to four beautiful children, one who was diagnosed with autism and one with tourettes. Grateful to all those moms who have shown me the way and provided me with hope and encouragement on this journey. I believe it is time to pay it forward and provide others with the same. Thankful for my husband who works tirelessly so that we can afford the recovery of our girls. Addicted to Pinterest, Paper crafts and Stamping.

Spartan (Maria O'Neil) — Hails from NY where she once worked in mainstream healthcare. Since marrying her Marine husband in 2006, she has been everywhere from North Carolina to Okinawa, Japan where she received her son's autism diagnosis at age 18 months. Since recovering her son Connor, now age five, her main focus is advocating for choices and different options in treating autism, along with keeping autism at bay in her youngest son Cash. Marine wives are often referred to as "Spartan Wives." Historically, Spartans are brave, undaunted warriors in battle — and battle this Spartan will until every parent she meets knows that they indeed have options and can treat the medical component of today's autism.

Sunflower (Laurie Connell) — I'm a mom of two wonderful boys. Our youngest is my focus and my mission is to heal and recover him from iatrogenic autism. Each day holds amazing surprises from our sweet, smart and funny little boy. In my former life, baton twirling was my passion. Now you can find me enjoying yoga, walks with our dog, outdoor activities with the family which include trips to Lego Land Florida, shopping at our local health food store, juicing and watching HGTV. I enjoy helping families newly diagnosed with autism to offer them HOPE. I am grateful for a supportive husband, family and for all of their help. My faith as a Christian keeps me going as well as wonderful friends cheering us on.

Zorro (Jill Rege) — Is a California mom with a point to make about autism (and ADHD and sensory integration dysfunction): It has biological underpinnings and it's treatable! Kids can improve and some can recover when their medical issues and nutritional deficiencies are corrected. Mom to three boys with issues including anxiety, autism (her son has recovered!), ADHD, epilepsy, dyslexia, and mild attachment disorder, Zorro spends her days looking for solutions, geeking out over neurobiology, juggling schedules, trying to feed picky kids with a billion food allergies, and keeping up with celebrity gossip. She blogs at Recovery Road (http://recoveryrd.wordpress.com/).

About the Authors

Helen Conroy is Executive Director of Team TMR and past president of the Thinking Moms' Revolution. After a 15 year career as a vice-president at a Fortune 500 financial services firm she made the transition to the not-for-profit sector and currently makes a difference in the lives of families living with autism. Helen is married to Doug and has three beautiful children.

Laura Hirsch, BA in Speech Communications, is the author of three books, including *The Other Side of Autism* and is the owner of the publishing company Rainbow Books. She advocates for children with autism and for food safety, and is featured in the documentary "Genetic Roulette: The Gamble of our Lives." She is married to Matt and has two incredible children, one with regressive autism.